The Maharajahs

By John Lord

Duty, Honor, Empire

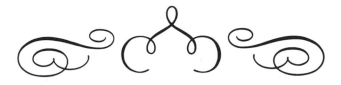

The Maharajahs

JOHN LORD

Random House New York

To Karolyn

May Ganpati, the elephant-faced one,
sweep away with his trunk all
impediments to my thoughts, and may
Saraswati, the goddess of wisdom,
put into my mind for every thought
its proper word.

Invocation for a
Sanskrit author

Preface

THE PRINCES of India were the last great anachronism of modern times, feudal barons living in the nuclear age. They were the only group of men to whom Francis Bacon's Elizabethan aphorism might still be applied. "Princes," he said, "are like to heavenly bodies, which cause good or evil times, and which have much veneration and no rest." By virtue of their position many of the maharajahs seem to have been larger than life; they held powers of life and death, commanded incalculable riches, pursued exuberant courses. A few lived by a stern code of honor outmoded elsewhere, others were better administrators than the British, some cultivated charming eccentricities, one or two indulged in luxuries and depravities remarkable in their ingenuity. Decadent or chivalrous, they were all colorful. Without them the British would not have won India and quite possibly might not have kept it for as long as they did.

The full and true history of the princes of India, if it can ever be written, will need a Gibbon and a series of volumes. The princes were numbered in hundreds, their roots stretched back a thousand years, their labyrinthine genealogies were kept only in the memories of Brahmin priests, their early records were either oral or unintelligible. The more intimate records of recent times were burned when the British transferred power to the new governments of India and Pakistan. In those flames disappeared much of the official record of some of the famous, and least reputable, episodes in the lives of the maharajahs: the Maharajah of Indore and the murder of the Mumtaz Begum's lover, the atrocities perpetrated by the Maharajah of Alwar, the blackmail case involving the Maharajah of Kashmir. Other records have been dispersed and in some cases altered. Nevertheless, enough remains in the archives of the India Office Library and in the accounts of former officers of the Indian Civil Service to piece together the better-known stories.

Though it was the princes exclusively who gave to India during modern times its peculiar magnificence, little was generally known about them. Even a British Cabinet mission arriving in Delhi in 1946 was not aware that the princes between them ruled one third of the subcontinent. There have been many misapprehensions about the maharajahs. Not all their wealth came from oppressing the poor; not all were decadent or tyrannous. The problems of India's proletariat lay far deeper than the personal extravagance of the princes. The princes have gone; the problems remain. During the time of the raj many of the British referred to the realms of the princes as "the real India." India meant splendor, glamour, wealth. The famine, the poverty, the desperate struggle of a vast people to become their own masters —that was another India.

J. L.

Acknowledgments

I MUST record my thanks to Miss Jan Aaron for guiding me on the road to the princes' India, and to Mrs. Bina Krishnamurti and Mrs. Vimala Sondhi of the India Government Tourist Office in New York for keeping me on it. Mrs. Gita Mehta was illuminating and helpful in London and New Delhi, and I thank her. I am in debt to Mr. Martin Moir, who first revealed to me the fabulous treasures of the India Office Library in London. As always, Mr. Robert D. Loomis of Random House has exercised an editorial judgment that brings light out of darkness; above all, to him I owe the idea of this book.

Contents

The Maharajahs

Prologue

◆《◆《◆《◆《◆《◆《◆《◆《◆《◆

The Mountain of Light

THE DIAMOND on the maharajah's arm was the size of a
hen's egg, and the fires within it winked with a cold, malevolent
light. It was a heavy oval, rose-cut, of the purest water, and of
a value once assessed as equal to all the revenues of India. It had
come to the Maharajah of the Punjab through a sea of blood.
Several of its princely owners had been blinded by brothers,
fathers or other competitors; one had died with a plaster crown
rammed on his head and filled with boiling oil, others more
mercifully under jealous knives. Found in a time beyond memory, it was first recorded in the possession of a king of Malwa
who, besieged by the Sultan of Delhi in 1306, had made a golden
replica of himself and sent it with a gold chain of submission to
the sultan's commanders with a message. "If precious stones,
gems and pearls are demanded," he promised, "I have a stock of
them such as the eyes of the mountains have not seen and the
ears of the fish have not heard. All of these will be scattered in
the path of the Imperial Officers." Among the tribute was the

biggest diamond in the world, the Koh-i-noor, the Mountain of Light.

A succession of Mogul emperors toyed with it. Nadir Shah of Persia carried it away from the sack of Delhi in 1739 with such a weight of loot, including the Peacock Throne, that the people of Persia were exempt from all taxes for three years. Nadir Shah went mad and was assassinated by his own body-guard. The huge stone tumbled glittering through the hands of several successors and aspirants until an Afghan king caught it and took it to Kabul. The king's grandson was blinded by a usurping brother, but before darkness fell on him, hid the dia-mond in the plaster wall of his cell. Because of his affliction he could not afterward retrieve it, but his jailer did so when it scratched his arm and gave it to another brother. This was Shah Shuja, erstwhile King of Afghanistan, from whose grasp it was prized in 1813 by Ranjit Singh, Maharajah of the Punjab. The maharajah wore the Koh-i-noor in a bracelet around his right bicep, set between two less significant diamonds about the size of pecans. There he was able to see it, for his left eye was a milky blank from smallpox. In repose Ranjit Singh was less than regal. Only five feet three inches tall, he seemed wasted; his arms and legs were thin, his left side was limp from paralysis and his skin was an unhealthy gray. He would hold the hand of a guest for half an hour at a time, squeezing it as if for reas-surance. But the diamond spoke of his power.

Bringing good luck to women but disaster to men, the Koh-i-noor was a symbol of sovereignty, and as the Maharajah Ranjit Singh well knew, of the danger that smoldered within the crown. He was not afraid. He had tasted his first battle in 1790 at the age of ten when his father, grown timorous during a winter siege, had anointed him his successor with a smear of saffron paste on his forehead. So busy was Ranjit Singh setting an ambush that he was barely in time for his father's funeral. Three years later he was ambushed himself, but his horse reared just as his adversary cut at him. The boy cantered home with a bloody head jammed on the point of his lance, a slightly belated celebration of his thirteenth birthday. Six years after that he captured the capital city of Lahore, and two years later, when he reached twenty-one, he was acclaimed Maharajah of the Punjab. Under him, this land of the Five Rivers became the strongest native state in India. It was entirely Ranjit Singh's creation.

The Punjab was a narrow triangle wedging through northern India with its base on the Himalayas and its apex pointing southwest. Its sides, when Ranjit Singh had finished extending his frontiers, were the Indus River in the north and the Sutlej in the south. These, with three other rivers, striped the Punjab with green, but the greater part was arid plain sown with coarse, persistent grasses and dry jungles of tamarisk and prickly bushes. Its only hills were bare red rocks glistening with salt leached out by the late-summer rains. The sun beat this dun landscape into a mirror of mirage. Heat filled the air so that the skin tightened and the eyes ached at the pressure. Before the monsoon, dust storms beat the land, towering black, yellow, red or brown from earth to sky, hissing and howling and dousing the light with a choking amber gloom. The rains hissed too, when they came, and drenched the unwary rider in a shining icy sheet.

Master of this land of extremes, the size of Kansas, the Maharajah Ranjit Singh took his ease in the Shalimar Gardens of Lahore among orange groves and pomegranates the color of wine, lulled by the plash and ripple of three hundred fountains, a silver mist against the white marble of his cool pavilions. It amused the maharajah in his later years to scatter clouds of gold upon his guests. He would signal to his dancing girls, pale Kashmiris with liquid eyes underscored with gold leaf, and they, giggling, would scoop up handfuls of bright powder, whirl away in billows of silken gauze and fill the air with motes. Sometimes the maharajah himself would fling a shimmering haze toward his intimates so that hair, skin, clothes and food caught the sheen and all became like gods, golden. His cups and decanters, the table on which they were set, his bed and the chair beside it were of solid gold. Plates of it chased with lotus shapes were nailed to the barrel throne where Ranjit Singh squatted on cushions of crimson velvet. The stud ropes of his favorite gray mare were of soft twisted gold, and her saddle and crupper both gleamed yellow. His body servants protected their beards with tissues of gold filaments and threw shawls of the same fabulous weave around their shoulders. When going to war, the maharajah covered his arms with gold bracelets, which he flung on the battlefield to deserving warriors. In peace he busied himself with pious acts, gilding the great dome of his people's shrine at Amritsar, the Pool of Nectar, so that it shone like a captive sun.

Gold seemed the natural ambience of this great prince. His enemies whispered that the years had turned him to avarice, the old man's vice. But Ranjit Singh was a man of multifarious vices, each more colorful than greed, and many virtues. He loved drink, jewels, horses, heavy cannon, women and lithe boys, but he lived for the exercise of power and used it superbly. He had unified the feuding clans among his people, the Sikhs, by guile and by the sword. He outfaced his former overlords, the Afghans, drove them back northward to the Khyber and set his border in their foothills. Learning from the successive victories of the British creeping up from the south, he hired French, Italian, English and American freebooters to drill his troops like regulars. He watched over the forging of his cannon with the devotion of a father and maintained a homeopathic doctor from Hungary to mix his gunpowder. This gentle healer also prepared a special potion that supported the maharajah in his later years, a draft of hard spirit doctored with herbs and ground pearls, opium, a touch of musk and orange essence, and the juices squeezed from any fresh raw meat but beef. Thus fortified, Ranjit Singh settled down to enjoy the fruits of thirty years of campaigning and intrigue. He could neither read nor write and his only means of calculation was a notched stick, but for his cruel times he was an enlightened ruler. He was the first and last resort of justice over eighty thousand square miles. Averse to shedding blood except in war, he punished theft and simple murder with fines. Offenses of a more baroque nature merited the amputation of a nose, an ear or a hand. Those incorrigible criminals whose complete withdrawal would benefit society at large were hamstrung.*

Since the majority of the Punjabis were Hindu converts to Islam, the maharajah was forced by circumstance if not by inclination to tolerate their institutions, which gratified them. They were farmers for the most part, eaters of wheat and drinkers of milk, big, hard men who could put a lot of weight behind a sword swing.

Comprising about one tenth of the total population, Ranjit Singh's own people, the Sikhs, came from the same stock but practiced a different religion. Sikhism was as different from Hinduism as Lutheranism was from the Church of Rome. The Sikhs deplored idolatry, hypocrisy, female infanticide and slander, and prohibited the use of wine and tobacco. To them, loyalty, justice, honesty, gratitude and philanthropy were supreme virtues, and they preached the sanctity of domestic bliss. Ranjit Singh's pronounced sins of the flesh prevented his becoming an object of devotion to the more orthodox Sikhs, but his saving acts of beneficence and his military genius made him popular with the general congregation. A Sikh was not born; he was baptized in water stirred with a dagger and made to bite from a wheaten cake passed indiscriminately from hand to hand to obliterate

---

* Some of Ranjit Singh's lieutenants favored a more Draconian approach to law and order. His Governor of Peshawar, Paolo de Avitabile, a six-foot Neapolitan, hanged fifty brigands and murderers a day when he first took over the city. After some days only liars and rumormongers were left: these had their tongues cut out. Then a surgeon appeared who claimed to be able to restore their speech. "I sent for him," Avitabile recalled, "and cut out his tongue also. After that there was peace, and in six months there was no crime in Peshawar."

Avitabile leased the more troublesome border areas to subordinates at rents paid in varying numbers of Afghan heads. He practiced impalement, flaying alive and the cliché of blowing men from guns. For variety he would daub a malefactor with honey and spread-eagle him on an ant hill, or strap him between two planks and saw him in half. His bedroom walls were covered with paintings of his "guardian angels," naked nautch girls. He made money on the side selling watches, artificial jewelry, musical boxes and obscene pictures. All who met him remarked on his cheerfulness and sense of fun. He retired to Italy, married a young wife, was cuckolded and shortly died, rather mysteriously.

caste. Five distinctions were ordained for him: he must not cut his hair (the hair piled atop the head deflected sword strokes) or beard, he must wear short drawers (for speed in attack) and an iron bangle on his right wrist (for virility), and he must carry an inseparable dagger (to strike down enemies of his faith). He emerged a member of the Khalsa—the Pure—and thereafter used the name Singh, meaning "lion."

The Lion of the Punjab, Ranjit Singh, commanded an army of forty thousand of these husky true believers, supported by a formidable weight of artillery. The force also included a few thousand fanatics called Akalis, about whom Ranjit Singh's feelings were ambivalent. One of them had tried to kill him. They were nicknamed Nihangs ("crocodiles") by their saner compatriots: they wore nothing but blue and their gigantic turbans were circled by steel quoits sharpened at the edge which they threw like whistling razors. Their original function had been to guard the temple of Amritsar, a place so holy that it was swept only with brooms made of sacred peacock feathers. Their consumption of hashish was conspicuous, and their savagery and reckless valor such that Ranjit Singh, while deploring fanaticism, gingerly deployed them against similar enthusiasts of other faiths.

Ranjit Singh loved his army. He was always ready for the field; he preferred to sleep in a tent on a campaign bed with his weapons handy and a horse saddled outside day and night. He had a string of these chargers, one dangling necklaces of emeralds and flaunting two stones on its saddlebow so big that they were framed like mirrors, another decked in diamonds and turquoises, a third rosy with coral and pearls. It was the maharajah's pleasure to ride out in the dews of early morning to watch maneuvers or artillery practice, with his round black shield slung over his shoulder and a heavy saber slapping his horse's flank. He had the thick neck and heavy shoulders of a cavalryman, and a quick, rough tongue for faults he spotted with his one rolling eye. He would stay in the saddle all day, under the beat of the sun or in driving rain. His devotion kept the army sharp even after the old enemies were vanquished, for one threat remained.

The British, for their part, considered Ranjit Singh a threat. But, being realists, they also saw him as an ally. Over the years they had sent him emissaries, one with five dray horses all the way from England, another with a selection of port, claret, hock, champagne and whiskey. Ranjit Singh ignored everything but the whiskey and went back to his own devil's brew, waiting for the British to show their hand. It was not a strong one, for its trump card was that same Shah Shuja of Afghanistan from whom Ranjit Singh had wrung the Koh-i-noor.

Shah Shuja was the last of his dynasty and there was that in his expression, as a contemporary put it, which "would betray to a skillful physiognomist that mixture of timidity and duplicity so often observable in the character of the highest order of men in southern Asia." By 1812 this unfortunate cipher had lost the Afghan throne and was a prisoner in Kashmir, whence Ranjit Singh rescued him, having been promised the Koh-i-noor by Shah Shuja's wife in return for her husband.

Shah Shuja was welcomed with pomp into Lahore one morning early in 1813 and settled in a small palace. But the Koh-i-noor was not at once forthcoming. A request for delivery was ignored on the following day. The maharajah reminded Shah Shuja's lady of her husband's price. Unfortunately, she said, dissimulating, the stone had been put in pawn with a moneylender in Kandahar, which was a long way off. Ranjit Singh controlled his anger and offered a token payment of one hundred and fifty thousand dollars and properties worth twenty-five thousand dollars a year. There was no response. Dropping subtlety, the maharajah marched four thousand troops into Shah Shuja's palace in the guise of guards, and twenty torchbearers to keep the reunited couple awake all night. Then he cut off food and drink for two days. Shah Shuja took the hint and indicated that negotiations might begin.

In summer mood Ranjit Singh galloped to the Shah's lodgings with six hundred Sikh horsemen. Shuja embraced him without much affection and led him to the royal audience chamber. The two princes sat at either end of a carpet, the one dark-faced, plump and uncertain, the other wrinkled and vital. Shah Shuja's beard was a deep-dyed black, while Ranjit Singh's was a thin, straggling white but there was no doubt which was the more aggressive. Each inquired politely after the other's health. There was a long silence until the maharajah reminded the shah of the business of the day. At a sad nod from Shuja a servant placed a roll of cloth in the center of the carpet. Fixing his good right eye on Shuja, the Lion of the Punjab once more inquired the price. "Its price," Shuja muttered, "is a heavy stick. My forefathers obtained it by this means: You have obtained it from me by many blows; after you a stronger power will appear and deprive you of it, using similar means." In this prediction Shah Shuja was inaccurate, though at last the stone was taken by force from Ranjit Singh's descendants.

Ranjit Singh wore the diamond for some years as an armlet, transferred it to his turban, then in a fit of boredom fixed it to his horse's harness and finally reset it to be worn once more on his arm. There its incomparable light dazzled Lord Auckland, Governor-General of India, when he came to the Punjab in 1838 to discuss with the Maharajah Ranjit Singh the last details of their scheme to launch Shah Shuja like a damp rocket into Kabul.*

Ranjit Singh's officers provided the visitors, who were numerous, with four thousand chickens and fifteen thousand eggs a day and gathered over eight hundred tons of wheat and nearly thirty tons of wine for the camp at large besides, in a last luxurious gesture, inviting every competent courtesan in the Punjab

---

* The British plan was to invade Afghanistan with the help of Ranjit Singh and his Sikhs, install Shah Shuja as a puppet on the throne in Kabul and thereby forestall its imminent occupation by Russia. Lord Auckland, a gentle Whig whose training in the law had given him a taste for drudgery but no capacity for imaginative leaps, was unable to discern the innate stupidity of the idea. Its instigator, the Political Secretary to the Government of India, disintegrated utterly in Kabul; his head and limbs were carried in carnival through the city while his trunk swung on a meathook in the bazaar. The British army of four and a half thousand men was annihilated among the black gorges of its escape route. Wisely, the Sikhs had not been present.

to grace the festivities. Lord Auckland was accompanied by his maiden sisters, Emily and Fanny. Miss Emily had been busy with an oil painting of the new Queen, Victoria, in her coronation robes (on whose bosom the great diamond on Ranjit Singh's good arm was eventually to settle), copied from a newspaper picture. Lord Auckland presented the portrait to the Lion of the Punjab set in a solid-gold frame picked out with diamonds and shells, together with an elephant in gold harness, an assortment of jewels and shawls, a string of horses and, best of all, two brass nine-pounder howitzers, each with Ranjit Singh's features embossed on its barrel, with two hundred shells. Lord Auckland received from Ranjit Singh a couple of blue Kashmir shawls so fine that they could be drawn through a wedding ring, and a solid-gold bed encrusted with rubies and emeralds.

In pride the maharajah paraded his army one crisp morning. The Governor-General rode the two and a half miles to the reviewing ground through an avenue of men in uniforms of yellow satin or gold brocade patterned in scarlet or purple. The sun glanced off collars of precious stones, coats of mail under silken tunics, shields and lances trimmed with gold, and off sharp, bright steel. Ranjit Singh's whimsical bodyguard of amazons curvetted around him on spirited Arabs, delicious girls all in daffodil silk and turbans worn aslant, like cupids armed with bows and arrows. Far off on the plain, Miss Emily sighted what seemed a long white wall capped with red tile. It was in fact a line of soldiers four and a half miles long, thirty thousand of the maharajah's infantry with the heaviest artillery in India.

Business over, Ranjit Singh threw a party in his city of deep-red tents. The moonlight, which drove Ranjit Singh into such rapture that he often honored it with a salute of guns, was shot with leaping fires. Rockets rushed and cracked in showers of green and gold, tourbillions spiraled for the stars like worms of flame. Tubs of Bengal fire, red and garish blue, pinwheels, maroons, candles popping multicolored fizzing orbs, vesuvian jets of gold sparks sent light glowing and cascading in a rolling cloud of smoke thunderous with gunpowder. Through the billows, not unimpressed, Lord Auckland and Fanny (Emily, wishing to conserve her strength, having retired) came to the maharajah's tent of audience. They found him in faded scarlet silk, cross-legged on a gold chair on a gold brocade carpet of ceremony, one stocking off to massage a rheumatic foot. Nautch girls swayed in tight trousers of silk, their hands and feet atwinkle with mirror rings, to the sound of flutes and drums. Buffoons pranced in bawdy antics fortunately not clear to Miss Fanny. The Sikh nobility crowded laughing around them, bearded and splendid in velvet and jewels, one in a breastplate of gold fleurs-de-lys given him by the hateful French. Miss Fanny was allowed to play with the Koh-i-noor and then with a necklace of impossible emeralds, whispering later to Emily that she hoped the maharajah had come by them honestly. She tried the maharajah's special liquor and it burned her lips, but being seated on His Highness' blind side, she was able to dispose of it under her chair. Impressed by her capacity, Ranjit Singh thereafter kept her goblet filled himself with what Lord Auckland's military secretary called "this abominable liquid fire." Nor was the food more cooling: meatballs spiked with pepper, and fat quail crammed with pungent spices relieved only by mounds of greasy sweetmeats and an occasional sticky pear.

It was said that the entertainment of Lord Auckland was the death of Ranjit Singh. He had already suffered two heart attacks. By the time Lord Auckland's caravan left after a month of debauches, Ranjit Singh lay dying of a third. On June 27, 1839, the Lion of the Punjab reached his end. His doctors, astrologers and his three gurus could find no remedy. He had swallowed compounds of powdered gems, he had donated two hundred tons of cooking fat to religious institutions and distributed five million dollars in coin to the common people, and he had been restrained with difficulty from giving away the Koh-i-noor to a temple. On a dais, raised like some sacrifice, he lay exposed to all and died in utter silence. He was carried on a golden bier shaped like a ship to the burning ground and stretched atop a six-foot pile of sandalwood logs soaked in sweet-smelling oil. Four of his wives climbed up beside his head and seven young concubines beside his feet. Reed mats were thrown over them and drenched with oil. Following the Hindu custom, Ranjit Singh's eldest son set a torch to the dripping, fragrant pyre which sent flame leaping twenty feet into the afternoon air. A blue pigeon flying overhead was caught in the whiplash of fire and instantly consumed. Then, when the moment came, the son tapped his father's skull so that the heat burst it and released his soul.

Ranjit Singh's legacy was the most powerful native army in India, a hundred camel loads of treasure, and anarchy. A holocaust of plots, poison and knives by night devoured his older sons and left a two-year-old boy, Dhuleep Singh, on the throne. The splendid Sikh army fought the Chinese in Tibet, then grew restless in the vacuum of power, threw up its own conspiracies and in December 1845 challenged the British. It was defeated in four battles within a month, but by no means crushed. The soviets that ruled the army (called *panchayats*, councils of five) muttered among themselves and two years later tried again. The Second Sikh War was a bloodletting on both sides. The British were outgunned and hampered by a commander in chief whose only tactic was frontal assault whatever the enemy's dispositions. He was popular with his troops, however, because in battle he affected a conspicuous white coat. The Sikhs had no fear of the foreigners; they said that when a British soldier was overcome he would put blades of grass in his mouth and cry, "Don't kill me! I am a cow—look, I eat grass!" The two major battles that decided the campaign in the white men's favor were the last fought in the fashion and uniform of Waterloo. The British came on shoulder to shoulder, dressed on their markers in rigid line, Indian and European battalions alike in scarlet coats, white crossbelts, tall shakos and white trousers. At Chillianwalla, when nightfall came and the fighting paused, the British commanders stopped the collection of their dead from the field because there were so many lolling from the camels and because each bore a hideous grin. The Sikhs had slashed across every dead mouth.

The new Governor-General of India, Lord Dalhousie, was an iron man with iron aides. On March 29, 1849, he annexed the Punjab to British India without bothering to seek approval from

London. His orders to the Sikhs were simple. Their army must be broken up, the twelve-year-old Maharajah Dhuleep Singh must abdicate and the proud country Ranjit Singh had carved out must submit to direct British rule by a white Council of Three. Moreover, the Koh-i-noor must be presented voluntarily as a gesture of good will to Her Britannic Majesty, Victoria. The boy Dhuleep Singh stepped down and came under the guardianship of Dr. John Login, surgeon in the Bengal army, and the Mountain of Light was handed for safekeeping to John Lawrence, the most responsible member of the Council of Three. Lawrence promptly forgot about it.

Queen Victoria did not. Six weeks later Lawrence was sitting in conference when a letter from the Governor-General arrived. In tones rather warmer than Lord Dalhousie's customary style, it reported that Her Majesty had been making inquiry of the whereabouts of her present. Lawrence's two peers stared at him. He stared blankly back. Suddenly he remembered. Taking care to hide his confusion, he excused himself and sauntered to his house. He recalled having dropped the Koh-i-noor in its cloth wrapping into a vest pocket. His body servant saved him. The old man had kept the package in a strongbox, so when Lawrence asked for it with a hint of agitation, he was able to deliver it at once, though what the fuss was about he could not imagine. "Open it!" Lawrence ordered. The old man unwrapped the cloth. "Sahib," he said, looking up, "there is nothing here but a bit of glass."

Carried to England by two stout British officers in the good ship *Medea*, the Koh-i-noor was presented to the Queen at a levee in St. James's Palace. Her Majesty expressed herself much gratified. Her more esthetic Consort felt, however, that the stone wanted refinement. A master diamond cutter was imported from Amsterdam and set up with all his requirements, including a four-horsepower engine, in Buckingham Palace itself. The Prince Consort adjusted the diamond, the grand old Duke of Wellington turned the wheel, and the world waited. Thirty-eight days later the Dutchman presented his work. The huge stone had been reduced from 187 to just over 109 carats without much enhancement of its appearance. The Prince Consort was not amused. He paid the cutting fee of forty thousand dollars and dropped the diminished Mountain of Light into a little box in Windsor Castle. From time to time it emerged to lend sparkle to the already impressive frontage of the Queen.

Queen Victoria was careful, however, not to wear it in the presence of young Dhuleep Singh, now seventeen and living in London on a pension of two hundred thousand dollars a year, and very much under her wing. Being a beautiful youth and having embraced Christianity, Dhuleep Singh was the very model of a deposed maharajah. He struck pangs in the sensitive hearts of Victoria's courtiers whenever he visited Buckingham Palace to sit for his portrait by the fashionable Winterhalter. One day the Queen asked his guardian if Dhuleep Singh ever regretted the loss of the Koh-i-noor, admitting that she felt "a certain delicacy" about wearing it when he was in the palace. Reassured that the maharajah had taken great interest in the recutting and would not be offended if the subject were raised, the Queen slipped the gem into the young man's hand during a sitting and asked whether he would have recognized it. Dhuleep Singh walked to a window and gazed at the jewel for a quarter of an hour without speaking. Even under the gray sky of England the Mountain of Light burned with an imperial fire. Bowing low, Dhuleep Singh at last returned it to Her Majesty, expressing his sense of pleasure at being able to place it in her hands. In private, Dhuleep Singh afterward referred to Her Majesty as "Mrs. Fagin." "She's really a receiver of stolen property," he would say. "She has no more right to that diamond than I have to Windsor Castle."

Dhuleep Singh's affection for the British was not immediately put to further test. In 1857 he gave his somewhat vicarious support to the British during the Indian Mutiny, the insurrection of the Bengal army. The British were grateful, for without the Sikh soldiery on their side they might well have been bundled out of India altogether. He was rewarded with the Star of India from Her Majesty's own hands.

In 1864 Dhuleep Singh married a German girl whose face had

fixed his attention while he was distributing prizes at a school in Alexandria. Their firstborn, Victor, became the Queen's godson. With a loan of nearly seven hundred thousand dollars from the Indian government, Dhuleep Singh bought an estate on the border of Norfolk and Suffolk, fine partridge country, and rebuilt its Georgian mansion at a cost of more than a hundred and fifty thousand dollars, including forty thousand for furniture. Four years of work on the house resulted in a golden dome and interiors in the Indian style. Here Dhuleep Singh entertained royalty to royal battues. He was the fourth-best shot in England, with an impressive technique. He fired sitting on a mat and whirling like a dervish. He made some reputation as a local antiquarian, and as a Christian gentleman owning land he supported the village church.

Buried in country matters, Dhuleep Singh might have spent the rest of his life in obscurity. But there was an oriental heat in his blood. There was a lady in London, a patrician blonde to whom he was so devoted that he required her to telegraph him in the country twice a day. She drank brandy and soda at her breakfasts with other gentlemen and had been a chambermaid in a hotel in Knightsbridge. In Paris there was another little friend whose conquests included, concurrently, Georges Clemenceau and the Duc d'Aumale, a catholic selection. All three liaisons languished when the lady acquired a handsome young hairdresser.

The expenses of Dhuleep Singh's life style led him into difficulties. When he could not persuade the Indian government to increase his allowance, he went so far as to write to *The Times* claiming that at the time of the annexation of the Punjab many of his personal possessions had been sold to pay prize money to the British army, and asserting his right to income from mines as well as other sources and, of course, to possession of the Koh-i-noor, or what was left of it. The maharajah's demands were rejected. Hoping to rally the Sikhs to his cause, Dhuleep Singh issued a proclamation to them and sailed for India. When his ship put in at Aden to coal, an officer of the Indian government was standing on the quay; he had orders to restrain the maharajah from proceeding to Bombay. Dhuleep Singh waited there in Aden in case the government of India chose to relent. It did not. But when he announced his intention of abjuring Christianity and returning to Sikhism, the government allowed some relatives from the Punjab to attend the ceremony in the Residency at Aden. In the end the iron faith of his forefathers could not prevail against the molten sun of Aden and his feeling of betrayal, and Dhuleep Singh's health broke.

Wandering through Europe, refusing to accept his pension from the British, Dhuleep Singh fetched up in Russia. Wanly he tried to persuade the Tsar to sweep over the Himalayas and restore him to his lost throne. He made less impression on the Russians than on the British, who were incensed. His wife died, it was said, of embarrassment and sorrow. In March 1891 Queen Victoria was vacationing at Grasse; Dhuleep Singh drove there one afternoon from his villa in Nice. The two were quite alone when the maharajah quietly began to ask Her Majesty's forgiveness, then, the years flooding back, he burst into tears and begged her favor. Never one to scoff at genuine sentiment, the old lady stroked his hand in her two plump ones and soothed him into stillness. Reinstalled to official grace, and reimbursed, Dhuleep Singh remained in the popular imagination, as the expression had it, a monster of the deepest dye. He died in respectability and luxury in the Hôtel de la Trémouille in Paris at the age of fifty-six. "The last thing the world heard of him," an obituary notice recorded, "was that he had, on the death of the Maharani, taken unto himself an English wife."

*   *   *

The fame of Ranjit Singh, last of the great independent maharajahs of India, now whispers only from a crumbling mausoleum on a dusty, once-heroic plain and is lost in distance. His throne, encapsulated in the Victoria and Albert Museum in London, seems no more than an ornate tub. Dhuleep Singh's antiquarian collection of portraits of Norfolk and Suffolk worthies survives in the Council Offices of the quiet town of Thetford, and his church is now best known for its memorial window dedicated to the men of the United States Army Air Force stationed there during the Second World War.*

The light of princes quickly fades. Diamonds, as a mistress of Louis XIV once remarked, are as durable as the sun. The Koh-i-noor passed down the line of England's queens from Victoria to Alexandra to Mary to Elizabeth, consort of George VI. It still sits in her crown, free of its ancient taint of menace, a footnote for explanatory beefeaters, amid the rest of the crown jewels in that stage set of a castle, the Tower of London. On the eve of the coronation of the present Queen it was dragged momentarily out of history. Mr. Lal Kureel, M.A., LL.B., a member of the Indian Parliament, chose to ask whether the government of India proposed to recover the diamond and the other art treasures and rarities looted by the British. Supporters rushed to Mr. Kureel's side, the government was embarrassed, and the British press, looking forward to an orgy of coronation sentiment, was briefly diverted into anger toward the Indians for their ill-timed piece of bad taste. A minister of the government of India tactfully revealed that the government had for some time been considering the compilation of a list of all the art treasures, antiques and rarities lost to India, but at no time had considered asking for the return of the Koh-i-noor because it was not an art object. The controversy lost impetus when the *Daily Express* tartly pointed out that if the Mountain of Light belonged anywhere outside London, its rightful home would be Lahore and that Lahore was now, of course, in Pakistan.

---

* Dhuleep Singh's shade also survived, thinly, until the end of 1970 on a menu in the Charles French Restaurant on the edge of Greenwich Village in New York. His portrait supervised one of the restaurant's five Grand Presentation Dinners, offered at $9.95 including champagne. There was a brief and inaccurate biography of him.

1

The Shadow of God

SOMEWHERE TOWARD the sunrise there was a land called
India. To the active, aggressive men of the Renaissance in Europe
it was as remote as the moon and existed, like the moon, chiefly
as a symbol. But India also presented to the collective mind of
that time much the same sort of challenge as would the moon
itself to a later generation. Herodotus had told strange, twisted
tales of it two thousand years before; two hundred years before,
Marco Polo had heard echoes across its border as he rode out of
China, and repeated them in Venice. Yet India herself remained
silent, her truths a matter of speculation and surmise. As the
Renaissance reached its peak and the hunger for knowledge
gnawed at the brains and guts of Europe, the quest for India
began. At the end of the fifteenth century Columbus sailed
toward the myth to make it real, and in 1497 Vasco da Gama
actually found the sea route to it around Africa and landed on
its western coast. Then the adventurers of Elizabethan England
at last took fire. For them India was the stuff of poetry, its

images flashing in their plays and limpid verses, mysterious, stupendous and infinitely distant. They determined to go there, partly to sack its riches, but also to satisfy a deeper appetite, to test the range of their imaginations against the facts.

It was a land of wonders. Its fabulous reefs bore rubies as big as pigeons' eggs, and emeralds, and oysters crept up its shores by night opening to the marvelous dews of its soft heavens and thus conceiving pearls. Mariners pressing eastward watched the dawn rise brighter daily as the sun's light reflected off the gold they believed was broadcast over its deserts. The only diamonds in the world were gathered in its mountains. Pepper, ginger, indigo, cinnamon and that precious medicine sugar grew there in profusion. Aromatic woods and the cured hides of unicorns and elephant's teeth were available for trade. It was a land of hyperbole. Its rats were as big as foxes, and exceedingly venomous. Its trees were extraordinary: some breathed so deadly an exhalation that travelers sleeping under them succumbed at once; one sprouted its fruit straight out from the trunk like russet bags of cold pudding tinged with rose water; the prodigious leaf of another was big enough to shelter half a dozen men from rain or heat and yet was as delicate as writing paper. There was a paradisal bird that flew always toward the sun, and being legless, never touched the ground, the male carrying the eggs in a hollow in his back, where the female hatched them. There was a wild ox which would stand stock-still if its tail were caught in a bush, "horribly vexed at losing a single hair"; thus the natives could cut off the tail and use it to decorate their horses and to swat flies. There were sheep with tails so luxuriously fat that they had to drag them on little carts behind them. It was a land dripping riches. There was an emperor who wore a priceless suit fashioned from the skins of a thousand salamanders whose wool, as was well known, extinguished fire and was called *asbestos* by the Greeks. The chamberlain of a king of Bengal became rich merely by recovering the camphor his master spat into the royal cuspidor. Some princes of the Indies were fed on poison from infancy to give them immunity from usurpers, so that flies biting them dropped dead on the spot.*

It was a land of bizarre dangers. The warm keels sliding for Cambay and Coromandel, Bengal the haunt of tigers and Malabar passed over sea snakes writhing like brown zones of weed in the ocean deeps. Monsters guarded the treasures of the land: manticores with a red-eyed human face, the body of a lion and a tail that shot a mortal sting, and dragons impervious breathing fire, and amphisbaenae—serpents with one head in front and one behind that rolled along like hoops, one head clasping the other. Semihuman species sought to plunder the land: men whose heads erupted below their shoulders, others with cyclopean eyes staring from their chests. The gold of its deserts was thrown up by burrowing ants, malevolent, nearly the size of dogs. Warlike tribesmen foraged after the gold, each man with one female camel and two male, descending at noon when the fierce heat had driven the ants underground, loading their she-camels with sacks of golden sand and rushing away with the ants in pursuit. The slower male camels fell prey to the ants.†

The country's diamonds were no less hard to come by. Serpents protected them, so the ingenious natives rolled hunks of blood-soaked meat down the mountainside to absorb the gems. White eagles, enemies of the serpents, seized the meat and bore it up to the plateau. By driving off the eagles the prospectors could collect the diamonds.

It was a land of unlimited possibilities. Knowing almost nothing of it for fact, except that it was ruled by the Great Mogul, that the Portuguese had gained a lodgment on its shores, and that riches proliferated there, some Elizabethan merchants

* Prompting Samuel Butler to the dubious couplets:
> The Prince of Cambay's daily food
> Is asp and basilisk and toad,
> Which makes him have so strong a breath
> Each night he stinks a queen to death.

† There were reports of the Shah of Persia presenting some of these spectacular ants as a curiosity to the Grand Turk. Later scholars identified the "ants" as pangolins, or scaly anteaters. Later still, by a piece of etymological clarification, the "ants" turned out to be Tibetan miners.

of London petitioned their red-haired queen to grant them a charter to adventure that far east. That she did on the last day of the sixteenth century "by the name of the Governor and Company of Merchants of London trading into the East Indies." There were one hundred and twenty-five shareholders with a capital of seventy-two thousand pounds. The ships in the Company's first two endeavors failed to reach India but made a profit on the way from ambergris and piracy. The third expedition sailed with a blustering wind in March of 1607. There were the *Red Dragon* of 700 tons, the *Hector* of 500 tons and the pinnace *Consent* of 115, the complement amounting to two hundred and eighty men. Seventeen months later *Hector* anchored off the coast of Cambay near the town of Surat, the first English ship ever to do so. It was August 24, 1608.

Hector's captain was one William Hawkins, a sometime trader in the Levant who knew how to shift for himself. His difficulties began when the jealous Portuguese kidnapped some of his men. Stiffly Hawkins protested, pointing out that he was commissioned an emissary from the high and mighty King James of England to the Great Mogul. The Portuguese commander returned a rough answer, as Hawkins reported, insulting his royal master, "terming him King of Fishermen and of an island of no import, and a fart for his commission." Abused by the Mogul officials on the coast but guarded by a hired band of fifty Pathans, Hawkins managed to reach the court of the Mogul Emperor Jehangir at Agra some eight months after his arrival in India. There, somewhat to his surprise, Hawkins found himself confronting the most powerful man in the world.

Jehangir the Mogul was the richest autocrat on earth, ruler of some seventy million, mightier than Charlemagne and at least the equal in power of any emperor since the Caesars. He was the fourth of the Great Moguls whose names—Babur, Humayun, Akbar, Jehangir, Shah Jehan, Aurengzeb—clanged like bronze gongs through the welter of the sixteenth and seventeenth centuries. Unique among dynasties for strength, magnificence and effect, their sway lasted for nearly two centuries. Theirs was the only word that mattered in all of India and they held the

title, among others, of "the Shadow of God." They were conquerors, the most recent of many Muslim waves rolling into
Hindustan from the north and west.

Long before the Moguls, there had been a civilization in the
Indus Valley, which ran through the Punjab. Two and a half
millennia before Christ, the people in the valley used copper,
bronze and gold, built their homes of brick and ran water into
them and sanitation out, wove cotton and wool, turned pottery,
met in vast halls to worship phalluses—and were overwhelmed.
The first known invaders of India were Aryans, charioteers and
cattle grazers, who began to flood the Indus and Ganges plains
of northern India about 1500 B.C. and crowded the dark Dravid-
ians to the south. Aryan and Dravidian mingled through the
centuries, following the way of Hinduism and evolving the system of caste the Aryans had conceived, and eventually produc-
ing the first native dynasty to command the whole subcontinent.
Its climactic king was Asoka, who trampled all his brothers on
his way to the throne and earned the nickname "the Furious."
When he died thirty-three years later, in 232 B.C., he was called
"the Loving-Minded." Part autocrat, part conservationist, part
prophet, Asoka had embraced Buddhism; it changed his life
and the life of India for ever. One of his edicts prohibited the
slaughter, among other creatures, of parrots, bats, queen ants,
twelve-pointer stags, tortoises and porcupines, boneless fish,
household vermin and rhinoceroses. Forests must not be burned
uselessly or in order to kill living things. "The living," he
ordained, "must not be fed with the living." Seventeen centuries
after his death Asoka's lion column became the symbol of a
free and reborn India.

Asoka ruled an area half the size of Australia. The Hindu
kings who followed him began a slow decline, dividing and
separating. From the eleventh century onward they faced the
crusading fires of Islam as successive waves of Muslims swept in,
questing for loot and souls, until in 1206 a sultan established
his rule at Delhi. His line enjoyed a limited rule. It was extinguished by the great Babur, descendant of both Tamerlane and
Genghis Khan, the first general to bring artillery to India and,

with its help, first of the Great Moguls and founder of the second dynasty to rule all India.

Babur had been chieftain of a petty kingdom in Eastern Turkestan, a place he always thought of as a land of milk and honey. "Its melons are excellent and plentiful," he wrote nostalgically. "There are no better pears in the world. Its pheasants are so fat that four persons may dine on one and not finish it. Its violets are particularly elegant, and it abounds in streams of running water. In the spring its tulips and roses blow in rich profusion, and there are mines of turquoises in its mountains, while in the valleys people weave velvet of a crimson color." In adversity Babur's mind often turned to a certain way they had in Ferghana of stuffing apricots with almonds. By comparison Hindustan lacked charm. Babur grumbled in his journal: "Its people have no good looks; of social intercourse, paying and receiving visits, there is none; of genius and capacity none; in handicrafts and work there is no form or symmetry, method or quality; there are no good horses, no good dogs, no grapes, muskmelons or first-rate fruits, no ice or cold water, no good bread or cooked foods in the bazaars, no hot baths, no colleges, no candles or candlesticks." On the other hand, the country was obviously rich in precious metals and offered an inexhaustible labor force. Babur set some of it to work destroying the Hindu idols that offended his Mongol sensibilities by their rather exuberantly sexual attitudes.

Babur had set out for India with the sun auspiciously in the sign of Sagittarius, and it continued to shine on him. He swept away the Afghan overlords of northern India in the spring of 1526, occupied Delhi and Agra, and began the Mogul Empire. Babur's next task was the subjugation of the proud princes of Rajasthan, no simple matter. Since Babur had planned to forswear drink when he reached the age of forty, he felt free to imbibe copiously and joyously in the meantime, ordering a pond twenty feet square to be cut out of solid rock for the keeping of his wine. By the time it was finished he was on the wagon, so it was filled with lemonade. Babur had overshot his target date by five years when the prospect of his final battle with the difficult Rajputs at last drove him to abstinence. He broke his golden goblets before his army and poured his stocks of wine into the dust. Then he won the battle and confirmed his empire.*

Babur's son Humayun lost the empire not long thereafter to an Afghan. Witty, generous and cultivated, Humayun had none of his father's brute vigor and compensated for the weakness of his will by retreating into a haze of opium. Reduced to swimming the Ganges on an inflated goatskin and leading his pregnant wife on a pony through the deserts of Sind, Humayun found refuge in Persia. Shortly before his death he regained the throne of Babur, but one evening in 1556 he slipped in a drugged stupor on the steps of his library after watching the sunset and crashed to extinction. His son Akbar, who had been born in exile fourteen years before, was proclaimed in a quiet garden on a makeshift throne of brick.

Akbar's inheritance was by no means sure. He made it certain on the same battlefield of Panipat that had given northern India to his grandfather Babur. The fight was going badly for the Moguls, outnumbered five to one, but a stray arrow pierced the eye of the enemy general and his troops deserted him. He was brought to Akbar's tent, where the boy struck off his head. Thus freed of competition, Akbar marched into Delhi, Agra and a life of magnificence the kings of Europe could not hope to match. What Babur had originally won, Akbar consolidated and extended southward. For the first thirteen years of his rule, however, it seemed he would have no successor, since all his offspring died in infancy. Akbar undertook pilgrimages but none bore fruit until he found a holy man in Sikri, twenty-three miles from Agra. This Muslim saint promised Akbar that his prayers would be heard and by way of guarantee allowed his own son of six months to be sacrificed. The outcome was Jehangir, the fourth of the Mogul emperors. Thereupon Akbar built a new capital, Fatehpur Sikri, around the site of his bene-

---

* Babur died, as he had lived, generously. His son being mortally sick, Babur offered his own life by walking three times around the bed in earnest prayer and begging, "On me be all thy suffering." The son shortly recovered. Babur was forty-six.

factor's saintly cell. The city was planted on a low ridge and surrounded by seven miles of triple walls, a red metropolis of sandstone. Within the dull-crimson courtyard of its great mosque, Akbar fashioned a little white mausoleum where the saint's sarcophagus lay under a marble canopy luminous inside with the gray and amber of inlaid mother-of-pearl and tortoise shell. From the canopy, as if halfway between earth and heaven, hung ostrich eggs symbolic of purity.

Akbar supervised the construction of the city, which took fifteen years, making the extraordinary figures of his fancy rise in solid stone. One courtyard was laid out as a parcheesi board; Akbar would squat at the center of the cruciform moving lithe girls in the moonlight through the hazards of the dice. Outside the walls a slender tower rose seventy feet over the grave of a favorite elephant; studded with stone tusks like slivered almonds on a candy stick, it culminated in a lantern where Akbar stood to shoot antelope driven past. After he vanquished the west Akbar added a great arch of victory one hundred and seventy-six feet high and titanic, and chiseled on its great curve: "Isa, on whom be peace, said, 'The world is a bridge: pass over it, but build no house upon it. The world endures but an hour: spend it in prayer, who sees the rest? Thy greatest richness is the alms which thou hast given. Know that the world is a mirror where fortune has appeared, then fled: call nothing thine that thine eyes cannot see.' "

Religion had become Akbar's preoccupation. The hall of private audience at Fatehpur Sikri was also a hall of disputation, and it was curiously constructed. Through its center rose a single massive octagonal pillar topped by a hollow capital, a round red vessel floating two stories up from which Akbar peered to scatter justice among the suppliants below. But he had designed the hall with a higher purpose. Four catwalks branched outward from the top of the central shaft to the four corners of the hall, ending in balconies from whose windows could be seen every part of the horizon, as though the thoughts and will of the emperor radiated to the very edge of the sky. To these balconies Akbar drew men of all religions, Muslims of various sects, Brahmins, followers of Zoroaster and Buddha, Jews and Jesuits. There they argued for hours on end, their voices carrying along the narrow catwalks to the secret emperor in his central chalice pondering the whereabouts of truth. They drove him first to distraction and then to conviction. In 1582 Akbar announced a new religion with but one god and with himself as regent on earth and exponent of the divine will. The sun, the planets and fire itself might be reverenced if some embodiment of the deity were needed, but there were to be neither priests nor places of public worship. It was a cult of reason encouraging personal virtue and condemning evil passions. A few of Akbar's more ardent courtiers embraced his synthetic faith, but to orthodox Muslims and Hindus alike it was, of course, anathema and it died with him.

The unusual architecture of the hall of audience afforded Akbar a number of advantages. It placed him out of reach of litigants, it channeled the waves of theology into his central cup and it also allowed him to arrive and disappear unnoticed. So, indeed, did most of the city's construction, for Akbar loved reticence. He had a house of dreams where he often slept alone. He could enter and leave it unseen for the house of his Rajput wife or that of his Turkish wife or for the palace of his concubines, where of an afternoon he would stumble laughing through labyrinths of passages and colonnades in a game of blind man's buff. The ardors of his spiritual quest did not reduce Akbar to any mortifications of the flesh. Five thousand women swarmed through the palaces and courts of his harem, costing him twenty thousand dollars a day for their upkeep.

Akbar's zenana differed from the regular harem only in the cosmopolitan provenance of its occupants: his wives came from as far afield as Constantinople and China and mingled in a heady cocktail of Christian, Buddhist, Muslim, Taoist, Hindu and plain pagan. Otherwise the harem was the secluded other-world of the oriental prince. It was administered by a female major-domo of reliable years answerable only to the emperor and aided by a secretary who kept a log of events within. Each occupant received a regular allowance partly in cash and partly in revenue from lands granted for the time being by the emperor. Naturally, there were also presents as warranted. Armed women guarded the perimeter from the inside, with eunuchs inside and out as auxiliaries. These were ringed by Rajput soldiery, who were prohibited the indiscriminate use of women by their caste. Squadrons of gentlemen-troopers stood ready outside the circle of Rajputs as a final deterrent. The precautions were necessary not only for the preservation of the emperor's nearest and dearest as well as the emperor's own person while in a peculiarly vulnerable position, but also because much treasure was deposited there.

Since they belonged exclusively to one man, the harem ladies enjoyed a certain amount of leisure. There were gardens and terraces for strolling through, pillared chambers and screened verandahs for lounging in, fretted balconies for mooning from, marble baths for soaking in. They could play chess, parcheesi or card games, smoke hookahs, or fly pigeons—Akbar had twenty thousand in his lofts—or kites. And there was always dressing and undressing. Fashion was kaleidoscopic in Akbar's harem but was divided into the two main categories of blouse and trousers for Muslims and bodice and long skirt for Hindus. Styles changed occasionally but only in minor degree, and little more than an ankle was ever visible, though a cleavage here and a midriff there might be more or less exposed. Decorations were lavish, setting off the multicolored silks and muslins and cloth of gold. Noses were pierced for rings; the shapes of flowers, peacocks and the crescent moon dangled from ear lobes; necks, upper arms and wrists were banded with jeweled gold and silver, waists with tinkling belts of bells, and ankles with hollow circlets filled with jingling beads. Pearls gleamed on foreheads, scattered in the hair, or in swags across the breast. Hindu wives stained their parting vermilion, Muslims dipped their fingers and toes in henna. Some glued on artificial eyebrows, some blackened their teeth with special powder, and most of them lined their eyes with collyrium, also handy as a contraceptive. Perfume was everywhere, in the smoke curling from strips of sandalwood, in the oils rubbed into the body before a bath, in the musky pastes smeared on afterward, in the flowers laced into coils of plaited hair, in the rose water sprinkled over shining brocades, in the betel leaf crushed between the lips for redness and sweet scent. Akbar delighted in it.

Akbar's appetites were extensive. He ate only one meal a day, at no fixed time, but he expected at least a hundred dishes within the hour when he called for them. They came to him on plates of Chinese porcelain, which was known to crack asunder in the presence of poison. He loved fruit, and it was brought to him from as far away as Samarkand. He drank fresh sherbets made with ice delivered daily from the northern Punjab, and ate special vegetables and plump waterfowl sent expressly from Kashmir. There was nothing he could not afford: he imported horses from Persia, coral and amber from the coasts of Arabia, European wines and Burmese gems, raw silk, civet, gums and quicksilver, broadcloth from England and brocade from France, ivory and slaves from Africa. The gold for his coinage, the finest in the world for purity and design, came from East Africa through Portuguese middlemen, the biggest piece a square worth a thousand dollars stamped with an admonitory "This coin is for the necessities of those who travel on the road to God." His hunting camp was as large as the London of his day. The Moguls took favorite ladies with them on sporting or warlike occasions in curtained howdahs or in palanquins shrouded in red velvet; the tents of this peripatetic harem and Akbar's purple pavilion alone stretched for nearly a mile. Beyond them the Mogul noblemen pitched their tents in order of rank, and beyond them again sprawled four bazaars. All night a great beacon burned where the emperor lay. Two of these camps were needed, for one was always on the march while the other was pitched.

Akbar hunted all kinds of game with spear and arrow, and even killed a lioness with a single sword stroke, but his favorite exercise was polo, which he loved to play in darkness with balls of smoldering wood so that he could gallop in a trail of sparks. He played fiercely and rewarded thrusters. Every day at noon when not afield, he would watch a couple of bouts of wrestling or boxing, and on Tuesdays he spilled blood, matching gladiators or crazed elephants whose riders were frequently swiped to the ground and trampled. Akbar was not wholly a man of peace: in a war with the Rajputs he put thirty thousand peasants to death for impeding his siege of the stronghold of Chitor, and once, in a flash of fury, he buried a girl alive for smiling at his son in the harem.*

By the standards of the time, however, Akbar was both clement and mild. Certainly his administration was enlightened. He prohibited the killing of female babies (an economical custom), and any marriage to which both bride and groom had not consented; a widow's self-immolation on her husband's funeral pyre was made a matter of choice, as was remarriage; animal sacrifice and trial by ordeal were discouraged. These reforms were not pressed home and later lapsed, but they were the inspiration of a humane and liberal mind. While Akbar preached to thousands in Fatehpur Sikri his doctrine of a universal faith rooted in tolerance, the stakes of bigotry were aflame all over Europe.

Akbar lined his roads with trees and punctuated them with rest houses every sixteenth mile from Agra, each populated by sixteen comfortable ladies and their servants. He made some caravanserais big enough to house a thousand men, at a time when the Queen of England could make a progress to the northern parts of her realm only with difficulty. Above all, he was a synthesizer, a combiner in religion, in social practices and in culture. Fatehpur Sikri, massively arched, pillared and domed in the Mogul style, was also decorated in the Hindu fashion, fantastically carved and brilliantly painted. Though most of Akbar's artists were Persians, they taught Hindus their methods. The emperor made all of them reduce their scale from the size of

---

* This was Anarkali, the Pomegranate Blossom. Akbar's son, Jehangir, raised a cenotaph to her at Lahore, carving on it the ninety-nine names of God and on her sarcophagus the lines:

> Ah, if I could again see the face of
> my beloved
> To the day of judgment I would give
> thanks to my Creator.

After annexing the Punjab in 1849, the British converted the tomb into the church of St. James.

wall frescoes to miniatures and imported the new medium, paper, for them to paint on. He was the first to engage a Rajput prince in the Mogul service, and the first Mogul to realize that he was not only commander of a conquering race but responsible ruler of the more numerous Hindus as well. His liberal policies and catholic tastes did not impoverish him. He died of dysentery at Fatehpur Sikri, which was then deserted forever, leaving behind a billion dollars' worth of coin* and, among his jewels, a couple of ruby prayer strings worth a quarter of a million. After Akbar there were no superlatives.

When Akbar quit one paradise for another, the Mogul Empire was already doomed, for everything depended on an Akbar succeeding an Akbar. His son, Jehangir, lacked the immense energy of mind that individual rule demanded. Moreover, he was too interested in bloody instructions. He tried and executed at speed, devising new forms of capital punishment by dogs, elephants and snakes, and taking pleasure in checking out their efficiency. He once passed in formal procession between lines of stakes as close as a thickset hedge on which he had impaled the rebel followers of one of his sons. The son rode beside him and afterward Jehangir had him blinded.

His favorite sport consisted of throwing a cordon of troops around a block of forest and drawing it tight: the animals caught in the noose were killed, the wild tribesmen sent to Kabul market for barter. His circuses were deadly; he had a Pathan wrestle a lion barehanded, and when the Pathan was killed, sent in ten more. Yet he was a man of refinement who could distinguish which of his painters had completed certain parts of a picture, even if only an eyelash had been contributed. He was also the first Great Mogul of whom there was any reliable report in England.

Jehangir received with evident pleasure the English sea captain who arrived at his court in the spring of 1609. Delighted by Hawkins' ability to speak Turkish, the family language of the

---

* In contemporary terms, Akbar's cash in hand alone was worth three times the value of Mr. Howard Hughes's entire estate.

Moguls, Jehangir made him an officer of his household and selected an Armenian Christian girl from his harem for a wife. But the jealous Portuguese and their Jesuit chaplains intrigued against Hawkins, and unwilling to bend to the soft compromises of the Mogul courtiers trying to smooth things over, Hawkins was at last excluded from the emperor's proximity. He was replaced by a proper ambassador, Sir Thomas Roe, who made Jehangir happy with a gift of two English war mastiffs so fearless that they would attack elephants. The famous walker Thomas Coryatt* witnessed an elephant fight in his palace. "They seem to jostle together like two mountains," he wrote, "and were they not parted in the midst of their fighting with certain fireworks they would exceedingly gore and cruentate one another by their murdering teeth." The impression gained in England from such accounts was of an immensely luxurious, powerful and barbarous tyrant.†

Jehangir contributed little to the continuing dignity of his house and spent his last years an addict in the hands of his wife, under whose name the imperial edicts went forth. Shah Jehan, his son and successor, bankrupted the empire by building the immortal monuments of the Mogul age. The hall of private audience within the Red Fort at Delhi was his, with its ceiling of beaten silver and its walls of precious stones bedded in marble, and so was the Peacock Throne of solid gold. Twelve pillars of emerald supported its canopy, two peacocks with spread tails of sapphire and emerald, and a tree between them dripping diamond and ruby fruit. Shah Jehan was very fond of jewels: he habitually wore ten million dollars' worth and stored or loaned the remaining fifteen million dollars' worth. He loved architecture. His wife Mumtaz Mahal (the Ornament of the

---

* Coryatt was known as "the English Fakir" but he was more like the first peregrinating hippie. *Coryatt's Crudities,* his account of an amble through Europe, was the first travel guide published. He set off from London on foot for India, allowing himself twopence a day for all expenses, which he intended to acquire by begging. The trip from Jerusalem to the Mogul's capital cost him twelve and a half dollars.

† Not all accounts of Mogul splendor were lyrical. A Jesuit traveling through Agra, Delhi and Lahore noted the narrow, smelly streets crowding the palaces. "When you have seen one city," he concluded, "you have seen them all."

Palace) died at the age of thirty-nine after the birth of her four-
teenth child. Every day for the next twenty-two years Shah Jehan
set twenty thousand men to work on her tomb; its brick scaffold-
ing cost twenty-two million dollars and the building itself as
much again, but when it was finished in 1653 it was one of the
wonders of the world. Shah Jehan's chaste miracle, the Taj
Mahal, was the summit of the Mogul style, vast in concept but
finished like a jewel box, yet his Pearl Mosque at Agra rivaled it
with white and pale-blue interior vistas that sent the spirit soaring in rapture. Delhi, Lahore, Kabul, Agra and Kashmir echoed
the hammering of the emperor's stonecutters as his palaces,
mosques and pleasure houses rose. Like all his family, Shah
Jehan was a master gardener. A classic simplicity distinguished
the Mogul garden: square or rectangular overall, it was divided
into eight sections (representing the eight parts of Paradise) or
into seven (signifying the seven planets). Often it was terraced,
with a pavilion for the emperor at the topmost level, and always
it was irrigated by a geometric web of canals, basins, shallow
waterfalls and fountains to bring life to its fruit trees, rose bushes
and bedded flowers. Masterpieces like the Shalimar Gardens of
Kashmir inspired not only poets but also the designers of the
magnificent carpets of Persia. Cool and brilliant, they remained
oases in a parched land long after their architects had departed.

Toward the end of his life Shah Jehan was deprived of the
enjoyment of his labors. When he fell ill in 1657, four of his
sons went to war to decide the succession. Within a year
Aurengzeb emerged, took the throne and imprisoned his ailing
parent. With his father immured within sight of the Taj Mahal,
Aurengzeb bound one brother in chains of gold and beheaded
a second. He wrapped up the head and sent it to his father, who
opened the package eagerly, thinking it a present. This was the
first of Aurengzeb's attempts to drive his father into a final
madness. Sporadically for seven years he sent troops to Shah
Jehan's prison to hammer on its walls, loose their muskets and beat
their drums for days and nights on end. Within, Shah Jehan got
drunk, called for a concubine and bawled down obscene songs.
His end came unexpectedly. Glancing into a mirror one morn-

ing, he saw two concubines behind him mocking his virility. He swallowed huge draughts of aphrodisiacs and soon became so comatose that, as an observer reported, he "could not smell the smell of an apple." So, unplanned, the great architect expired.

Aurengzeb was quite unlike his predecessors, and he had to be, for the Mogul Empire was falling apart. Calling himself "Grasper of the Universe" and wearing an iron disemboweling claw on his arm to prove it, Aurengzeb managed by bigotry and oppression to preserve the empire for fifty years, and even, in the second half of his reign, to extend it to cover the whole peninsula. He ruled by the Koran, crude cunning and fear. He prayed incessantly, kneeling on a rug of Persian lamb spread over a smooth black stone, and read the Koran throughout the night, often sleeping for no more than a couple of hours. He made copies of the Koran in his own hand and gave the profits from them to the poor. Campaigning, he slept on the bare earth with a tiger skin for covering. He was a thin and acid vegetarian, and a stickler; his police patrolled his cities carrying scissors to ensure that no man's beard grew longer than the regulation four fingers' breadth. He built nothing. Music was forbidden at his court. His only use for painting was to have a portrait made from time to time of a son he had shut up in the Gwalior fort, thus saving himself the labor and embarrassment of a visit to inquire after his son's health. He covered the carved figures on his grandfather Akbar's tomb with whitewash. A flat and unprofitable conservativism settled over the Mogul Empire, and even Aurengzeb knew he was only marking time. Anticipating Madame de Pompadour by half a century, he murmured, "*Azma ast hamah fasad baqi*" ("After me will come the deluge"), and prepared himself for immortality.

In 1707, in his ninetieth year, Aurengzeb, the last of the Great Moguls, felt death upon him. "Carry this creature of dust to the nearest burial place," he ordered, "and lay him in the earth with no useless coffin." He had directed that his funeral expenses were not to exceed the amount he had made sewing and selling some little quilted caps (a sum in the region of five dollars), but his wishes were disregarded to the extent of a simple marble sepulcher open to rain and sun, as Muslim law decreed.

Aurengzeb's austerities were not enough. His predecessors had emptied the treasuries. Their taxation had destroyed agriculture and industry, and their territories and responsibilities had grown too large for one man to handle, though they had left behind a standard of magnificence against which any prince might measure himself. Within twenty years of Aurengzeb's death the whole structure of the Mogul Empire disintegrated. The Mogul governor of Bengal stopped paying tribute, the kingdom of Oudh and the huge province of Hyderabad declared themselves independent. The Marathas occupied the Mogul capital of Delhi, and after them the Persians and then the Afghans. Within a century the inglorious heir of the house of Babur and Akbar was taken under British protection and left like a living effigy with only the Red Fort at Delhi for his kingdom. When the last of the Moguls was captured by the British after the Mutiny, those male relatives unfortunate enough to be taken with him were shot in cold blood outside the gates of Delhi by a highly irregular captain of irregular cavalry. Some more distant kinsmen survived to be presented to Edward, Prince of Wales, when he visited Benares in 1876. There were six of them, all wearing black caps, all very poor and all admirably dignified. The last descendant of the heroic strain of Tamerlane and Genghis Khan to be noticed was also alive and living in Benares in 1884. In a faint memory of the princely style he would entertain guests to a cockfight in his yard, but it could be seen that the spurs of his birds were bandaged, for he could not afford replacements. However, the mighty shadow of the Moguls was not quite erased when the last of them to occupy the throne died in exile in Rangoon. In 1944 the Indian National Army marched in review past his tomb to pay homage, and perhaps for luck, before they invaded India in behalf of the Japanese.

*   *   *

As the Mogul Empire died like some exploding sun, its fragments took on a radiance of their own. Hyderabad glowed among the debris, already a great princedom. In all, about a dozen states spread over modern India might have claimed a part of the Mogul inheritance if only because their rulers were Muslims, not a few of them descendants of Afghan freebooters. Such was Bhopal, ruled by three women in succession, and the second Muslim state in India. The esthetics of Islam also survived in smaller courts, like that of Rampur, a tract two-thirds the size of Rhode Island spreading over a fertile part of the Ganges valley where the Himalayan foothills sank into it. Rampur's library was one of the finest in the East. Some of its manuscripts were six or seven hundred years old; it contained not only a little book of verse annotated by Babur and Shah Jehan but an invaluable collection of Mogul paintings and a stimulating collection of erotica. The exquisite taste of the library did not pervade the rest of the palace, made somber by teak paneling and vulgar by recent copies of European masterpieces. The contrast suited the character of the most remarkable prince of the Rampur line. His Highness Sir Syed Mohammed Hamed Ali Khan Bahadur (1875–1930), religious leader of the Shia sect in northern India, was an acknowledged scholar and a gourmet of note. His fastidiousness extended even to the bathroom, where he spent much of the day dispensing justice and advice from a toilet seat specially designed by his chief engineer not only for comfort but to give the impression that he was formally enthroned. His Highness prided himself on the variety of his curses; challenged once at dinner, he not only quickly silenced all competition but continued solo for another two hours without repeating himself in Urdu, Punjabi and Persian.

Though the majority of the population of Rampur was Muslim, the state was peacefully absorbed into the new Hindu-dominated India of 1947. Bahawalpur, third largest of the old Muslim principalities, sank equally quietly into the arms of its co-religionists of Pakistan and became one of the border states of that new nation on the west of the Indian Desert. The Muslim state of Junagadh, however, created a problem. At the time of partition, when each state was given the option of joining either

Pakistan or India, Junagadh preserved a long silence which no official noted. Suddenly it opted for Pakistan. That was awkward indeed. Though its ruling house was Muslim, 73 percent of its people were Hindus and it held common borders with purely Hindu states. Since it had a seaboard and a port, Junagadh was accessible by water from West Pakistan. Most important of all, Junagadh was a microcosm of Hyderabad, the most powerful of all states, where an old and accomplished Muslim oligarchy ruled a Hindu peasantry, and a mirror image of Kashmir, where a Hindu ruled Muslims. What might happen in Hyderabad and Kashmir was not yet clear. The spotlight suddenly burned down on little Junagadh and its prince, a man of quicksilver.

In thirty-six years of rule, His Highness Sir Mahabat Khan Babi Pathan had succeeded in establishing himself as the leading dog breeder of the Orient and a noteworthy sadist. At its height his pack numbered eight hundred or so, but by the time of independence, perhaps foreseeing hard times ahead, he had reduced it to a mere three hundred. The accommodation for favorites was luxurious, consisting of a room apiece with servant, electric light and telephone, and including a tiled hospital of three wards supervised by an English veterinarian with canine specialties. Those dogs that died despite all medicare went to their happier hunting grounds to the sound of Chopin's funeral march. The upkeep came to about thirteen thousand dollars a month, or 11 percent of the entire revenue of the state, but the cost was nothing to the pleasure the prince experienced watching deliberately starved hounds setting upon a captive and crippled antelope. The prince had first caused a stir by marrying Roshana, his favorite bitch, to a handsome golden retriever called Bobby in a state ceremony graced by fifty thousand guests, though the Viceroy disappointed everyone by declining the invitation. The bride was perfumed and bejeweled in the usual fashion, and the groom, to set off his gold bracelets, wore a cummerbund of embroidered silk. Elephants and a guard of honor took part in the solemnities, which were attended in force by the press and filmed. At the bridal banquet the happy couple were seated on the prince's right hand. The bride spent the rest of her life on air-conditioned velvet but was separated from her husband shortly after the consummation. He was returned to the kennels.

It was not easy for the new government of India to divine Sir Mahabat Khan's likely reactions in a political crisis. There were rumors that Pakistan had promised him money and troops. More-over, below the political consequences of Junagadh's defection lay weightier concerns, for the sacred river Saraswati watered it, and the relics of an ancient Hindu culture (not least a granite boulder on which the immortal Asoka had chiseled fourteen edicts) and two holy mountains made it a place of pilgrimage.* Accordingly, the Indian government hemmed in Junagadh with infantry and a few light tanks and sent a squadron of fighters howling over its mossy sandstone battlements. His only artillery a couple of sixteenth-century bronze cannon of Persian make, the prince thought it politic not to order his lancers to the attack. With four of his dogs, all his jewels and three of his four wives, leaving the last lady to follow next day when she found a child she had mislaid, he boarded his private plane to take up residence in Pakistan. Junagadh was incorporated into India.

---

* Junagadh was also the last refuge of the Indian lion. Its hills encompassed the Gir Forest, five hundred square miles of dry thorn scrub that blazed scarlet in the spring with the arrogant blossoms of the flame of the forest. Though the princes of Junagadh obliged visiting nobility with a shot or two, they did protect the lions, so that today some three hundred survive for the pleasure of tourists and to the annoyance of local farmers, upon whose bullocks they sometimes leap.

2

✦❧✦❧✦❧✦❧✦❧✦❧✦❧✦❧✦❧

So Bright a Jewel

THE WRIT of the Great Moguls ran from the Arabian Sea to the Bay of Bengal and from the Himalayas to the tide race at the tip of the peninsula. Great Hindu princes paid them tribute or were replaced by Mogul viceroys, and some, the Rajputs, served the Moguls directly as generals and ministers. The mines of Hyderabad and Mysore sent them diamonds and gold, Kathiawar bred horses for their cavalry, the deserts of Bikaner supplied camels for their baggage trains, from the teak forests of Assam came elephants for their siege operations, Travancore and Cochin farmed ginger and pepper for their dishes of boned duck baked in butter, Malwa harvested the opium for their drinks, and the hills of Jodhpur and Alwar gave up the white marble of their mosques and tombs. Though predominant, the rule of the Great Moguls had one fatal flaw. Its only law was the word of the emperor: if the emperor failed, all else failed.

The declining power of the Moguls was beset by two forces, one native, one foreign. The first grew from the genius of

Shivaji the Grand Rebel, who led his people, the Marathas, out of their dragon's-teeth mountains of the west in a flood of hardy, plundering horsemen. The far-flung but amorphous Maratha confederacy lasted for over a century until the British crushed it. The foreign force emerged (after Asoka and the Moguls) the third universal government of India. It had been foreseen. Aurengzeb had held captive a guru of the Sikhs, Tegh Bahadur, and accused him one day of peering through the shades of the imperial harem from the roof of his prison. Tegh Bahadur denied the charge. "I was looking," he said, "toward the Europeans who are coming from beyond the seas to tear down thy curtains and destroy thine empire." Scoffing, Aurengzeb beheaded him. But there was a prophecy older even than the guru's which foretold that the children of the monkey god Hanuman would inherit India. The British were soon recognized by their irritable habits, the color of their skin, their love of destruction, and their propensity for taking things over, as "the monkey people." The first of the monkey people to arrive had hardly seemed a threat to the Moguls, who lounged in their fretted audience chambers with forty executioners ranked behind them and a thousand horses at instant call. The first ambassador of England, Sir Thomas Roe, hated them and their country, and advised the East India Company: "Let this be received as a rule, that if you will profit, seek it at sea and in quiet trade; for without controversy, it is an error to effect garrisons and land-wars in India." Heeding him, the East India Company trod delicately at first, contenting itself with trading posts (or "factories") in Bengal, Madras and Bombay, and making a steady but modest profit out of chintzes and calicos, spices and sandalwood and an occasional jewel.

But by the end of its first century of business the East India Company had lost its preoccupation with trade and had begun to scheme for real estate and power. It acquired both piecemeal, fighting and beating the French in the middle of the eighteenth century and thereafter concerning itself only with native potentates, who were many and varied. Some were Hindus of antique southern lineage who had not been greatly disturbed even by the Moguls, some were descendants of officers of the Moguls who had acquired sovereignty during the decay of their masters. Some dynasties were new, others so old that their members claimed descent from Indra the sun god, and had papers to prove it. The Company spun a web of treaties with these princes, beginning with the immensely wealthy Nizam of Hyderabad in 1759, using one state against another or merely regularizing a sort of *mariage de convenance*. Its policy of dividing and conquering was never more effective than during the Third Maratha War of 1817–1819: the proud leaders of the Maratha confederacy in its prime had reckoned that the British would have to increase their strength tenfold before they became a threat. The Company subdued the Maratha princes one by one and thus became master of India.

In spite of the cost of its wars, the Company had thus far shown a profit. In the early days it paid dividends of 12½ percent and never paid less than 10½ percent. At home, the Company pursued a vigorous public relations policy using influence and stunts, once attempting to draw its opponents away from a crucial vote in the House of Commons by arranging a tiger-baiting in Whitehall. But the Company lost its trade monopoly at the beginning of the nineteenth century, and in 1833 a new charter changed it completely from a commercial organization, making it the agent of the British Crown in India and assigning it administrative and political powers held "in trust for His Majesty and his heirs and successors, for the service of the Indian Government." In short, the Company was now the great landlord and tax collector of India.

About one third of the area and a quarter of the people of India were ruled by their own princes, supervised by the British. The rest was British India, which consisted of the provinces of Madras and Bombay (each ruled by a Governor) and Bengal (ruled by a Governor-General with some jurisdiction over the Governors). The Governor-General reported to a Court of Directors in London, as he had when the Company still engaged in trade, but since the government of India was now vested jointly in the British Parliament and the Company, the Court of

Directors was answerable to Parliament. This arrangement provided the perfect instance of the flag having followed trade, but
a more cumbersome system of government could hardly have
been devised. It came rattling down overnight in 1857 at the first
gusts of what the British came to call "the Devil's Wind."

Having sown the wind themselves in ignorance, the British
reaped the whirlwind when the Company's Bengal army mutinied throughout a vast area stretching from the foot of the
Himalayas to the mouth of the Ganges. In 1857 the British in
India had some reason to feel complacency. Their countrymen
had proved their commercial and esthetic supremacy when the
Great Exhibition of 1851 at the Crystal Palace failed to produce
any article of foreign manufacture or art to challenge what had
been made in England. More recently they had soundly trounced
the Russian Bear in the Crimea by a striking use of cavalry at
Balaklava and a little help from the French. Landseer had completed his *Monarch of the Glen*, Tennyson his *In Memoriam*,
and the Queen twenty years of a rule that in style promised to
eclipse the products of the paintbrush and the pen. The grand
heroic tales of India were already in the past—Clive at Plassey,
Wellington at Assaye, Gough at Chillianwalla—and what now
remained was the spread of middle-class standards and Victorian
civilization over a benighted peasantry. The smugness was blown
away on the evening of May 10, 1857, when some troopers of
the 3rd Native Light Cavalry boiled out of the bazaar in Meerut
and began to cut down their white officers, spit their white
officers' wives on wooden stakes and club to death their white
officers' children. They did similar things to white civilian families.

Their hysteria had old and complex causes, of which the
chief was the British abhorrence of the Hindu faith. "The great
majority of the population of India consists of idolators,"
Macaulay had thundered, "blindly attached to doctrines and
rights which are in the highest degree pernicious. The Brah-
minical religion is so absurd that it necessarily debases every
mind which receives it as truth; and with this absurd mythology
is bound up an absurd system of physics, an absurd geography,
an absurd astronomy. Nor is this form of paganism more favor-

able to art than to science. . . . All is hideous and grotesque and ignoble. As this superstition is of all superstitions the most irrational and of all superstitions the most inelegant, so it is of all superstitions the most immoral." Those British intelligent enough to seek the meanings of Hindu culture were blinded by their education in Greek and Roman forms; those inquisitive enough to search for the qualities of Hindu life were blocked by their Victorian Christianity from enjoying its sensuous warmth and peace. None thought of learning from India, all strove to change her. They shuddered at the sight of goat's blood glistening on the shoulders of a grinning black god and turned away, never comprehending that to the Hindu, religion was life.

The British had never been able to elucidate the mysteries of caste, which were partly religious, partly economic and partly sociological. "Caste" derived from a Portuguese word, translated as "breed, kind, or race," though it was none of these things. The concept had arrived with the Aryans and evolved into a system of dividing a society into strata or groups according to function or profession. There were four main "castes," the highest the priestly Brahmins, then the warriors and rulers, then the merchants and artisans, then the farmers. Outside the castes came the untouchables, whose duties were degrading and unspeakable. The restrictions of behavior imposed by the system became rigid as rock, and if a man flouted them, consciously or not, he became an outcaste and could only be reinstated, if at all, after rituals expensive enough to make him destitute. If a man lay with his wife while an outcaste, he might suffer castration. It was every man's prayer to achieve, through his deeds in successive reincarnations, the level of the Brahmin, for the Brahmins' eternal reward was oblivion. The ramifications of the system were beyond calculation; each caste contained scores or hundreds of subdivisions, each with its particular codes and prejudices, to a grand total of over a quarter of a million. The result was to make some of the transactions of daily life extraordinarily difficult: the mere shadow of a man of inferior caste falling on a Brahmin's cooking pot rendered his food unclean. Nowhere were such problems more evident than in the Bengal army, where a senior noncommissioned officer would bow before an ordinary soldier because of the latter's higher caste. In 1857 the Bengal army shivered with the fevers of religion.

The East India Company had three native armies, one in each province, totaling a quarter of a million men. They included Muslims as well as Hindus, but their officers were British. Of the quarter of a million *sepoys* (infantrymen) and *sowars* (cavalrymen), more than half were in the Bengal army, and of these, one-third were high-caste Brahmins and intensely devout. There was also a political problem, for half of the Bengal army's sepoys came from the ancient and independent kingdom of Oudh in the north of central India. In 1856 Lord Dalhousie, the Governor-General, had deposed its imbecile ruler for incapacity and depravity, and annexed the country to British India. The valuable privileges the sepoys from Oudh had enjoyed thereupon vanished. The youngest man to be appointed Governor-General, Dalhousie in his eight years of rule annexed in all a quarter of a million square miles, roughly the equivalent of absorbing Texas. In doing so he extinguished two great kingdoms—the Punjab and Oudh—and some smaller states, dispossessed thousands of landlords, made the princes apprehensive and spread insecurity everywhere. Fluent and adamant, Dalhousie explained it all as for the good of the Company and the peasants.

The sepoys thought otherwise. They complained at being blamed for not obeying orders when their British officers did not know how to give commands in the native language. They resented having to shave off their mustaches and wipe the caste marks from their foreheads. They hated the pressure to bring their women out of the harem, "which," as an apologist put it, "tended to disrupt their peaceful family life." Above all, they believed there was a conspiracy to convert them to Christianity by destroying the distinctions of caste. Rumors and distorted facts began to circulate in the night. New recruits would be sent to serve overseas though crossing the black water made a man an outcaste. The princes were to be married to white women widowed by the Crimean War so that their heirs would be Christian. Flour brought to Cawnpore to relieve the current famine had been adulterated with the ground bones of cows, sacred to Hindus, and pigs, forbidden to Muslims. And now, the last infamy, the British were issuing Enfield rifles with a new cartridge that was smeared with pork and beef fat. The end of the cartridge had to be bitten before the charge could be poured. It became the spark that ignited Dalhousie's powder train.

Normally, for security, some units of the British army proper were stationed in India on loan to the East India Company and paid for out of the Company's revenues, but in 1857 there were fewer of them than usual because the Crimean War had drained troops away. In all there were slightly more than forty thousand English soldiers in India; they were outnumbered six to one and they were lamentably short of cannon. Moreover, the princes were an unknown quantity. The great maharajahs maintained their own armies, including an elite corps of Ethiopians and Arabs at the disposal of the Nizam of Hyderabad and regiments of well-drilled Sikhs owing allegiance to the princes of the Punjab.

Two and a half centuries of British endeavor were put in the balance when fifty-four of the Bengal army's seventy-four regiments of native infantry mutinied and were joined by regiment after regiment of cavalrymen, many of whom were Muslims. Delhi fell instantly to the mutineers, complete with its armament and the rheumy old Mogul Emperor Bahadur Shah, at eighty-two hardly capable of thought or action and living in an opium twilight. The British thought him a cipher and in return for a modest pension had persuaded him to limit his empire to the environs of the Red Fort. Nevertheless, he was the nineteenth of a mighty line and a man of some dignity and cultivation, and it was by no means impossible that the mutineers could reconstruct his house. For a few weeks everything depended on the other princes, supposed allies of the British but hardly their debtors. The biggest of them, Hyderabad, stood firm. The Maharajah of Patiala in the Punjab gave the British five thousand men to guard their supply lines, but even he wavered toward the old Mogul until the British bluffed him with a tale of troopships hastening from England. The Sikh Maharajah of Jhind marched in person at the head of his troops, and the crafty

Maharajah of Kashmir, who had bought his state from the British, sent men and money over the mountains. A few princes sympathized with the mutineers and one or two were overwhelmed by them, but most sided with the British, forty of them actively with troops and treasure.*

In suppressing the rebellion, the British made many martyrs. In a few of the British, fear turned to sadistic fury. On the road to relieve Cawnpore, Colonel James George Neill held kangaroo courts day and night and hanged men for so much as glancing away in his presence. Condemned Hindus were splashed with bullocks' blood, Muslims smeared with lard. Some were slung up by the heels to die over slow fires. Neill swore to bury all Hindus and cremate all Muslims, thus consigning them to everlasting perdition. "I cannot help seeing that God's finger is in all this," he announced. His troops christened him "the Butcher," not out of affection.

Atrocity bred atrocity. There were two hundred and six English women and children held prisoner in Cawnpore. Their captors, seeing such retribution as Neill's, and believing them useless as hostages, put them to the sword. The British took Cawnpore the day after the massacre: in a little single-story building they found a line of children's shoes, containing feet, a tree gray with the spattered brains of infants, and a well crammed with severed heads and limbs and hacked torsos to a depth of more than forty feet. The house was two inches deep in congealing blood. Neill himself dragged many of the two hundred and seventy sepoys taken captive there over the floor, forcing each man to lick clean a square yard before he was led away to be hanged.

At the storming of Lucknow, Colin Campbell's Highlanders called their bayonets "Cawnpore dinners" as they jabbed them into sepoy bellies. After their charge, a lieutenant counting the

---

* The sepoys of the Madras and Bombay armies also fought for the British. Nearly eight thousand of the eleven thousand troops besieging Delhi, the crucial battle, were natives. The mutiny cost the British upward of two hundred million dollars, two thousand white men killed in battle, and nine thousand more dead of disease. The total of Indian dead on either side is not readily available.

enemy dead in what had been a rose garden was delighted to find they amounted to a symbolic 1,857. Breaching the walls of Delhi, the British sabered civilian and mutineer alike, drove out the population, dressed the streets with dangling corpses, ransacked homes and stores for booty, branded and flogged and blew from guns and banished to penal islands. They dragged the enfeebled emperor from the tomb where he was hiding, tried him in sackcloth for forty days and exiled him to Burma. They had put down the mutiny and they had changed India, and themselves.

Shocked, the British in India now had to see themselves as a minute autocracy, a few thousand ruling scores of millions, settled in enclaves and isolated, in many cases incapable even of communicating adequately with those surrounding them. They thought they had brought enlightenment, but they had bred hatred. They had been driven into courses foreign to their national inclination toward procrastination and compromise; they felt their guilt and yet they could never again trust their Indian subordinates. The Indian masses were still so ingenuous that many believed the sahibs were born from eggs that grew on trees in a far-off island; an Englishwoman passing through a remote village might still be taken for a fairy. But the growing Indian middle class recognized the raw force the British could exert so ruthlessly, acknowledged it, and remained subservient and resentful. One of them, three times president of the Indian National Congress and the first Indian to be elected to the British Parliament, told a learned society in London in 1871: "The natives call the British system *Sakar ki Churi,* the knife of sugar. That is to say, there is no oppression, it is all smooth and sweet, but it is the knife notwithstanding." The savage extremism of the mutiny had hopelessly polarized these vastly disparate elements of society in India; after 1857 the Indians never doubted that they must free themselves. That was to take them ninety years.

Fortunately for the immediate future of both sides, London held cooler heads than Delhi. Mr. Benjamin Disraeli had argued for three hours in the Commons that the government was faced with a national revolt, not a mere military mutiny. Prime Minister Lord Palmerston, discarding his habitual flippancy, perceived religious fears at play. The Queen herself felt a pressing anxiety and confided to her uncle, the King of the Belgians, "Altogether, the whole is so much worse than the Crimea—where there was *glory* and honorable warfare." After much debate a bridge over the abyss was conceived. The Honorable East India Company was dissolved at once and Her Majesty assumed the government of India. The Queen signed her proclamation to that effect while the fighting was still going on, and it was read out all over India on November 1, 1858. It was specific about religious tolerance. "Firmly relying ourselves on the truth of Christianity," it declared, "and acknowledging with gratitude the solace of religion, we disclaim alike the right and desire to impose our convictions on any of our subjects. We declare it to be our royal will and pleasure that none be in any wise favored, none molested or disquieted, by reason of their religious faith or observances, but that all shall alike enjoy the equal and impartial protection of the law; and we do strictly charge and enjoin all those who may be in authority under us that they abstain from all interference with the religious belief or worship of any of our subjects on pain of our highest displeasure." In principle the proclamation extended to Indians the status of British citizens: "We hold ourselves bound to the natives of our Indian territories," it promised, "by the same obligations of duty which bind us to all our other subjects," and continued with the usual democratic promises of responsible employment, regardless of race or creed. Of course, there was a gulf between theory and practice, but at the end of 1858 the Queen expressed her pleasure at the proclamation's effect. "It is a source of great satisfaction and pride to her," she wrote, "to feel herself in direct communication with that enormous Empire which is so bright a jewel in her Crown."

That Crown was now represented in India by a Viceroy, a title replacing the former one of Governor-General. The Viceroy had a double function. Directed, if not always controlled, by a Secretary of State in London, the Viceroy executed British policy over British India. As the personal delegate of the monarch he also stood in relation to the princes of India as the Queen to her nobility, part arbiter, part parent, absolute authority. Queen Victoria's proclamation had been warm toward the princes; it accepted all the treaties made with them by the East India Company, renounced all territorial ambition and continued comfortingly: "We shall respect the rights, dignity, and honor of native princes as our own; and we desire that they, as well as our own subjects, should enjoy that prosperity, and that social advancement which can only be secured by internal peace and good government." Lord Canning, the first Viceroy, was laudatory. He wrote: "These patches of native government served as a breakwater to the storm, which would otherwise have swept over us in one great wave." Commenting on the result of the proclamation, he reported: "The Crown of England stands forth the unquestioned ruler and paramount power in all India and is for the first time brought face to face with its feudatories. There is a reality in the suzerainty of England which has never existed before and which is not only felt but eagerly acknowledged by the Chiefs." In short, the golden age of the maharajahs had dawned.

It was some time before the improved condition of the princes after the Mutiny became widely recognized, even by themselves. Though they owned a third of India, the only representative of their order at all familiar to the English was the deposed Dhuleep Singh, formerly of the Punjab. The first ruling prince to visit London was the young Maharajah of Kolhapur, who did so shyly and briefly in 1870 and left in some bewilderment toward an untimely death in Florence.

In 1875 all was changed by a single stroke of splendor originating in the lavish mind of the Prince of Wales. It was a happy conjunction that portly Edward should be heir apparent at this turn in the princes' fortunes. His opulent figure and broad features, his passion for minutiae of dress, decoration and ceremony, his disposition to luxury, his bonhomie iced with a touch of regal distance, and the absence of any intellectual pretensions whatever, made him the image of a budding emperor. With unaccustomed deviousness Prince Edward wrung permission from his mother for an official tour of India to seal the new relationship between the Crown and the maharajahs by bestowing favors and receiving homage. Since he was penniless and his mother penurious, he persuaded Disraeli to beguile five hundred and sixty thousand dollars out of the House of Commons and five hundred thousand more from the government of India, a total not thought extravagant for an imperial occasion.

Two decks of the troopship *Serapis* were gutted and refurnished in solid oak and brown morocco leather, including a horseshoe dining table to seat sixty. The hull was painted white with a belt of gold, and the insignia of the order of the Star of India, of which His Royal Highness was Grand Master, were picked out fore and aft. The Prince's entourage was small and workmanlike and included a zoologist, a botanist and an artist; Mr. Isaacson, a clerk in the India Office, to keep a record of gifts given and received; and as official historian, Dr. William Howard Russell, the famous correspondent of *The Times*. The Duke of Sutherland, a private guest of the Prince, naturally brought along his personal piper, an unexpected advantage.*

Dr. Russell was prevailed upon to design a uniform for himself, the lower and posterior part of which gave way one day as he was boarding an elephant, releasing a festoon of white linen. Happily, the Indian princes took it to be a part of his design, so he suffered no loss of face. During the voyage His Royal Highness paid attention to some other matters of dress. He decreed that in view of the heat, mess uniforms and swallow-tail coats for dinner might be replaced by a short dark-blue jacket with black trousers and a black bow tie, thus inventing the dinner jacket.

The royal party's arrival in India was perhaps most elegantly reported by a Persian gentleman. "His Honor of High Title, the Star of the Sky of Wealth and Fortune, the Great Star of

---

* The bagpipe was the sole item of Western musical culture enthusiastically absorbed by the Indians. It enchanted them. When a Viceroy's escort of Highlanders piped through Lahore in 1860, an old Sikh chieftain sighed, "That is indeed music! It is like that which we hear of in ancient story, which was so exquisite that the hearers became insensible."

the Firmament of Glory and Prosperity, the Generous One of the Age, the First One of the Time, the Essence of the Family of Honor and Loftiness, the Prop of the Dynasty of Might and Pomp, possessing the dignity and rank of Saturn, of exalted honor, the Cream of the Princes of the Age, the Glory of the Nobles of England, Albert Edward, Prince of Wales," he announced, "landed in Bombay." A humbler pen saluted the Prince with

Beautifully he will shoot
Many a royal tiger brute;
Laying on their backs they die
Shot in the apple of the eye.

It was the first and last state visit to be greeted with such universal and unstinting enthusiasm. Triumphal arches of bamboo or steel trellis soared everywhere. TELL MAMMA WE'RE HAPPY trumpeted one in Bombay; WELCOME TO OUR FUTURE EMPEROR proclaimed another. In Baroda they raised an arch of palm leaves and perched ten little naked urchins in it for cherubs, frozen in angelic postures, each wearing gold wings tied on with string and a long auburn wig on his shaven head, and all dripping whitewash from a billsticker's brush. The effect, far from innocence, was of such bizarre depravity that His Royal Highness wept from the pain of suppressed laughter. The will to please was everywhere and the Prince answered in kind.

The maharajahs astonished him constantly. There was the twelve-year-old Gaekwar of Baroda in jewels worth three million dollars, exquisitely beautiful in face and figure, presenting six cannon of pure gold (later discreetly returned to his treasury). There was Jung Bahadur of Nepal bringing five thousand men and a thousand riding elephants to a camp in the jungle where the Prince shot six tigers before lunch, took a hot bath and held a formal dinner party. There was the short, stout Maharajah of Patiala wearing the jewels he had bought from the Empress Eugénie of France for a million and a half dollars, pleading for two more guns in his salute to bring him level in importance with the Maratha princes of Gwalior and Indore. There was the tall Maharajah of Rewa in a turban flashing with diamonds above a face strangely red as if worked with a dull tattoo all over; he was a leper. There was the Maharajah of Gwalior proudly showing the palace he had driven seven thousand workmen to finish in time for the Prince's visit, with gold bed and toilet articles, baths of solid silver, perfume bottles labeled "Prince of Wales's Own Bouquet," fifty thousand dollars' worth of lighting fixtures, and a Persian carpet in the drawing room that could hold two thousand people standing. There was the Maharajah of Kashmir leading the Prince into his winter capital of Jammu, all white and red stone, where thirty bands warbled thirty different tunes of welcome, all off key; and the designs painted on the elephants' ears, of whales battling tigers and other fantasies, looked like pages in the coloring book of some crazily talented child. There were howdahs of gold on the elephants worth two hundred thousand dollars, princely barges shaped like swans, palanquins of precious metal, chairs of ivory, fans of peacock feathers, umbrellas of cloth of gold, carpets of pearl and turquoise. There were wild pig to be ridden down, tigers and numerous game birds and leopards to be shot, cheetahs to be slipped at running black buck, hawks to be flown at whirring grouse, wild elephants to be corralled. There were troops to be reviewed, glittering cavalry and bullock guns, and medieval infantry in casques and breastplates of brass. There were jugglers, wrestlers, snake charmers, nautch girls, eaters of fire to be applauded, and fireworks exploded everywhere. The Prince was a connoisseur of fireworks, and his time was the heyday of the art.

Magnificent as the maharajahs were, none could outshine His Royal Highness in his field marshal's scarlet tunic and the great blue cloak of the Star of India, the Royal Standard borne before him by Sir Dighton Probyn, a black-bearded hero of the Mutiny. In state Prince Edward carried an imperial aura; informally he poured forth charm. The princes took to him for his grand style and his love of sport; though he was not a good shot, he always fired away lustily and he was a fearless horseman, if inelegant.

For his part, he looked on them as members of the same trade union and complained to the Queen that some political officers bullied "the princes and chiefs upon whom they were appointed to *attend*." He loathed racial and religious prejudice. "Because a man has a black face and a different religion from our own," he wrote home, "there is no reason why he should be treated as a brute." This plainness infuriated the redneck element of British officialdom, but it won him the devotion of the princes and of those among the masses who understood it. After the Prince had left, a harbor, hospitals and schools were built with the maharajah's money and in his name.

Serapis brought him to Portsmouth after seventeen weeks in India in time to find his mother officially Empress of India, enthusiastically signing her papers and even postcards "Regina et Imperatrix" and demanding a bodyguard of Sikh cavalry for the fun of it. *Serapis* and the attendant royal yacht were loaded with gifts including a menagerie of tigers, baby elephants, leopards, a Kashmir stag, two bears and some others of the maharajahs' creatures. In the holds were crates of swords, antique armor and flintlocks, shields of rhinoceros hide, tea sets, goblets and boxes of gold, necklaces, fine shawls, carpets and jewels and bracelets, all received in royal trade for picture books of England, fire engines, snuffboxes, organs and riding crops, rifles and watches and binoculars. One of the Prince's chefs carried a subtler treasure—the secrets of thirteen curries and eight chutneys learned in the spicy kitchens of the Madras Club. The Prince of Wales at once delivered the presents he had received in his mother's behalf, including a waist belt of pearls from the thrifty Maharajah of Indore. The souvenir the Queen liked most, however, was a copy of her own literary work, *Leaves from the Journal of My Life in the Highlands,* rendered into Hindustani and bound in inlaid marble.

She was also aware, with a twinge of jealousy, that her son had brought back something less tangible but of immensely greater value. He had secured the trust and admiration of the princes of India, and he had left behind a sense of the solemn presence of the British Crown. Having tasted of the Prince's cup, the maharajahs began to flock toward it before long to take another sip. Their gorgeous figures were a focal point at royal occasions like jubilees and coronations. And thus they learned the rich pleasures of the London season, the delectable savor of a Parisienne's laughter in the suave luxury of the Hotel Bristol and the gentle austerities of Marienbad. They became an indispensable part, like orchids and champagne, of the Edwardian age.

3

A Pride of Princes

To the mass of British at home, who saw them only distantly, the individual maharajahs who came to London—elegant Cooch Behar, bow-legged Sir Pratap Singh of Jodhpur, portly Gwalior—seemed like majestic puppets sharing certain characteristics, all commendable, like wealth, bravery, loyalty to the Crown, martial expertise and perhaps potentially a touch of oriental wickedness. The first Indian of any kind to become universally known and popular throughout England was His Highness the Maharajah Sir Ranjitsinhji Vibhaji, Jam Sahib of Nawanagar, whose nickname at Cambridge had been "Smith." He owed his fame not to the fact that he was a prince, but to his brilliant unorthodoxy on the cricket field. "He moved as if he had no bones," a fellow player wrote. "One would not be surprised to see brown curves burning in the grass where one of his cuts had travelled, or blue flame shimmering round his bat as he made one of his strokes." He began to play at the turn of the century and in a couple of seasons was a legend. He played so well for England against Australia in 1899 when the rest of the team failed that the newspapers trumpeted "RANJI SAVES ENGLAND!" In this golden age of cricket Ranji shone like a meteor, and the British, always ready to attribute more to the game than merely athletic qualities, saw the prince as a symbol of knightly grace and his bat as an avenging sword. Even his color was an advantage. "They would have admired Ranji as a white batsman," a contemporary shrewdly wrote, "but they worshipped him because he was black." When Ranji's stroke play flashed in conquest, it spoke of the power and glamour of India, jewel of the Empire. In fact, not one in ten thousand of his fans could have placed Ranji's state of Nawanagar on the map.

The British were aware only of the more westernized among the princes; few could distinguish the great differences in race, religion and tradition that kept the maharajahs from being anything like a homogenous body. There were Muslim princes, mostly relics of the Mogul Empire, some ruling Muslims, some Hindus, scattered all over India except the far south. There were Hindu princes of different races and propensities. The most familiar were the Rajputs, fiercely mustached warriors and polo players, clustered around ancient fortresses in the dry lands south of the Punjab and professing for the most part a regular but not too arduous practice of Hinduism. On the edge of the Punjab were a few Sikh states, militant Hindus of a more ascetic sort, at least theoretically. Spreading across central India were the remains of the Maratha empire that had briefly challenged the British for dominion. In the far south, in Travancore and Cochin, ruled Hindu dynasties tracing their descent as far back as the third century B.C., beyond which the details became a little indistinct. There the throne passed through the female line, sons of the maharajah's sisters succeeding. The maharajahs of Travancore were particularly devout; Brahmins themselves, they were regularly weighed against gold which was then broadcast among the priests, and were so assiduous in their observances that they would not receive an Englishman after dawn, which was the hour at which they took their ritual bath of purification. Variations in behavior, customs and beliefs were great. There were no standard universal guidelines of religion or race by which the princes could be collectively measured. Moreover, the semiautonomy of the Native States meant that each prince remained fairly free to develop his individuality as he pleased. There were monsters and near-saints among the maharajahs, martyrs and eccentrics, heros and shams, but there were no nonentities.

Aware that all that glistened was not gold, the British officials in India were very definite about who was a maharajah and who was not, and emphasized their definitions with a protocol of iron. Over six hundred and seventy princes and "independent" chiefs were recognized by the British, the majority of them masters of small and insignificant domains. Five hundred were administered by one or other of the provincial governments and seldom came to notice. The remaining hundred and seventy-odd, the most important, came directly under the Viceroy's suzerainty, which His Excellency exercised through the Foreign and Political Department of the Government of India, the portfolio for which he himself retained. The principal device by which the British distinguished the greater princes from the smaller was the allotment of gun salutes: about a hundred of the Viceroy's hundred and seventy princes could be greeted on formal occasions by the thunder of nine or more guns; those enjoying a minimum of eleven guns or more (about eighty princes out of the hundred) were also entitled to be addressed as "Your Highness." No prince was ever thought of as royalty.* Those at the lower end of the scale of bombardment were mostly rajahs, those with thirteen guns or more were maharajahs, and those with the most prolonged reports of all, twenty-one guns, were grandees by any standard. These last were Hyderabad, Mysore, Baroda, Gwalior and Kashmir. Official pleasure or disfavor could quickly be registered in the ears of all India by adding or subtracting a

---

* The size and design of crowns used on princely notepaper was scrutinized. A coronet, proper to a prince or peer, was in order, but a closed Tudor crown such as that used by a king or an emperor was out of the question. One maharajah overcame this prohibition, or at least mocked it, by writing on notepaper from the George V Hotel in Paris, embossed with a crown fit for a giant.

couple of guns. So jealous were some princes of their noisy privileges that they would arrange the arrival of their private trains into Delhi at a quiet hour when the guns might speak with maximum effect but never on Sunday, which was a day of silence. In addition to the list of salutes, a little black book was kept in Government House to advise the Viceroy of the exact honors due to each of his nobility: the Nizam of Hyderabad must be met at the front door and escorted through all the public rooms, but a minor prince was entitled to only a couple of cursory steps to the edge of the carpet in front of the Viceroy's throne. Obversely, when the Viceroy went visiting, a twenty-one gun prince need only advance as far as the door of his drawing room, but a lesser potentate must await His Excellency at the border of his state. The observance of all these rituals was rigid, for they were not empty symbols. A Viceroy's stumble on the steps of his palace could betoken the fall of an empire.

The less formal business with the princes was conducted by some fifty officers of the Foreign and Political Department, all but half a dozen of whom lived and worked in one state or another. Three-quarters were soldiers on secondment, the rest civil servants, and all were hand-picked by the Viceroy. The twenty-one-gun states enjoyed the permanent presence of a senior "political" known as the Resident, who lived in palatial style behind Corinthian porticos with a staff not much inferior to an ambassador's. Lesser states, like the desert states in Rajasthan or the little jungly ones in central India, were grouped under a Resident (also known as Agent to the Governor-General) assisted by two or three Political Officers, each stationed at some point convenient for the oversight of his remote charges, some of whom he might see only once a year after a long perambulation on horseback. Though most of the important princes held powers of life and death over their subjects and were above the law, even in British India, the terms of their treaties denied them any direct dealings with another state or a foreign power. Such matters were conducted by the British representatives of the Viceroy.

It happened, unfortunately for some of the princes, that these luminous years coincided with the appearance in India of her most formidable Viceroy. He had been characterized in an undergraduate review at Oxford with

> My name is George Nathaniel Curzon,
> I am a most superior person

and though ironically meant, it was a just assessment. Calculating, ruthless, brilliant, and inspired by a soaring idealism, Curzon became very largely responsible for the destiny of India in 1899 at the age of thirty-nine. He had worn a steel back brace for eleven years already and lived in pain, but he worked at his desk insatiably; reluctant to delegate, he set out to revamp the whole machinery of government single-handed. He built thousands of miles of railroads, irrigated millions of acres, set up a program of agricultural research and a department of archaeology, and antagonized his more conservative subordinates. The Orient dazzled Curzon and fired his vigorous fancy, but he was adamant in corseting it in the systems of the West. One moment he wooed the princes, the next he lectured them like a schoolmaster. "The Native Chief," he declared, "is concerned no less than the Viceroy or the Lieutenant Governor in the administration of the country. I claim him as my colleague and partner." Yet in a circular letter he claimed that in return for its support his government was entitled to expect "that the ruler shall devote his best energies not to the pursuit of pleasure, nor to the cultivation of absentee interests or amusements, but to the welfare of his own subjects and administration." The result of European tours, he declared severely, was "more often a collection of expensive furniture in the palace and of questionable proclivities in the mind of the returned traveller than an increase in his capacity for public or political service." Curzon forced, cajoled, enacted, studied and preached with the single-mindedness of a zealot.

With all he had hoped for in personal glory tarnished by a pointless political feud, he left India still saying, "Let it be our ideal to fight for the right, to abhor the imperfect, the unjust or the mean, to swerve neither to the right hand nor to the left, to care nothing for flattery or applause or odium or abuse, never to let your enthusiasm be soured or your courage grow dim— but to remember that the Almighty has placed your hands to the greatest of His plows, in whose furrows the nations of the future are germinating and taking shape. . . . That is the English-man's justification in India. It is good enough for his watchword while he is here; for his epitaph when he is gone." Such senti-ments might have marked Curzon for an American.

It could not be said that Curzon's exhortations were taken to heart by the princes as a body; some had no need of them, others scorned them, a few grand old dynasties ignored them as more gibberings from the monkey people. Curzon's successor, whom Curzon despised, reflected a quite opposite opinion when he instructed his officials in the states: "Administrative efficiency is at no time the only or indeed the chief object to be kept in view. This should specially be borne in mind by officers charged temporarily with the administration of a state during a minority. They occupy a position of peculiar trust and should never for-get that their primary duty is for the *conservation* of the cus-toms of the state. . . . Unless misrule reaches a pitch which vi-olates the elementary laws of civilization, the Imperial Govern-ment will usually prefer to take no overt measures for enforcing reform."

In comparison with British India, all the Native States re-mained to some extent repositories of the traditional way of life. For there was one prime distinction between that third of the subcontinent and the two-thirds under alien rule, a bond between prince and peasant that liberals and nationalists could only abhor. Curzon spoke of it in Jaipur: "The Native States have that in-definable quality, endearing them to the people, that arises from their being born of the soil." When Lord Lytton was Viceroy twenty years before, he had written about it to Disraeli, more pragmatically: "Politically speaking, the Indian peasantry is an inert mass. If it ever moves at all, it will move in obedience, not to its British benefactors, but to its Native Chiefs and Princes, however tyrannical they may be. . . . The Indian Chiefs are not a mere *noblesse:* they are a powerful autocracy." Lytton was proved wrong in the end only because the princes failed or declined to capitalize on that relationship. In fact, the princes never formed a really cohesive group. There were too many differences between them, racial, religious and cultural; old antipathies lived on, traditions would not die, there were too many petty spites. There was no leveling. About the only generalization with any truth to it was that in the Native States both taxation and the level of civilization were lower than in British India. An Indian colonel once lamented: "It is a regrettable but definitely established fact that democracy is bad for elephants." There were always plenty of elephants in the pyramidal world of the maharajahs while it lasted.

There were times, however, when certain of the princes felt the British yoke. Though the British professed not to meddle in the internal affairs of the Native States, they would not tolerate a rule that was, by their standards, depraved, incompetent or inflammatory. They were more severe about incompetences than about a depravity which in any case was difficult to define in the curious Orient, and were always reluctant to act unless matters became flagrantly public. They knew, for instance, that a certain maharajah disported himself of an evening in a shallow swimming pool which he entered down a line of steps on each of which he was welcomed by a couple of naked ladies. In all, there were some forty ladies, each holding a candle of peculiar shape. When the maharajah and all the ladies were in the water, which came up to mid-thigh, the candles were adjusted in the orifices for which they had been designed, and lit. A watery dance began, with each lady striving to protect her candle from the consequent splashings. The last to retain her flame had the pleasure of being pleasured by the prince. Innocent diversions of this nature, so long as they remained within the harem, were no cause for interference by the British. When, however, a maharajah's peccadilloes created a common scandal, he was doomed.

Such was the case of the Maharajah of Indore and his dancing girl the Mumtaz Begum. One of the three great Maratha states in central India, Indore was prosperous and advanced, having long enjoyed a substantial portion of the opium trade based on the favorable conditions of the Malwa plateau for the growth of poppies.* In 1925 the Maharajah of Indore was a thin, green-eyed man of thirty-four who had betrayed no eccentricities. Among his hundred or so concubines was a young beauty from Lahore called the Mumtaz Begum. The maharajah was infatuated with her but his feelings were not reciprocated. The girl jumped off his private train while the Indore menage was being transshipped to a hill station, and went home to Lahore. Her mother took her to Bombay, where she attracted the attention of a rich merchant and accepted his protection.

One evening the couple were taking an evening drive outside the city when their car was stopped by a group of men. As the men opened the car doors, the merchant opened fire with a revolver. The men shot him dead and dragged the Mumtaz Begum toward their own car. Two British army officers had heard the shots. They ran up and began to belabor the girl's assailants with their sticks. The men fled. Of course she had recognized her attackers: they were servants of the Indore court and their leader was the chief of police. The crime could not be ignored. The extent of the maharajah's participation in the affair was never made public but he was soon given the choice of abdicating in favor of his son or of giving evidence at an official inquiry. He abdicated, subsequently married Miss Nancy Miller of Seattle, Washington, and spent most of his time thereafter in France† in his château at St. Germain or his villa at Cap Ferrat.

This Maharajah of Indore was dealt with more summarily by the British than the thirty-fourth Maharajah of Rewa. In 1942 the prince of Rewa was suspended while two charges against him were considered. The first was of complicity in a murder

---

* Malwa opium was rated the world's best by the experts of China. It was processed and exported by the government of India, and the proceeds formed a vital part of the revenue. The drug was used extensively in India in the form of pills, but in China was smoked, with more harmful results.

† He thus set something of a style in Indore. His son married two American ladies in succession and spent the greater part of every year in the United States or Europe, provoking the British Resident at Indore to suggest changing the state's national anthem to "Some Day My Prince Will Come."

—it was believed in Rewa that the prince was guilty of twelve such crimes—and the second of sending spies into the Resident's office. Within a year, the charges unproven, the maharajah was allowed to resume his throne. He continued his old habit of appropriating a generous part of the revenue of his state and sending it to his own private account in the Bank of England. The British knew that although he had more than six million dollars in London by the end of the Second World War, he did nothing to recover the money and use it to improve the lamentable condition of the people of Rewa. Despite this lenient attitude the maharajah openly despised the British. Nevertheless, when he was dying he sent for a British political officer and dictated to him the terms of his will, asking him to make sure his son followed them. In view of the maharajah's hatred of the British, the official asked why he was being honored with this request. The maharajah said simply that he could not trust anyone else to carry it out.

The magnificent world of the maharajahs achieved its Augustan age in the period between the visit of one Prince of Wales (later Edward VII) in 1875–1876 and that of another, his grandson (later Edward VIII) in 1921–1922. In the interim a third Prince of Wales made his royal tour in the winter of 1905–1906, then returned to India in 1911 in the King-Emperor's full majesty for the greatest ceremony of state ever held on the face of the earth. George V's Imperial Durbar at Delhi, a formal assembly of all the leading men in India, was mounted from a camp of forty thousand tents sheltering three hundred thousand people in a concentration of wealth and power not even the Tsar of Russia could equal.

All three Princes of Wales were entertained privately and in splendor by the leading maharajahs, who received enough marks of royal condescension to encourage them in their opinions of themselves. They became aware, with Edward VII and George V, of an affinity springing from a faint but commonly held memory of the ancient divinity of kingship: the more spirited among them were emboldened to take a firmer stance in their dealings with the government of India, and the many who deserted traditionalism copied the imperial style they felt was suited to their rank with houses in London, Paris and Delhi and creamy villas on the French Riviera.

Their minor eccentricities became a source of light entertainment wherever gossip was prized. One conducted all his business sitting on the lavatory. Another bought two hundred and seventy automobiles. One was so devoted to dogs that he built a three-ward hospital for his pedigree retrievers. One would use only bank notes fresh from the presses of the mint and paid 10 percent extra to get them. Another filled one vast room of his palace with packages containing the entire stock of a hardware store he had bought outright in England in reaction to a fancied slight from its bucolic proprietor. The princes pursued their passions with simple enthusiasm. One refused to have a railroad run through his territory because it offended his religion to think of passengers wolfing down beef in the dining cars. Another, enamored of the tartan, bought Highland uniforms for his household troops perfect in detail from kilt to feathered bonnet, and even including pink tights to lend to dusky knees an illusion of Scottish integrity. One, desiring a dish of quail at the Savoy Hotel in London, caused cables to be sent to the four corners of the earth and so discovered six in Egypt, too late for dinner. Another occupied an entire floor of the same hotel, satisfying his esthetic sense with three thousand fresh roses a day. Opening his morning paper, one heir apparent fell full shock in love with the leggy photograph of a current beauty queen, located her, pressed his suit and swiftly married her, though she was merely the sixteen-year-old daughter of a railroad porter from Crewe. Another prince, insatiable for tigers, accused of tying up live infants as bait, excused himself with the observation that he had never missed a tiger yet, which was true. The same maharajah protected a duchess hunting by night with a precautionary searchlight and a machine gun mounted on an elephant.

All the maharajahs were great hunters, players of games, and superb hosts. In one state thirty ortolans might be killed on the rise with a single shot, to be eaten later in a pie a hundred at a time. Another state prided itself on its golf course, groomed by convicts, where the maharajah was attended by an official whose duty it was to remind him in a subdued but unremitting chant to be kind enough to keep his eye on the ball. In another, croquet playing in the indigo night was made possible by a system of hurricane lanterns flitting hither and thither like lunatic fireflies in the hands of scurrying, noiseless servants. In variety and extent, the sports were limitless. So was the hospitality. It was not unusual for a solitary guest to find at his absolute disposal a staff of a hundred and a guard of a score or more state policemen, with his supplies of champagne and French bath oils replenished night and morning.

Generous as the princes could be in private they were capable of even greater munificence when it seemed that their King-Emperor needed their services. One or two fire-eaters were always dashing off in person to some frontier war or other, but the maharajahs' greatest contributions were made for the two world wars. At the first gunshot they offered money and men: troops from the maharajahs' private armies fought in Flanders, Egypt, Palestine, East Africa and Mesopotamia during the first world war, and all over the Middle East and in Eritrea, Italy and Burma during the second. The Jodhpur Lancers swept into Haifa at the charge as General Allenby pressed his crusade against the Turks toward Jerusalem; a generation later the Jaipur infantry endured in the Apennine snows before the bloody rage of Cassino. Loyal, trusting, proud, the soldiers of the Native States merely mirrored the single-minded code of their princes. It was, of course, an outdated chivalry. When, as their stars dimmed, the maharajahs had some right to expect of the British some moral recognition of the bond they had honored, they were disappointed. By 1947 the world had become egalitarian; the ideal of service no longer relied on a fierce sense of personal honor. As the last Viceroy saluted the new flag of India, unfurled in Delhi on August 15, 1947, a rainbow touched the sky with glory. Radiant, brave, ineffably beautiful, it was obviously an augury. But for a remarkable and medieval nobility it was the last romantic emblazonment on their outdated shields.

4

✦❰✦❰✦❰✦❰✦❰✦❰✦❰✦

The Richest Man in the World

THROUGHOUT THE FIRST HALF of the twentieth century, His Exalted Highness the seventh Nizam of Hyderabad was thought to be the richest man in the world. He probably was not, but certainly he could lay his hands on more ready cash than any man on earth, before or since. The eight million dollars' worth of bank notes that the rats had secretly gnawed away in the bowels of his palace hardly affected the intricate arithmetic his heirs were put to in 1967. Their sums revealed seventy-two million dollars in gold bars and gold coin and nearly a hundred million more in jewelry, though not all the jewelry was easily negotiable. Two of the diamonds alone, each the size of a lime, weighed over 180 carats apiece,*and potential buyers on that

---

* For comparison, the blue Hope diamond weighs a mere 44½ carats and was insured for a million dollars when Mr. Harry Winston mailed it to the Smithsonian Institution in 1958. The Regent diamond in the Louvre weighs 140½ carats and was valued, when owned by Napoleon, at about four million dollars. The diamond bought from Messrs. Cartier in 1969 by Mr. Richard Burton for Miss Elizabeth Taylor weighed 69.42 carats and cost him something more than one million, fifty thousand dollars.

scale were not numerous. Fewer still were the connoisseurs who would want to put one of the diamonds to the same use the Nizam's father had: it had been his paperweight. Estimates of the Nizam's personal wealth at his death swung wildly from just under half a billion dollars to just under one billion and three quarters. The Nizam himself had had no idea of the total, though it was the overriding concern of his last years to keep it as high as possible. To this end he restricted himself to an expenditure for his own needs, which were cigarettes, betel nut and opium, of slightly more than a dollar a day.

Lieutenant General His Exalted Highness Sir Osman Ali Khan Bahadur, Regulator of the Country, Victorious in Battle, the Aristotle of his Age, Shadow of God and Faithful Ally of the British, to give the barest hint of the Nizam's titles, was not in appearance the image of a king. His thrones when he occupied them always seemed too large for him, like other men's coats. Five feet three inches tall, and slender to the point of delicacy, fine-boned and smooth-skinned, he retained the look of youth long past middle age and through decades of rule. Immaculate in public, in private he affected the rumpled cotton pajamas of the common people, camel-skin slippers bought for a few shillings in the nearest bazaar, gray socks of inadequate length, and a disgraceful old fez that he kept for thirty-five years. He was revered as a religious leader by Muslims throughout India and beyond, and as a prince by the millions of his Hindu subjects. Those who were close to him feared him. His style was elegant and spare, and he moved in quietness. Yet there was about him something dangerous and strange, something incalculable. It was in his eyes, black and adamantine behind his cheap steel-rimmed spectacles: they stared without blinking and without a hint of expression. It was impossible to tell what lay behind them, whether it was lust or aloofness, piety or hate. In the end it could have been a sort of madness.

The heart of kings, the Proverbs say, is unsearchable. Though the true person of the seventh Nizam lay inaccessible, he was by lineage and appointments undeniably a king. The house of Asaf Jah, the first Nizam, began in 1724 when that great warrior

took over the Deccan as viceroy of the Mogul emperor. Of
Mogul descent himself, Asaf Jah had commanded an army for
Aurengzeb, last of the Great Moguls, and when that ascetic
tyrant died, strode through the wreck of the Mogul Empire and
installed himself prince of the Deccan—that is, of virtually all
the south. To the Moguls, the Deccan proper was an immense,
flat rock plateau stretching practically from the Bay of Bengal
to the blue Nilgiri Hills. Politically its boundaries could run
wherever Asaf Jah chose to put them, for he was unchallenged.
They crystallized during his reign to delineate an area more than
half the size of France. It was a dry land for the most part, dotted
with great gray boulders round and wrinkled like petrified elephants. There was a legend that they were the debris left over
by the Creator when he had finished making the world, but
there was irony in that, for the Deccan was a rich prize.

Completing a stone wall around the delicate white city of
Hyderabad, Asaf Jah settled down to the enjoyment of his spoils,
officially only the Mogul emperor's viceroy but in fact a sovereign
prince. Nervous of his power, his nominal master the emperor
encouraged the governor of Hyderabad city to revolt. Asaf Jah,
whose cunning was enriched by a dark sense of humor, shortly
wrote in the tasteful style of the Mogul court to congratulate
the emperor on a victory over the forces of radicalism, enclosing
the governor's severed head. By such dramatic correspondence
and by exercising his quite immoral wits, Asaf Jah survived
and prospered while the subcontinent boiled with change as the
Marathas challenged the dying power of the Moguls. He remained secure in Hyderabad in the shadow of his menacing
rock fortress of Golconda. Golconda was also the market for all
the diamonds in the world. The mines of Kollur were not far off,
worked by sixty thousand men, women and children spewing
out a brilliant stream that would amount to twelve million carats
before the pipes were exhausted. One man alone, a former commander of the armies of Golconda, counted his diamonds by the
sackful, including perhaps the Koh-i-noor itself.

The glitter of accumulated wealth lay over the Deccan. Canals
irrigated its hot earth carrying water from vast man-made lakes.

It abounded in cattle, rice, corn, sheep, fowl and fish of uniquely delicate flavor. Hyderabad itself, named by a former king "the Fortunate City," was as big and bustling as any town but the capitals of Europe. Foreign merchants came there to buy hides and gems, and iron to fashion the sharp blades of Damascus. A stone bridge not inferior to the Pont Neuf in Paris crossed the river outside its walls, and over it trotted daily five or six hundred packhorses bearing palm wine for the thirsty gullets of its busy population. Hyderabad's great mosque was a marvel, even to visitors from Mecca, for it included a shrine hewn from a single slab of granite; five hundred men had labored for five years to quarry it, and fourteen hundred oxen had been conscripted to drag it into the city. Hyderabad had gardens and orchards and music and twenty thousand ladies of easy virtue and even easier access, each one registered in the books of the chief of police.

Providence allowed Asaf Jah twenty-four years of comparative ease until, at the age of ninety-one, he was called to Paradise. He left a last will and testament running to seventeen clauses and packed with sound advice about the treasury (keep it mobile at all times), the troops (allow them enough furlough to propagate), the inhabitants of Kashmir (never believe what they say) and war (avoid disputes and enmities). Those to whom it was addressed paid no heed to it, being occupied in a murderous scramble for the throne.

Between the death of Asaf Jah in 1748 and the accession of Osman Ali in 1911 there were five Nizams. Each of them enjoyed the magnificent and somewhat mysterious state of an oriental monarch, and each saw his dominion slip further and further into dependency on the British. Since Hyderabad was the first Native State to enter into alliance with the East India Company, it was also the first to have the honor of accommodating a British Resident within easy reach of its court. The succession of Residents included a number of formidable characters and a leaven of eccentrics. Colonel James Achilles Kirkpatrick flaunted a scarlet beard and fingers dyed with henna to the first joint in the Persian fashion; encouraged by his father to study

oriental manners and tongues, Kirkpatrick showed enough enthusiasm for the indigenous to marry a Muslim princess. Except
for the pallor of his skin, he appeared in every respect one of the
noblemen of the court and conducted himself toward the Nizam,
as a colleague reported, not without misgivings, "like a native
and with great propriety." Later came Colonel John Low, a
hard Lowland Scot who had once blown in the gates of the
Lucknow palace to get at a king and unseat him, and who in
retirement enjoyed the distinction of being the only member of
the Royal and Ancient golf club allowed to pursue his ball
astride a pony. More powerful still was Charles Theophilus
Metcalfe, one of India's greatest administrators, an awkward,
chunky little Etonian with a pimply face, a brilliant record and
a stubborn will to see right done. When traveling, he preferred
elephants to horses because the elephant's more deliberate motion
allowed him to read. Most of Metcalfe's colleagues supported
"sleeping dictionaries" but few married these local girls, as
Metcalfe did his. She was a Sikh or Kashmiri girl whom he had
met on a mission to Ranjit Singh, lord of the Punjab. She bore
him three sons, whom he schooled in England. Metcalfe had
few illusions. "Empires grow old, decay and perish," he wrote
in 1820. "Ours in India can hardly be called old, but seems
destined to be short-lived. We appear to have passed the bril-
liancy and vigor of our youth, and it may be that we have
reached a premature old age."

Kirkpatrick, Low, Metcalfe and their like forced or cajoled
the Nizams into following British policy and rescued one or
two from the results of their own folly. Though it was never
the Resident's function to govern, in some ways, at least, he
was given the appearance of a ruler. To begin with, the Resident
lived in a palace some two miles outside the city and seldom
left it without a decorative escort of cavalry. The site was a gift
of the Nizam. The construction funds, also a gift of the Nizam,
allowed a lieutenant in the Madras Engineers to draw up rather
lavish plans for the new Residency. The curved stone portico
was sixty feet long and twenty-five feet deep. Twenty-two
granite steps emphasized by two couchant but colossal lions led

up to its Corinthian columns. Its principal room was a durbar (reception) hall sixty feet long, more than half as wide and with ceilings fifty feet high. Private apartments were distributed east and west of this vast throne room, with vistas of enormous fig trees and tamarinds where a population of flying foxes roosted by day, tumbling off one by one as the sun set to flicker toward some juicy orchard. The grounds spread over sixty acres. If not a sermon in stone, the Residency at least suggested a text: the choice of the Palladian style was at once modish and significant, for pillars spoke authority and permanence. The Residency made it clear that the British were in Hyderabad to stay. Unfortunately, at least one of the British should never have arrived. Henry Russell, Resident during the time of the third Nizam, was the son of a great Indian judge* but proved that probity was not hereditary by joining a conspiracy to suck the Nizam's territories dry.

After Asaf Jah the finances of Hyderabad had fallen into ruin. The third Nizam, the target of the conspirators, was a man uniquely inclined to folly who had been dealing with the banking firm of William Palmer and Company. Its principal, Palmer, was "a gentleman not of pure European blood" (he was the son of a British general and a princess of Oudh), and on those grounds some might excuse his villainy. Palmer was merely the front man for one Sir William Rumbold, who, though of unsullied European blood, was by no definition a gentleman. Rumbold had married the Governor-General's ward and had come to India expressly to make his fortune. Though the government of India had a law prohibiting Europeans from lending money to Indians, Rumbold somehow persuaded his quasi–father-in-law, the Governor-General, that the law might be ignored, since the Indian to

---

* Sir Henry Russell (1751–1836) was Chief Justice of the Supreme Court of India. On January 8, 1808, he brought honor to the memory of British justice in the case of John Grant, cadet in the service of the East India Company, who had been found guilty of maliciously setting fire to a native's hut. In sentencing Grant to death, Sir Henry observed, "The natives are entitled to have their characters, property and lives protected; as long as they enjoy that privilege from us, they give their affection and allegiance in return."

whom he wished to make loans through Palmer and Company
was on sovereign Indian, not British Indian, soil. Sophistry, or
perhaps nepotism, triumphed. Rumbold, as a partner of William
Palmer and Company, invited Russell, the Resident at Hyderabad, to join the firm. He did so, secretly, and the bank began its
operations blatantly in the Residency garden.

Their game was quite simple. The Nizam's business was conducted by a Hindu Prime Minister foisted on him by the British.
Rumbold suborned him. The Prime Minister, who took a share,
permitted any measure that would wring money from the
peasantry to give Rumbold the interest on his loans to the
Nizam. The state's tax gatherers clipped heavy weights to delinquent ear lobes or pulled out fingernails with heated pliers to
encourage early payment. It became a commonplace in Hyderabad for farmers to turn brigands out of desperation, then to be
hunted by bewildered and reluctant British officers intent on
restoring law and order.

In 1819 Palmer and Company pressed on the Nizam an additional loan of seven million dollars. In reality a paper transaction,
its interest would be hard-enough currency, to be split between
Palmer and Company and the Prime Minister. The Nizam was
unwise enough to murmur that he did not need another loan
from Rumbold. Rumbold reported the Nizam's ingratitude and
lack of financial acumen to the Governor-General. Brushing all
that aside, the Governor-General countered through his official
channel, Russell the Resident, with a brusque demand for an outright gift from the Nizam of over eight hundred thousand dollars, "for public purposes connected with the city of Calcutta."
Perhaps out of delicacy, the Governor-General did not mention
that the "public purposes" he had in mind were the building of
an Anglican cathedral and a palace for its bishop. The Nizam
was the leading Muslim in India, descendant of both the Caliph
and the Prophet Mohammed, so it was hardly the kind of charity
to appeal to him greatly. The stink of graft at last began to
percolate so far that the East India Company's board in London
smelled it. It refused to approve the loan and Russell was replaced as Resident by honest John Theophilus Metcalfe. Met-

calfe quickly uncovered every detail of Rumbold's shoddy adventure, reduced William Palmer and Company's total claim on the Nizam to seven and a quarter million dollars, and despite the Governor-General's vigorous opposition, enabled the Nizam to pay it off.

Metcalfe reformed the system of taxation, but even he, selfless and experienced as he was, could effect nothing permanent. One of the causes of Hyderabad's insolvency was that the Nizam was required to support a contingent of "British" troops (in reality Indian regiments) "ready to settle the affairs of His Highness' government in everything that is right and proper, whenever required." This had been one of the provisions of the treaty between the Nizam and the East India Company, the first alliance between the British and an Indian prince. The treaty also stipulated the rather curious means by which the Nizam would pay for the troops' upkeep. He would rent five of his provinces to the East India Company for about a million dollars a year, and the British would deduct from that rent the cost of the troops. Even a novice in accounting and politics could have predicted that the cost of the troops would come to about a million dollars a year. The net result was that the Nizam got no money and had to live with foreign troops in the middle of his country, and the British made a pleasant profit through their better administration of his five provinces. They were even able to lend the Nizam money.

The troops remained, the Nizams came and went, the financial swamp spread wider. By the end of 1850, the balance of the current Nizam stood at four and a quarter million dollars owed to the British. They pressed him for it. He scraped half of it together. The British then proposed a deal. There was a province called Berar, sixteen thousand square miles of rich cotton soil, the most productive land in Hyderabad. The Nizam could see, from their administration of the five rented provinces, that the British were more efficient administrators than his own people. The British would take over Berar in perpetual trust, paying back to the Nizam any surplus profits they might make by their superior management. Of course, the cost of the troops would have to be deducted as usual. The accounting was now a little more complicated, with Berar and the original provinces in one scale and the rising cost of the troops in the other, but the balance always seemed to come out much the same. There was a yearly dispute between the Nizam and the British about the expensive way in which the British ran his divorced territories and the resulting meagerness of the surplus.

This minor irritation was not enough to turn the Nizam against the British during the Mutiny, though when it started in 1857 the British in Hyderabad telegraphed fearfully: IF THE NIZAM GOES ALL IS LOST. A group of fanatics demonstrating outside the Residency was swept up by the Nizam's own troops, who then marched with the British. In 1860, with a grace occasioned by profound relief, the British wrote off the Nizam's current debt of one and three-quarter million dollars, bestowed a sweetener of thirty-five thousand dollars in cash, a jeweled sword, a diamond ring and a few other trinkets, restored to him a part of the territories they had been administering worth more than a quarter of a million dollars a year, and finally hung on the appropriate parts of his person the star, badge and collar of the Order of the Star of India. Berar, however, remained in British hands, so the ungrateful Nizam had cause to murmur to a confidant, "Generosity is uppermost in the minds of my British allies, even though their mathematics are a trifle weak." Not a few of the pounds sterling of his vanished debt had gone to fight the British war against the mutineers.

All Hyderabad's public affairs were now handled by a man of imposing bulk and impressive ability, the Hindu Sir Salar Jung. Sir Salar crushed the Arab condottieri who had bedeviled Hyderabad, created a police force and a judiciary, and organized a workable system of revenue. The British called him a statesman of genius but he embarrassed them by amassing enough millions to buy back Berar; they were hard put to it to find a good reason to refuse. He had already antagonized some of Hyderabad's men of ancient lineage by usurping their powers. In 1859, while he was leaving a gathering at the Nizam's palace arm in arm with the Resident, a would-be assassin fired a shot without effect and rushed in with drawn sword, but was indiscriminately hacked down by Sir Salar's bodyguard before it could be ascertained which of the two gentlemen had been his target. It was charitably assumed that the Resident had been the mark. In 1868 a second assassin missed and this time was set upon by the Nizam's guards. Sir Salar survived these mishaps with every appearance of good fellowship and robust well-being. But in 1883 he was the only member of a picnic party to die of a surfeit of canned oysters, though others were unwell. One Residency doctor certified cholera as the cause of death and the other disagreed, creating fertile ground for rumor, for while there might not be much proof of poison, there were plenty of motives.

Sir Salar had served three Nizams as minister, quite overshadowing the fifth of the line. When Sir Salar died, the sixth Nizam was still a minor whom he had served and governed for close to fourteen years. Outside his palace the sixth Nizam was a diffident young man who never smiled and seldom spoke because, the whispers said, there had been an accident with a pistol in the women's quarters and a child had died—sufficient cause, they said, for the young prince guiltily to think that the Resident might imprison him at any moment. A few months after Sir Salar's death in 1883, the British declared the boy to be officially of age at eighteen and placed him on the throne with ceremony and homily in the Chow Mahalla palace, once the pleasure house of Asaf Jah. The Chow Mahalla was a complex of four massive buildings and three quadrangles linked by angled passageways permitting no more than three people to walk abreast, thus discouraging mass movement in the event of a palace revolution. One of the sixth Nizam's occupations was the decoration of innumerable apartments of state with chandeliers and wall lights of Levantine or Venetian opulence, glowing ruby, purple, pink, green and, inevitably, gold. Thick silk was everywhere, on the walls, swathing windows, covering Louis XIV and Victorian chairs. In each of the public rooms there was a wrought-iron gallery obscured by a veil of fuchsia so that the ladies of the harem might hear and dimly see the affairs of the great world without sacrificing their religious anonymity. On February 5, 1884, two thrones stood ready in the durbar hall of the Chow Mahalla, one for the sixth Nizam and one for the Viceroy, who carefully arrived at the same moment. The Viceroy, a devout Roman Catholic, and a liberal as deeply dyed as his master Gladstone, preached a gentle sermon full of good advice, then buckled a diamond-hilted sword of state around the Nizam's slim waist—on the wrong side.

Unfortunately, the advice was not applied and Hyderabad's finances slid once more into their familiar pattern of Micawberish economics. The Nizam's tastes were in keeping with his Edwardian times. He was perhaps the finest shot in India and once proved it to the doomed Archduke Ferdinand of Austria by repeatedly hitting a coin spinning in midair. His wide estates offered great sport, and in the heat of April or May when his jungles were dry, the Nizam would order his special train on a whim and rattle away to bag a tiger. The Nizam's longings could always be answered, since the train would keep up a head of steam and since all his palaces and shooting boxes were kept fully staffed. This was the best system, for it was his habit to announce a move without designating the location. He dressed in an English suit of unimpeachable cut, glossy button boots, full cravats and suede gloves, and like the portly Edward, Prince of Wales, frequently carried a gold-topped cane. He might have been taken for an English gentleman of breeding, side whiskers and all, but on one occasion he behaved in a manner unbecoming to a gentleman and a ruler.

One summer afternoon in 1891, as the worst of the heat was lifting, a soft, plump little black-haired man dressed in white duck came to the Chow Mahalla palace. In the inside pocket of his coat he carried a diamond of rather more than 162 carats. His name was Alexander Jacob and he was to be characterized in three popular novels.* Jacob was notorious, from Simla to the

---

* Marion Crawford made him the protagonist of *Mr. Isaacs:* Crawford had described Jacob over dinner at a New York club to his uncle Samuel Ward and had been encouraged to write the story. Colonel Newnham Davis drew Jacob's picture in his less familiar *Jadoo,* and Kipling turned him into Lurgan Sahib, the maker of spies in *Kim.*

fashionable spa of Homburg, for his powers of magic. The gullible credited him with the ability to walk on water and even the least credulous granted him powers of mesmerism and telepathy. It was generally believed by British and Indians alike that he practiced white magic, and it was variously supposed that he was a Jew, an Armenian, a Russian agent, a British agent. It was obvious to all that he was the most important dealer in jewels and antiquities in India, and known to a few that he had in fact undertaken missions for the Secret Department of the government of India. He traveled by private train. His little store in Simla was a pantechnicon of riches, blazing with gold and smoky with incense, and in it Jacob squatted, pale and subtle, keeping a diary full of secrets.

Jacob had agreed to purchase for the Nizam a famous diamond, kept in England, then called "the Imperial" (and later "the Jacob"), for the sum of three hundred thousand pounds, half of which His Highness had paid as a deposit. Now Jacob delivered the diamond in person with only the Nizam's valet as a witness. He left, with the Nizam still owing half the purchase price. Unknown to Jacob, the Resident had heard about the transaction. A worthy, wordy man whose lust was legalities and propriety, the Resident sought to save the Nizam's almost bankrupt government from the folly of buying yet another bauble. The Nizam froze. He was not allowed to pay the rest of the money and he would not return the diamond. He wrapped it in an ink-stained cloth and dropped it into a drawer. Jacob was forced to defend his investment by suing in a Calcutta court; though he won the case, he was broken. His legal expenses were great. No prince in India would deal with him again and he died in penury, even his magic spent, in Bombay. After his father's death the seventh Nizam discovered the diamond in the toe of one of his father's slippers and had a base of gold filigree made for it, the better to serve its purpose as a paperweight.

Hyderabad's financial well-being remained a matter of concern to the British and in 1902 the sixth Nizam bowed before Lord Curzon, the most imperious, most efficient and most selfless of all the Viceroys. Curzon had come to Hyderabad with an escort of hussars to settle the intricate affairs of that state. At dinner he was feted with pies which, when opened, released frantic little birds; one settled on Lady Curzon's tiara and another with relief on His Excellency's noble head. The flutterings stilled, Curzon pressed the Nizam to sign a letter which it was thought would bring to an orderly conclusion all his financial problems. Under its terms, Berar would be leased in perpetuity to the British for a quitrent of nearly a million and a half dollars; the Nizam would fix a budget for his personal expenses and hold to it, and would accept the advice of a British financial expert. Out of deference to his guest, the Nizam signed the letter of agreement. The next morning he sent his minister to the Residency to get the document back and destroy it. At the Residency, the minister seized the letter of agreement and loyally swallowed it. His action did not force Lord Curzon to regurgitate Berar, however. When the seventh Nizam raised the question of Berar twenty-one years later he was snubbed, though in the interim he had done the British Crown much service.

Osman Ali, the seventh Nizam, came to the throne in 1911 a mere Highness. The title of "Exalted Highness" was one of the rewards for his aid in men, treasure and moral support in the First World War. He was the product of a childhood spent in the harem in the company of women, and of a youth guided by a British tutor. He spoke Persian and Urdu, had been instructed in the precepts of Islam and knew the silken places of the palace where intrigue bred; he also practiced the manly exercises of a clean young Englishman, riding at a gutted sheep slung from an upright pole and bisecting it with a single cut. He was thin and vigorous, this premier prince of India, and preened himself in long, smooth coats buttoned with pearls or emeralds or rubies, or even diamonds. His father had taught him the elements of royalty, such as leaving dropped coins where they lay to demonstrate a king's disdain for money, and had set him up in his own quarters, a small palace bought from a noble kinsman. This place, King Kothi, became Osman Ali's permanent home.

Of his larger palaces, the old Purana Haveli was an abode of women, and Chow Mahalla was used only for formalities when the Nizam built a durbar hall among its cypresses and fountains which was enclosed on three sides and open on the fourth behind a triple colonnade. A bolster of yellow satin and a Persian rug thrown over a white marble dais, with a crystal column at each corner blossoming into clusters of golden lights, served as a throne. Guards stood by the walls in blue tunics splashed with gold and headdresses barred with the bold ochre of Hyderabad, their drawn swords liquid with the light winking from Bohemian chandeliers. Evening durbars were the custom. The noblemen would advance one by one, bearing in outstretched hands the prescribed gift of gold coins. Offering was obligatory in Mogul courts; acceptance or remission was the prerogative of the prince. It was becoming noticeable that as he grew older, the Nizam Osman Ali was remitting less and accepting more. He would hand the money to an official, mingle briefly and pleasantly with the crowd and drift away into the night to the mysteries and delights of King Kothi.

His fourth palace, Falaknuma, he thought of as a gigantic guesthouse for the eminent. A visit by royalty cost him thousands in refurbishing. When the glamorous young Prince of Wales came by for three or four days in 1922, the polo ground was completely returfed and a squash court was built for the good of His Royal Highness' liver. He did not use it. Once the huge bed in the principal suite was lengthened for a Viceroy who, as a servant explained, "was a very tall Excellency." Falaknuma's style was Edwardian abundance, velvet plush and wine-dark glass crammed into a Grecian case of marble walls and staircases. There was even a smoking room, retreat of the male from the world of corseted propriety, paneled in oak and equipped with chairs of dark leather with brass studs, a vast hookah with golden silk tubes, and a large painting of a local naked maja sporting shocking red toenails. The Nizam placed hidden cameras in his guest bathrooms. One of his legacies was a unique assortment of candid photographs of the famous performing their toilets; it eventually joined his notable collection of more commonplace erotica in a back room of the Hyderabad Museum. The durbar hall at Falaknuma held two chairlike

thrones on tiger skins, one for the Nizam and the other for the
Viceroy, but the Nizam used it more often in his more carefree
years as a ballroom. Captured by the waltz and the strange
new rhythms of the fox trot, he entertained Hyderabad's society
once or twice a week, and the room's thirty-six chandeliers
would stir and shimmer, flecking the long mirrors on the walls
as "I'm Forever Blowing Bubbles" bounced in a wail of saxo-
phones from one gray, pink and gold panel to another.

Despite the supposed rigidity of Muslim law, social life in
Hyderabad was of a refinement described by one Resident as
second only to Peking's. Scholarship, the pursuit of poetry, the
collection of fine art and the practice of brilliant conversation
were commonplaces among the noble families, whose homes
equaled the Nizam's for splendor, and whose sons went to the
best English private schools as a matter of course. Armies of
servants and guards—a troop of amazons in the case of the
Nizam's formidable aunt—ministered to them, and their own
bands of musicians amused them nightly, frequently with "The
Eton Boating Song" in a local and fortuitous arrangement.
These grandees were mostly Muslims, descendants of Afghan
and Arab mercenaries ennobled by former Nizams, but some
were Hindus and in the 1930s one of these still followed the
ancient custom of Hyderabad of scattering largesse as his Rolls-
Royce drove him to his office. Gossip and intrigue coursed like
adrenalin through the body politic of Hyderabad, so that the
best advice of a senior British official to a newcomer was, "Keep
your mouth shut and your bowels open." Fear was, of course,
the great laxative, and the greatest object of fear was His
Exalted Highness the Nizam, whose powers within Hyderabad
were not inconsiderable. He had a nasty habit of singling out a
nobleman at the dinner table by sending him a glass of champagne from the princely bottle, at which the nobleman would
stand and bow, hiding his annoyance, because the gesture meant
that the next morning he would have to present himself at the
palace with a suitable gift lest ill befall. The shadow of the
Nizam's omnipotence was not enough to darken the daily life
of the city, however. It was at times so gay and glittering a

place, its multitudinous domes like a cluster of fabulous balloons out of a fairy tale, that visitors could imagine it floating away into a never-never land of privilege and style.

The Nizam himself displayed a number of contradictions. He owned one of the world's finest collections of Grecian silver, jade so rare it could scarcely be valued, crystal of peerless quality, but it was all distributed about his palaces more for form's sake than for ostentation. He amassed things in a fever of possession. No new luxury car was safe in Hyderabad, for the Nizam would ask its owner if he might take a ride in it; he would order his chauffeur to drive it straight into the palace garage and have it stored. In the end the Nizam had collected more than two hundred great limousines, none with any mileage to speak of. For many years the Nizam himself used a 1934 Ford tourer or a 1910 Rolls-Royce. At formal dinners in the Falaknuma palace even the crumb scoops were of solid gold; there was enough plate to feed three hundred, and the fare, because it was paid for out of public funds, was lavish, but an invitation to tea in private would mean only a frugal cookie. The Nizam was a heavy smoker of local cigarettes bought in the bazaar for a few cents for a pack of ten, but his guests were offered more expensive brands, probably left behind by previous visitors. It was his habit to dump ashes and stubs in a neat pile on the floor by his side. Yet he could be fantastically clean. In his last years he washed his hands after every letter or state paper he handled, though many had been touched only by a secretary of hygienic habits. He was a meticulous man, and of all who examined his possessions—appraisers, jewelers, civil servants, privileged visitors —none was more able than he to come to a correct assessment. If he achieved one he never revealed it.

The Nizam collected people as well as things, mostly women. It was commonly thought that he exercised a sort of jubilant droit du seigneur in his dominions, a custom both ancient and codified. The procurement of ladies was managed in two ways, the first being more circumspect and hallowed. In the part of the harem where the Nizam's mother held sway, there were women who were neither slaves nor servants. They were dependents, frequently the product of some complicated liaison, and must be cared for. They were called *khannazads* and they were numerous. On some festive occasion, like her son's birthday or a public holiday, the old dowager might select from among them a fair maiden, have her bathed, oiled, perfumed and dressed in gauzes and gold, and send her off as a surprise package. Since a son could not refuse a mother's gift, the girl willy-nilly became part of the Nizam's household and lived thereafter as a concubine in the harem.

The second stream of entry into the harem was more general. A family blessed with a pretty daughter might conceive of her as a means of advancement. Whispers would pass from courtier to courtier until the good news reached the ear of His Exalted Highness, and an inspection by some competent woman of the entourage would be arranged. On some few occasions a family might be honored without any formality at all. Such was the case with Leila Begum, a singing girl whose beauty struck the Nizam dumb while he was touring the provinces. She became his favorite and bore him five sons and two daughters.

More formally, the Nizam had four wives, the maximum allocation of Islam. His first, a local aristocrat, he married at the age of twenty, in 1906. She had two sons, who survived him, and a daughter who by custom was not allowed to marry lest, as the superstition had it, her leaving the household bring on her father's death. The Nizam's first wife became a poet of some distinction and an expert grower of roses, and made the pilgrimage to Mecca. The third wife was a niece of the Aga Khan, and the two others were drawn from the nobility of Hyderabad. The Nizam's entire female establishment was extensive, but an exact tally was difficult to achieve. At the height of his pomp the Nizam was probably the proprietor of some two hundred concubines and in the 1920s took most of them with him by special train when he visited New Delhi for a few days. At the end of his reign the total was reduced, for economic and other reasons, to forty-two. The children (a total of between fifty and one hundred and ten) remained a charge, of course, as well as some scores of *khannazads* and a thousand servants, and there was a particularly painful problem with one daughter whose kleptomania necessitated having her followed around the rambling bazaars of the city so that what she stole could be paid for or replaced.

All his life the Nizam was in close proximity to women who had little to occupy them but matters of hypochondria, a consideration which may have raised in him his own intense interest in matters of health. His chief relaxation in old age was watching surgical operations. But for many years his passion was a far gentler therapy, the medical system of ancient Greece, known as *unani*. As a result, Hyderabad became the only place in the world with a hospital and free public clinics following this practice. *Unani's* basis was the action of powdered jewels administered in infusions of herbs or in syrups. A teaspoonful of crushed pearl mixed with honey, for instance, was a remedy for ailments of the heart. With some reason, as a gemophile, the Nizam believed in such specifics.

The Nizam's principal belief, however, was in his God, and his observance was strict and deeply felt. He applauded the work of the Ecclesiastical Department of his government, an unusual and powerful agency charged among other things with guarding the sacred name of the Prophet. The law of Hyderabad forbade the destruction of legal records or newspapers in which the name of Mohammed had been published. Since many devout citizens bore that name, the amount of the department's paperwork was prodigious. Great wire baskets were placed in the streets in which the public carefully deposited all papers bearing the sacred name. The Nizam's personal religious regime was rigorous. He regularly rattled down to the great mosque in an old car and worshiped there among his people without seeking or being given any distinction. Every evening at six he prayed alone beside his mother's grave. His religious knowledge and stature were widely respected. There was sound reason for the British to believe that after the end of the Ottoman Empire in 1918 and the discrediting of the Sultan of Turkey, the holy mantle of the Caliphs might fall on the Nizam. This possibility, obvious to millions of Muslims in India, made the Nizam's good will very valuable to the British.

The Nizam served the Imperial Crown most faithfully. He had been on the throne for three years when the First World War began: he sent two regiments of Lancers to guard the Suez Canal and to march with Allenby against the Muslim Turks and into Christian Jerusalem, and he poured treasure into the British coffers for bonds and as gifts to a total of one hundred million dollars. In 1919 he was made an "Exalted Highness" and "Faithful Ally." A quarter of a century later his troops again went to war for the British, and his money bought a squadron of Hurricane fighter planes for a start. Not long after the end of the Second World War the British deserted him as well as his fellow princes. He had given them decisive moral support for thirty-six years in all their problems with India's Muslims and while they had fought his co-religionists in the Middle East and later in Afghanistan. When he needed theirs in his opposition to the new Indian government of 1947, the British could find no comfort in their hearts. The Indian Independence Act of August 15, 1947, transferred power from London to the new native governments of India and Pakistan. But there was one principle that could not be transferred and it was, some thought, a matter of honor.

The relationship between successive Nizams and the British had rested on the recognition by both parties of the paramount interests of the latter. By accepting the principle of British paramountcy, the Nizams (like all other princes) acquired the right to expect British guarantees of their frontiers, the security of their thrones and the continuance of their dynasty. Quite suddenly the British announced that the principle of paramountcy no longer existed and suggested that the princes, including their own faithful ally the Nizam, make what terms they could with the new governments of India and Pakistan. The Nizam was in an interesting position. His state was the second largest in area in India, the most populous and the wealthiest, and he was a Muslim ruling Hindus. From the Indian government's point of view, if Hyderabad were allowed to accede to Pakistan, as principle at least permitted, India would have an alien presence twelve times the size of Israel sitting in her vitals. In the Nizam's opinion the British withdrawal had left him an independent sovereign, as his ancestors had been before the British came to Hyderabad. He therefore requested from the British and Indian governments the return of the territories leased to the British through the years and refused to accede to either India or Pakistan.

For a year a fog of rumors and alarms drifted over Hyderabad: Communists were infiltrating from the south, the Nizam was nourishing Pakistan with a flow of gold, Lancaster bombers were running in cargoes of arms by night, the Nizam was in the grip of a group of fanatics who were about to take over the state in the name of Islam and Pakistan. There was some truth in all these tales, but the ethos of Hyderabad's real mood was expressed by a lady at tea in a quiet garden in New Delhi. "Delhi is not what it was," she sighed. "There are no Mogul emperors now."

Knowing that the fatalistic Nizam might never bring himself to accede, the Indian government ordered its 1st Armored Division over his rocky escarpments. The Nizam acceded. A little apprehensively he welcomed General J. N. Chaudhuri, the divisional commander and new military governor of Hyderabad, who had set up his headquarters in the old British Residency. The Nizam had been seeking the general's antecedents in the local social register; when the general was able to confirm that he was indeed one of the Chaudhuris of Bengal, the Nizam was relieved. "We will look after this situation together," he proposed in his fluting voice, "and we need not be bothered by the riffraff either here or in India."

An agreement was reached which confirmed His Exalted Highness as a constitutional monarch with such continuing privileges as his salute of twenty-one guns. But the gold was carted away to modern banks, the jewels were sorted and valued, and the Nizam graciously accepted a pension for life of over two million dollars a year. The Nizam was not exactly reduced to penury by the fixing of this allowance, for he had already relieved himself of some expenses by forming a number of trusts—for his two sons and other kin, for various religious endowments and for the maintenance of the jewelry, and one to make sure his grandsons would enjoy an adequacy of candy and ice cream. For some years the Nizam occupied an official position in his former state, but it was empty of real power and there were constant skirmishes with the government of India about the payment of the pension and allowances, neither side being notably pacific.

At the end of 1956 the Nizam retired and disappeared into the obscurity of King Kothi. There he found plenty to do. Every morning his daughter woke him at five o'clock with the first of his forty or fifty cups of coffee a day. By seven he had composed the menus for all his household, issuing them from his cramped white-painted bedroom like imperial writs. He had more time for his old interests, including poetry, which he had once written with great elegance in the Persian style, full of the lover mortally struck by a glance from dark eyes, the anguished heart classically unrequited, a formal approach required by the genre and not related to his real life, in which, of course, womenfolk were not inaccessible. He still followed with interest the progress of the university he had founded, the first in India to teach in Urdu. He roused himself enough, when China came boiling over the Himalayas, to donate to his country's National Defense Fund forty-two thousand dollars in ready cash and eleven antique rifles. He mused on the history of his line and refurbished the ancestral monuments of his famous house. No doubt he reflected from time to time on the forecast made to Asaf Jah by an old seer. Asaf Jah as a young wayfarer had sought shelter and food; the old man had offered him loaves of unleavened bread, pressing them on him one after another. Asaf Jah had eaten seven before his appetite failed and the seer then revealed his future: he would rule a kingdom, and after him, his sons to the seventh generation.

The seventh Nizam's retirement lasted a little more than a decade, years that were lightened by the presence in his ménage

of a small white goat. It had been injured by his car and nursed
back to health by the best medical facilities of the palace. Now
it sat by the Nizam's side on his verandah, munching turnips
while he nibbled betel nut and drank the dark juice of poppies.
Shortly after it died in mature age, the Nizam too expired. He
was eighty-one. His body, which weighed less than ninety
pounds, lay all night swathed in Kashmir shawls on the verandah
with tubs of ice beneath it, three fans and an air conditioner
playing on it and incense burning, for it was not embalmed.
Then it was taken to the main mosque, smothered with the
petals of the musky roses of that place, and in the hot white
streets half a million of the people in Hyderabad mourned the
passing not, perhaps, of a man, but of a symbol.

5

❖❖❖❖❖❖❖❖❖❖❖❖❖❖

The Relatively
Liberated Woman

THE FIRST LADY of India at the end of the nineteenth
century and the beginning of the twentieth was a stout little
party. Her Highness Nawab Sultan Jehan Begum of Bhopal was
the only woman ruler in Asia and a mixture of Queen Victoria,
the Great Mogul and a lady editor of *Home Notes*. She was
known throughout the world from photographs as a dumpy
white truncated cone in the forefront of all great imperial occasions. A couple of breaths over five feet tall, she had strong
ankles, plump arms, a motherly bosom and a slightly fleshy but
pleasant face from which two direct dark eyes beamed upon the
world with merriment and shrewdness. None of these features
was ever revealed in public, however, for as a strict Muslim, the
Begum observed the rules of purdah with severity. At all times
she wore the *burqa*, a sheet of creamy muslin spraying down-
ward to the ground, anchored by a round boxlike cap, and
breached only by a slit across the eyes covered with lace. At
various points on this frail bell-tent, corresponding to the appropriate whereabouts of the Begum's anatomy, were pinned

superb jewels and the honors and decorations by which her long life of service had been recognized. What the Begum wore beneath the *burqa* only Allah knew, but there were reliable reports that it was silk and brocade of the most elegant quality and design. She attended the coronation of George V in London and all occasions of state in Delhi. Surrounded by her courtiers all in solemn black frock coats, she gave the impression of a small ruffled white owl being mobbed by rooks. What was also hidden was a very efficient beak and claws.

By descent the soft little Begum was an Orazkai Afghan. Her roistering ancestor Dost Mohammed Khan, a sword slinger for Aurengzeb, had murdered his way to the little principality at the beginning of the eighteenth century. His successors managed to hold off the Marathas, though at great cost, and were glad to make a formal treaty with the British in 1818. The then prince was shortly afterward shot with a pistol by his brother-in-law, a child of eight, an accident which, as an early historian lamented, "deprived Bhopal of her ablest ruler and worthiest citizen." His widow took over the state and there followed a hundred years of rule by women under whom Bhopal became one of the most progressive states in India. The first of these Begums, the widow Sikander, appointed herself regent in behalf of her daughter over the protests of the British by a *fait accompli*. She presented herself to her people unveiled, on horseback, and in the costume of a Muslim prince topped by a jeweled Mogul cap. The shock of all this was enough to convince the people that she would make a vigorous and virile ruler. In appearance boyish and thin-faced, Sikander's strongest feminine instinct seems to have been her love for her daughter and heir. Sikander Begum rode all over Bhopal pressing reforms and development schemes and roughing it in a tent. The dagger in her belt was not for ornament. Working twelve hours a day, in ten years she paid off the state debt of four million dollars and nearly tripled the revenue. She built dikes and roads, reorganized her army and the judiciary, and created a police force. When the Mutiny came she crushed the disaffection of her own troops and led them off to fight beside the British. Coming of age in 1859, her daughter immediately abdicated in her favor, so Sikander Begum pressed on with her reforms, establishing schools and orphanages and abolishing slavery and (perhaps as a feminist) the making of eunuchs. In 1863 she made the pilgrimage to Mecca and had hoped to voyage to London, but was so harassed by marauders near Islam's holy city that she returned instead to Bhopal, where she could personally guarantee law and order. She died there five years later and her daughter returned to the throne.

Sikander Begum's daughter was much under the influence of her husband, in whose veins ran the arrogant blood of Afghan tribesmen for whom it was lawful, if a wife spoke to any man but her husband, father or brother, to cut off his foot and her nose.*

The husband expected to be enthroned next to the Begum on formal occasions, ignoring the prerogatives of her heir, a daughter by a previous husband. In fact, he kept the daughter and her husband prisoner in their palace for close to ten years while he himself enjoyed the status of a prince. One day, however, he got a nasty shock. There appeared without warning at the Bhopal court no less a dignitary than the Viceroy's Agent for the Central India States, dressed ominously in his best uniform. The Agent asked kindly after the health of all and invited the Begum to assemble her durbar. The Agent, as representative of the Viceroy, of course merited a seat of majesty beside the Begum, displacing the husband. When all the ceremonies proper to this formal occasion had been completed, the Agent leaned toward the Begum's ear. It was the Viceroy's wish, he imparted, that her husband be stripped forthwith of all his titles, his salute of guns and his priorities in seating arrangements, and denied any voice whatever in the government of Bhopal.

Now the daughter, Shah Jehan Begum, freed of her stepfather's tyranny, had merely to wait for her mother's throne. Shah Jehan Begum came to that throne in 1901, when she was forty-three and a widow. She occupied it strangely like the

---

* It was not unusual for British hospitals south of the Khyber to be visited by repentant husbands accompanied by wives in need of radical plastic surgery.

Queen-Empress Victoria, whose remains lay newly buried at Windsor, and ruled for a quarter of a century, becoming rightly famous.

Bhopal, only slightly smaller than New Jersey, formed a part of the Malwa plateau in central India, long celebrated for its opium poppies. Half broken plain, half jungly hills, the state was populated by some seven hundred thousand peasant farmers, three quarters of them Hindus, and a number of those primitive dark Gonds whose hunting with a ring of troops had been a sport of the Moguls. Until recently it had been the Gonds' habit at the appropriate season to kidnap a Brahmin youth, stick him with a poisoned arrow, sprinkle his blood over their vestigial fields for fertility, and eat him. In the Begum's time, dressed in red, the Gonds had degenerated into dancing for visiting personages and mingled in the bazaars of Bhopal city with the scented Muslims who carried their sabers wrapped in muslin shawls and whose long hair wafted the sweetness of rose water and sandalwood. The city was set on a slope like an amphitheater. The first intimation of it from a distance was twin minarets reaching like rockets to the sky. Its roofs were red tile and its houses washed white, pink and blue. In the poor quarter, squalid alleys were blackened with smoke and stinking with urine but the overall impression was one of delicacy and light. The sun shone openly even on the jail, where the convicts wove careful rugs in the shade of banyan trees. The white walls of the Begum's principal palace dropped plumb and dazzling into the sapphire waters of a lake six miles long. Flowering vines covered the walls and tangled through the town, all green and white. The onion domes and the spikes of Bhopal's minarets, gold and sugary above a patchwork of verdure, breathed romance, as well as the certainties of a rigidly dogmatic religion.

Sultan Jehan Begum was the most devout of Muslims. Three years after her accession she made for Mecca; then, in 1911, after lending her picturesque and tentlike authority to the consecration and crowning of George V, Emperor of India and Defender of the Faith, ended a tour of Europe with a sojourn in Constantinople, city of the Caliphs, custodians of Islam. Wherever she was she began her prayers at dawn and continued them throughout the day at the stipulated intervals. Like her grandmother and mother, she built a mosque in the city. When the First World War began she placed her faith, like the Nizam, at the disposal of the British, who sorely needed it, and published a manifesto to that effect giving causes for fighting the Muslims of Turkey. She later supplied copies of the Koran and religious pamphlets for the encouragement and comfort of her co-believers fighting in the Middle East.

The depth and strength of the Begum's religious convictions were equaled by her desire to improve the condition of women, though her keenness for emancipation was somewhat blunted by what she had observed in liberated Edwardian London. Back in Bhopal she lectured the Princess of Wales's Ladies' Club she had founded. "I am sure that our purdah ladies have no idea of the extent of the liberty of the women of Europe," she declared. "I have no hesitation in saying that that liberty is entirely unsuited to the conditions of this country, and particularly in the case of Muslims." However, her fundamental belief remained. She concluded her address: "Female education is the foundation of all national success and progress." But it was education only within the very clear limits defined by the Koran and its interpreters. While, as purdah ladies were quick to point out, the Koran had been the first document to acknowledge the existence of Eastern women and attribute souls to them, it still set forth a rather forbidding concept of their utility and rights. "And one of His signs," the Prophet had announced, "is that He created mates for you from yourselves that you might find quiet of mind in them." And moreover: "O ye women of the Prophet, ye are not like any other women; if ye fear God then be not too complacent in speech, or he in whose heart is sickness will lust after you; but speak a reasonable speech. And say still in your houses and show not yourselves with the ostentation of the ignorance of yore." The Begum was a frequent speaker at the ladies' club and stated the roots of her conviction very plainly. "It is self evident that when God has divided humanity into two sections," she wrote, "the very division is proof positive that He must have marked out different fields of activity for each sex. For the physically stronger of the two the field is larger and wider, and for the weaker it is proportionately smaller and more restricted." Purdah, she believed, was created for the protection of women and was a boon, not a hindrance. Given that, all else followed: "With the existence of this natural difference in the sexes, it is but obvious that the meaning and import of the words 'progress' and 'advancement' when used with reference to men and women cannot be identical." How much uplift was pumped into the bosoms of the Begum's rather captive audience was never measured, but perhaps it did not matter, for the Begum had other than intellectual claims to their attention. The majority of ladies in the club were relatives, rich or poor, of the Begum and she explained cheerfully to a Viceroy's wife, "What I tell them to do, they do, and they are very happy."

The Begum had recruited a daughter-in-law as vice president of the club, whom she had chosen at the age of six to be betrothed to her youngest son and had tutored from then on. Either her choice was lucky or her methods of education were very effective, for Maimoona Begum turned out to be beautiful, intensely loyal, highly intelligent and devoted to the Begum's principles, helping her with the ladies' classes in Home Nursing, Art, Hygiene, Gestation, Games, and Child Nursing. With the ladies' support, which was hardly vital, the Begum and her daughter-in-law established in Bhopal a women's hospital, state schools for girls in which languages, religion, the usual academic subjects and cooking were taught, and an industrial school offering instruction in Mogul embroidery in gold and silver, basketwork and other crafts that could be practiced in purdah. For the Begum's entire design was to liberate her sex only within the boundaries imposed by God. Even so, she was ahead of her contemporaries.

The struggle left its mark on her. In her later years there was a notable weariness in her generous face, a down curve to the full lips. She had worked selflessly and hard, often until three in the morning, but the apathy and superstition of her peasant subjects were immovable. They would not even allow themselves to be inoculated against a plague that had killed hundreds of thousands across the Punjab. There were still carefree moments, however; she adored her two granddaughters, who were addicted to water pistols in the rose garden. She got a good deal of pleasure out of reading American women's and educational magazines. "I admire and like the English," she told a visitor, "but you Americans are more energetic, more progressive. You have a broader vision."

By 1924 the Begum's hair was snow-white and her teeth were black stumps from chewing betel. She often wore a Kashmir shawl against the cold and she was tired. She was sixty-six and she thought of retiring. Two of her sons died in that year; the survivor, her youngest, was thirty and she had trained him carefully, sending him to the university and then keeping him beside her as her chief secretary. The Begum wanted to abdicate in his favor. But there was a snag. There was a surviving son of her eldest son, and the British, adhering to the law of primogeniture, had assumed he was her heir. She spent Christmas of 1924 with her friend the Viceroy talking about her problem and trying to enlist his aid. She was briefly diverted by the lovemaking in an Italian opera to which she was taken, but got no solution to her dynastic problems.

Early in 1925 the Begum began to go through official channels and presented her case to the government of India. She stated a principle of Islamic law by which the nearer in degree excluded the more remote in the order of succession, and extolled the popularity, fitness and experience of her son. Blinded by the law of primogeniture, the government of India balked and countered with the vague observation that it felt keenly its responsibility for settling all matters of succession in dispute and noted that the Begum had been unable to quote any precedent in support of her claim. In private, being fair and thorough men, the officials of the Political Department examined the Begum's principle and began to riffle through their files for a precedent. Unaware of their researches and fearing the worst, the Begum picked up her skirts and some grandchildren and went to see the King-Emperor in London to seek his support. The Indian government's files went back no further than the Mutiny, so the search was continued in the archives of the India Office in London. The Begum was kindly received at Buckingham Palace, met the Secretary of State for India and took three of her grandchildren to tea with his lady, where she managed between lamentations to cram down a good deal of hot buttered toast. The India Office clerks labored and brought forth a miracle the Begum had not dreamed of. There was precedent. Her principle had been invoked in the succession of several of the later Mogul emperors and of one king of Oudh. The Begum dried her tears and the Secretary of State wrote somewhat uncharitably to the Viceroy: "I should imagine the old lady is in her seventh heaven; but I hope she will spend what remains of it in her own country."

In May 1926 Shah Jehan Begum abdicated and gave Bhopal a male ruler for the first time in a century. His Highness the Nawab Mohammed Hamidullah Khan's style was that of an English country gentleman. His guesthouse at Bhopal contained a billiard room, a library, and bedrooms stuffed with flowered chintz. Even his temporary quarters were on the solid side; a guest quartered in one of his many tents could expect a sitting room twenty feet square with morocco-leather armchairs and sofas on Kermanshah carpets, walls covered with silk, writing tables, a humidor stocked with Havana cigars, a pile of newspapers and magazines, an English dining table of gleaming mahogany, silver bowls of roses, three brands of Scotch (none of them the sort of muck blended by wine merchants) and the same of champagne, a dressing room and a bathroom, and reading lights over the beds. Handsome, slim and always immaculate in a pale-blue turban, the nawab was a great one for simplifying matters. He once astounded a very experienced and senior British official who had just refused a lunchtime invitation to shoot a tiger on the grounds of an urgent appointment. The nawab assured him the delay would be minimal, certainly not more than half an hour, pressed him to finish his coffee, then whisked him away on a very brief drive to the edge of a little clearing in the teak jungle. As the official was wondering why there was none of the usual tumult of distant beaters, the nawab tapped

him on the shoulder. A tiger had walked into the clearing. The
official shot it. Dazed, he asked the nawab his secret. It was all
a matter of organization, the nawab explained. One studied the
lay of the land, one judged the probable action of the tiger and
one arranged for half a dozen chaps to make some discreet clicks
here and there in the jungle. In fact, he was thinking of doing
the whole thing with electric buzzers, so all one would have to
do would be to press a button.

The nawab's efficiency made him Chancellor of the Chamber
of Princes in 1931, and again from 1944 to 1947. When the
British prepared to withdraw from India in earnest he resigned,
complaining not without justice to the last Viceroy that the
British were deliberately evading their responsibilities. His attempts to organize some of his fellow princes into an effective
bloc in the new India failed, and when the time came he acceded to India, despite his religion. His standing in the Muslim
world was so high that in 1948 he was tapped to become governor-general of Pakistan, but he stayed in Bhopal and died there
in 1960. In the tradition of Bhopal his heir was his eldest daughter, a petite, unsmiling girl who had endured a brief, sad marriage and given up purdah. Like her father, she was a fine polo
player and would use a bicycle for it when ponies were not
available. She drove fast, shot well, and piloted her own plane.
But the *burqa* of sturdy little Shah Jehan Begum did not fit her,
and abdicating in her sister's favor, she went to live in Pakistan.

6

❖⟨❖⟨❖⟨❖⟨❖⟨❖⟨❖⟨❖⟨❖⟨❖⟨❖⟨❖

The Heir of Sadness

BETWEEN THE GREAT Maratha king Shivaji and Sir Tukoji Rao III, Maharajah of Dewas Senior, lay three centuries of
leveling, the British and a world of faded dreams. What bound
them across time, and across differences in social degree and
personal character, was that both were Marathas sharing a pride
of blood. In the eighteenth century the Marathas had spread
through all of central India to challenge Moguls and British alike
for supremacy over the whole subcontinent. Both Shivaji and
Tukoji Rao were idealists, but Shivaji was practical and forged
an empire, while Tukoji Rao died in poverty seeking a love that
perhaps did not exist. Both had small beginnings.

Shivaji's family were Maratha landowners, squires or at most
barons, proprietors of a tract crunched between the Mogul territories proper and the sultanate of Bijapur, a dependency of the
Moguls in the west of India. Shivaji's father was in the Bijapur
service when the greatest of all the Marathas was born on April
16, 1627, and received the sacrament of honey dropped through
a gold ring into his innocent mouth, like any Hindu infant. The

family's lands near Poona in the Western Ghats had been over-run by the Mogul Shah Jehan, marching in wrath to punish Bijapur, and had been abandoned by the father, together with his wife and children. A fugitive in a wasteland, Shivaji spent the first ten years of his life hurried from kinfolk to kinfolk by way of savage canyons and over mountain slopes where the sea fogs billowed, through the tempests of the monsoon and the twilight of summer jungles, always hidden and always pursued. Shivaji learned the tracks through these harsh mountain fastnesses of the Marathas, the Western Ghats. He came down from the mountains for the first time in 1637 to return in peace to the family home in the village of Poona. It had been razed. The Moguls had plowed its ruins with asses and sewn it with salt and set a rod of iron in the earth to mark it destroyed forever. The Marathas threw down the iron, furrowed their land again with a plow of gold pulled by white oxen and rebuilt their homesteads. Shivaji bought himself a seal ring and inscribed on it: "Although the first moon is small, know that it will grow great." He hid his anger.

The stories of Shivaji's manhood read like those of Robin Hood or Davy Crockett. He was a sharpshooter, a trickster, a bluffer, a winner. He would penetrate the enemy camp at will, cheekily, once merely to hear a recital by his favorite poet, once for loot, dressed as a drummer in a fake wedding procession. He was fearless, and adored, and as crafty as a weasel. Aurengzeb, the Mogul in lofty Agra, called him "the mountain rat" and the Europeans "the Grand Rebel." He was neither. Shivaji was the Maratha messiah, without the martyrdom. He began his crusade modestly by taking some frontier forts from Bijapur, employing a mixture of daring and duplicity. Once he was through the gates with his small Maratha band, he used bribery and sweet talk to fend off retribution. His successes annoyed both the Sultan of Bijapur and the Moguls, but when the latter marched against him, Shivaji stole a thousand heavy horses from Aureng-zeb's cavalry lines to replace his own light Maratha ponies. His ochre banners, the mark of Hindu pilgrimage, flapped in defiance of the Mogul and the Sultan of Bijapur alike. His bases were hill forts on the peaks of granite scarps, and his light horse-men struck, vanished and struck again.

The Sultan of Bijapur sent an army to root him out. Its com-mander, a huge Muslim called Afzal Khan, built a cage for Shivaji and carried it in his baggage train. But that was bravado, for Afzal Khan had seen his own death through the eyes of a Muslim priest. Glancing at Afzal Khan at prayer in a Bijapur mosque, the priest had been horrified to see a prostrate, headless trunk, conceived it an omen and warned Afzal Khan. Afzal Khan had ordered the slaughter of his sixty-four wives as a pre-liminary to his own death and set out to tempt providence. Shivaji was in the hills protected by a glacis of impenetrable jungle. Afzal Khan camped below him with the ready cage, a train of twelve hundred camels, a hoard of treasure, sixty-five war elephants, four thousand horses and ten thousand men. Shi-vaji went silently and alone through his guards in the night to reconnoiter. He found a Brahmin in Afzal Khan's service who, being a fellow Hindu, revealed Afzal Khan's plan to call for a truce and kill Shivaji at the parley.

Shivaji had his men cut a road through the jungle up to the plateau where his tents were spread. When Afzal Khan invited him to the parley, Shivaji said he was too scared to venture down the mountain. Would Afzal Khan climb it by this new path? Afzal Khan did so, through Shivaji's mountaineers hidden all around him in the jungle. Shivaji greeted him among the silks and carpets of his tent, dressed all in white, with a jeweled dagger at his belt, no sword. Shivaji was short, but his arms were abnormally long and he had the chest of a bull. A ringlet of black hair fell from one side of his turban and his large dark eyes were melancholy and guileless. But under the white tunic he wore a coat of mail and in his closed left palm he hid the *baghnakh*, the tiger's claws, four knives of steel. His decorative dagger had a Genoa blade eighteen inches long.

Afzal Khan loomed over Shivaji and behind him stood a giant, his bodyguard, a man with butcher's arms. The host vol-unteered to dismiss his attendant if Afzal Khan would send his bodyguard outside. When they were alone the Hindu and the

Muslim embraced, arms circling, in the universal gesture of friendship. But Afzal Khan moved a powerful arm up Shivaji's back and took him in a neck lock. Shivaji opened his left hand and struck with the *baghnakh* for the kidneys, then as Afzal Khan shrieked, slid the dagger into his left side. The bodyguard was hacked down when he rushed in, the rest of Afzal Khan's men were overwhelmed, and as the priest had foreseen, Afzal Khan's head was cut off. Shivaji sounded his war horn, and his Marathas poured out of the forest and took all the sultan's horses, all the sultan's men and all the sultan's treasure.

Not even the Mogul emperor could quench Shivaji's fire. He blazed back and forth across the Maratha country, a triangle stabbing into central India from its base in the coastal mountains of the west, raided north and south, and gazed down on the hundred trading ships—dhows, galleons, junks—at anchor in Surat, and pillaged the town. By now he had not only united the Marathas, he had given them a sense of nationhood and a taste for winning. On the last day of September, 1664, Aurengzeb sent against him his most formidable general, a professional, the Rajput Maharajah Jai Singh of Jaipur. Jai Singh, as Shivaji knew, was another matter. They reached an accommodation. Shivaji rode softly through the mulberry trees to Aurengzeb's court at Agra, where impassively the emperor broke his pledge and imprisoned him. Smuggled out in a fruit basket by some daring followers, Shivaji regained his mountains and made his next treaty with the Moguls from their safety. In 1672 he began foraging again, this time as far afield as the diamond mines of Golconda in the Nizam's dominions. The Maratha army could cover fifty miles a day, day after day, for its horsemen carried nothing but an iron ration, and for their mounts a few balls of black peas spiked with garlic and pepper. Shivaji's power was reaching its climax and he decided to crown himself king of Hindustan, the vast and ancient land of the Hindus. Among his honorifics he assumed that of Chhatrapati (Lord of the Umbrella, symbol of paramount sovereignty), marking it with the gift of a solid-gold umbrella to the temple of his patron goddess. During the month-long ceremonies Shivaji prayed incessantly and at last fell into a trance. An alien voice spoke from his mouth, foretelling the fall of Delhi to the Marathas, the long rule of his descendants and their end in a tide of red-faced strangers. The red-faced British did subdue the Marathas, but not for over a century.

Shivaji pushed his frontier as far south as Madras, but after his death in 1680 the Marathas could not hold. Aurengzeb tore out the tongue of Shivaji's son, blinded him and thus put him to a slow barbaric death. The Moguls flooded over all the territories Shivaji had taken. But Shivaji had left more than land. He had bequeathed to the Marathas both a belief in themselves and a system of government. Shivaji had been supported in his rule by the Cabinet of eight ministers, chief of whom was the Peshwa (Prime Minister). During the temporary decline of the Maratha fortunes the office became hereditary and successive Peshwas wielded power until the line ended in the Nana Sahib, a prime instigator of the Indian Mutiny.* Besides the Peshwas other Maratha dynasties grew, of equal or greater power, some in the blood line of Shivaji, others descendants of his officers. They crystallized into the ruling families of Baroda, Gwalior and Indore, who dominated central India and challenged the British at the end of the eighteenth century and the beginning of the nineteenth for the mastery of India. Had they not also quarreled among themselves they might have won it. The Maratha confederacy survived two wars with the British, including a grim day with Sir Arthur Wellesley at Assaye in 1803. Over eight thousand of both sides were killed or wounded, for the Marathas would not break. The future Duke of Wellington himself lost

---

* The Nana Sahib was the adopted son of the last Peshwa, a deposed pensioner of the British. The intractable Lord Dalhousie refused to transfer the dead Peshwa's yearly allowance of forty thousand dollars to the Nana Sahib on the grounds that the Peshwa had received twelve and a half million dollars in all from the East India Company and must have invested at least some of it for his successors. But the Nana Sahib had inherited well over a thousand dependents and was accustomed to having his groceries shipped regularly from Fortnum and Mason in London. As he sank into debt he grew quietly but savagely bitter. He intrigued, he joined the mutineers and he ordered the Cawnpore massacre. The British never caught him and assumed without much conviction that he died in the jungles of Nepal.

two chargers. In his old age, with the Peninsula and Waterloo behind him, he was asked which of his battles he considered his best. He answered in a word: "Assaye!" In a third war, from 1817 to 1819, the Marathas were defeated piecemeal. The treaties after it left their great chieftains with their lands and titles but acknowledged the British interest as paramount.

The Maratha princes—of Baroda, Gwalior, Indore—retained much physical power but spiritually they were inferior to Sir Shri Rajaram, Chhatrapati Maharajah of Kolhapur. His family claimed blood descent through two centuries from Shivaji's second son. For this reason thirty million Marathas regarded the Maharajah of Kolhapur as the doyen of their princes, and mighty heads were bowed to touch his feet in reverence. An unlikely-looking successor to Shivaji, he was gross, excessively fleshy, though his height and huge frame relieved it partially. He loved the hunt and horse racing and imported cheetahs from Africa to course his black buck, but he lived for intrigue and he was a past master at it. His heavy face with its thick mustache and sharp nose betrayed few emotions, though he was capable of tears and even more capable of avenging them. He used men, showing them nothing, gaining their trust and discovering what they knew, giving them back not even affection. He believed in corruptibility as a fact. He was a very clever and misleading man, powerful, rich and surrounded by sycophants, whom he recognized as such, and spies, whom he uncovered and duped. He had a very beautiful daughter with whom the Maharajah of Dewas Senior fell in love, which began his tragedy.

Dewas was a curiosity among states. It had been founded in the early 1700s by two Maratha brothers, descendants of a servant of Shivaji, who had discovered dual rule impracticable and therefore decided to divide their eight hundred square miles and establish a senior and a junior branch. The division was very thorough and unbelievably confusing, for it split fields and gardens, the city of Dewas, facilities and even houses. When the conquering British arrived to fit Dewas into their pattern for the Central Indian States, they were baffled; the general principle was explained by an obliging resident with "If a lime is presented to a villager, it must be cut into two equal parts and divided between our two princes." The system was accepted, though it settled in some bizarre patterns; the school had two headmasters, one appointed by Dewas Senior and the other by Dewas Junior, and the flagpole crowning the famous hill of Devi was the property of Senior at the top and Junior at the bottom, so that the flag, impartial, flew forever at half-mast. The British took the place under their beneficent wing in 1818 and nothing much happened in Dewas until the advent of Tukoji Rao III as Maharajah of Dewas Senior eighty years later. He succeeded to the throne at the age of eleven in 1899 and assumed full powers in 1908.

Tukoji Rao's realm was no paradise. Its crumbly black soil was good for cotton but affronted the eye; its chief lake was pretty enough when full but was often dry, when its mud cracked like the skin of a crocodile. The city seemed quaint to a newcomer but soon revealed itself as merely ramshackle. The chief feature of the place was a brown conical hill blackened at the top and looking curiously, like much in India, as though it had been caressed endlessly by millions of greasy hands. On it sat the shrine of Devi, the titular goddess.

Tukoji Rao's pride was raw. He would flinch at any slighting of his Maratha dignity as if cut by a whip. This, and an unquenchable longing for affection, was his undoing. He had been the star pupil at the two chiefs' colleges to which the British had sent him for the proper education of a young gentleman, and even official reports (which distrusted brilliance) described him as "of good character and reputation and very intelligent." Tukoji Rao was also highly neurotic, and might even have been a genius. He was short and lightly made but lithe and pleasantly proportioned, his face was smooth, regular and active, and his heavy, drooping Groucho Marx mustache might have given it a quizzical look had his dark eyes not countered it. They were hooded and opaque. Much became known of this melancholy prince because he was the subject of two remarkable books, E. M. Forster's *The Hill of Devi* and Sir Malcolm Darling's *Apprentice to Power*. Forster was His Highness' private secretary for a while and always his friend, and Darling was his tutor and virtually his brother.

Malcolm Darling came to Tukoji Rao's diminutive empire, four hundred and forty-two square miles supporting six thousand people, armed with all the certainties of Eton and King's College, Cambridge, the consciousness of the superiority of his race, a couple of years' experience as a junior official in the Punjab, and all the vigor of young manhood. The captain of cricket was meeting the effete little oriental. Dewas changed Darling, and what he learned there helped make him one of the greatest servants India ever knew. Darling had been appointed tutor and guardian to the young prince in February 1907, and charged with teaching him administration in preparation for his assuming the full powers of the throne. Darling fell back on Mill and Bagehot, and more gingerly on Aristotle and Plato, but which of the two young men learned more from the other is debatable, for the air of Dewas was not that same cold wind that fanned the Athenian plain.

By way of practical teaching, maharajah and tutor took a three-month tour of the subcontinent designed to broaden the prince's mind and to impress on it the weight of British power and the modesty of Dewas compared with, say, a twenty-one-gun state. Tukoji Rao, fifteen guns, was cold-shouldered by the far grander Highnesses of Udaipur and Jaipur, Rajputs not condescending to a mere Maratha, and graced with a five-minute interview by a kindly Viceroy wearing a white rose in his buttonhole, a pink shirt and an air of candor tempered with indifference.* At Benares, Darling watched the priests throw into Mother Ganges with suitable incantations all the hair cut from Tukoji Rao's head since his accession. It would have been a proper moment also to commit to the waters the one small bone rescued for that purpose from the funeral pyres of each of his recent ancestors, but Tukoji Rao, who had ten such mementos in

* This particular Viceroy was greatly envied by the horsey set for the distinction of having broken his neck riding in the Grand National steeplechase.

his keeping, had left them at home, for reasons that remain inscrutable.

From the British point of view the tour was a great success. Tukoji Rao's experience had indeed been broadened: he had been snubbed more than once and he had been forced to realize that Dewas was not a universe. Still, Dewas was home. Prince and tutor were welcomed back by a delighted populace as the children of the diarchic Victoria High School chorused:

> "Let us clap and let us sing
> Let us form a merry ring;
> God has safe our Master brought
> Home with precious lessons fraught."

How far the lessons were applicable in Dewas was not yet clear. Tukoji Rao's pride had been badly bruised and he might well retire within himself.

Fortunately Tukoji Rao had early found a confidante in Darling's mother, who had been vacationing in the capital for a while. Riding in a dog cart through the thin smoke of Dewas' evening fires, the prince had poured out his dreams, his fears and his fantasies, and so, consciously or not, had indirectly given Darling the key to his mind. It was not a simple mind and it was not a happy one; it longed for affection and yet was too proud to solicit it. He had been adopted by his newly widowed aunt, the maharani, after his predecessor's death. Since then he had seldom seen his real mother lest the maharani accuse her of interfering in affairs of state. The maharani he painted was an elderly ogre; in fact, she was still quite a few years short of thirty and gave occasional vent to an innocent lightness of heart. She was known to dress her women attendants in male costume at festivals and dance with them, and she stretched the rules of purdah to allow herself picnics on the palace lawn during which she moved about in a sort of rabbit hutch covered with white muslin. Tukoji Rao believed that his aunt intended to poison him and tested all his food on a mongrel dog, once with immediately fatal effects. Nor was he alone in sensing something sinister in Dewas: Forster had not been there long before he noted uneasily in his diary: "Land of petty treacheries, of reptiles moving about too cautious to strike each other." Part of the tension came from the Brahmins, whom Tukoji Rao had detested ever since they tried to force him to make his mother burn herself on his father's funeral pyre in the custom of suttee, long illegal. Also, the Brahmins' scorn of his low caste humiliated him: though he was a prince, he had to bow to them. He told Darling's mother that he had not been happy since he was named to the throne at the age of eleven. Already he had asked if he might abdicate. Yet one thing brightened his future. He was engaged to the only daughter of the Maharajah of Kolhapur, a girl of thirteen.

The Maharajah of Kolhapur's attitude toward his daughter Akka Sahib was ambivalent. His great bulk could quake with weeping at the thought of losing her, but Tukoji Rao told Darling's mother, half jokingly, "My father-in-law says that if she is disobedient, I am to beat her with a shoe, and that the shoe shall have nails. But I shall not do this. If she is disobedient I shall send her back to Kolhapur and the maharajah can beat her. He beat her once."

The first time the lovers were allowed to meet, for twenty minutes, Akka Sahib bent to touch Tukoji Rao's feet in worship, but he stopped her, taking her hand. There was already a conflict in him: he respected her devoutness and her submission, yet he wished to lead her into the modern ways of the West. They were married early in 1908, when she was fourteen and he twenty. The court of Dewas in all its splendor came south to Kolhapur by special train, with the ten-man state band in new uniforms of red and green blasting forth "Oft in Danger, Oft in Woe." The court of Kolhapur, being much richer, overwhelmed the Dewas contingent with scarlet Lancers and gilded elephants, and standard-bearers chanting the honorifics of their gigantic prince as heir of Shivaji and Emperor of Hindustan.

The ceremonies took days, following the long customs of the Hindus. First the Maharajah of Kolhapur bathed Tukoji Rao's feet, making him a god. During the first part of the marriage itself, bride and groom were separated by a red curtain; it dropped and he saw her face for the first time. She was beautiful. Three days later Tukoji Rao still had done no more than gaze briefly at his bride, for her father had forbidden the two to meet and secluded Akka Sahib as soon as the rites were over. He himself, he explained, had not seen his wife for two years after his own marriage, and the time for Akka Sahib and Tukoji Rao was not yet ripe. The womenfolk, meeting in purdah, backed him. Tukoji Rao's blood raged and that night his fever soared to a hundred and five degrees. He left Kolhapur without seeing his wife again.

The arguments and intrigues continued at a distance. Six months later, at the end of 1908, Tukoji Rao was allowed to come back to Kolhapur to claim his wife. Kolhapur was famous for its hunting and Akka Sahib loved the sport, so a final grand shikar was arranged. They went out with gun and rifle, with falcons and boarhounds, and most notably with cheetahs, which the maharajah imported from Africa. These were used to course the black buck that grazed in little groups all over Kolhapur's flatlands. The party would set out in bullock carts like those driven by farmers so as to allay the bucks' suspicions. In some sat the spectators, in others, a couple to a cart, the slender cheetahs in blue coats, hooded in scarlet like hawks. The carts would trundle slowly in tightening circles around a likely group of bucks; then, closing to within a hundred yards, a cheetah would be readied. The hood flicked off, the luminous alert eyes locking onto the prey, the cheetah would riffle silently to the ground and stalk in a long continuous stream of charged muscle and nerve until a buck raised his head, startled, and careered away. It was never a long chase. The cheetah's bounding spurt would end in a leap and jaws clenching on a throat or a hind leg, holding until the huntsman came with the knife and only loosing for the smell of warm blood held out in a wooden spoon. Then back into the cart, black lips still glossy with blood, and on to the next little herd.

Akka Sahib's farewell hunt was a great one, but it ended in

tempests of tears so distressing to her father and mother that they could not see her off at the station. It was not a good omen. Tukoji Rao brought his beloved after sunset into a Dewas decked with light, riding in state upon an elephant. Together they worshiped at his family shrine in the old palace in the middle of his city, and there he installed her and loved her. It was a dark place, neglected, a honeycomb of little rooms where intrigue festered. Akka Sahib lived there like a captive bird.

By now Tukoji Rao had been formally installed as ruler with full powers, so Darling's position had changed. He had become the maharajah's adviser and private secretary, occupied with matters of business. On the surface, life at Dewas was entertaining enough. There was tea with the English companion of Tukoji Rao's aunt, the sinister maharani, a thin spinster of a certain age very fond of her mistress, her three small dogs, her blood-red parasol and anything growing in a garden. There were long discussions of Hindu metaphysics with the black-bearded superintendent of education as Orion burned in the clear Dewas nights. A holy man came by periodically in pink muslin and ochre socks, distributing his plentiful earthly bulk on the tennis court and discoursing blithely and lengthily on the unimportance of the flesh. *Ping* would go the racquets and *pong* would go the sadhu's holy thoughts. But behind the diversion, the machinery of state crumbled; there were corrupt officials, the revenue was no more than a quarter of a million dollars a year, and time had no meaning. And Tukoji Rao was mercurial.

He could be practical enough, but he lived much in the lands of the spirit. His daily observances were thorough and long, and during festivals lasting a week or more he came close to experiencing divinity itself, dancing ecstatically and remote in the persona of a god. He thought deeply and lucidly, once explaining to Forster his endearing concept of the relationship between God and man. Everything, he said, was a part of God. But we must not expect God to recognize that at all times, for just as a man might, if concentrating momentarily on some difficulty, forget the existence of his own hand, so God, His energy engaged elsewhere, might not for a time be conscious of men as

parts of Himself. Salvation, Tukoji Rao told Forster, is the thrill
we feel when God becomes conscious of us again. Forster felt
much enlightened, but he could not follow when Tukoji Rao's
mind ventured into areas infinitely more abstruse. "He was certainly a genius and possibly a saint," Forster later wrote, "and he
had to be a king." He also had to be loved, but that was not easy.
Close as he was to Darling, and later to Forster, his pride sometimes kept him apart. He once said to Darling, "We have a feeling that the English in this country do not belong to the most
aristocratic class." Darling and Forster both gave him affection
and he returned it as well as he could, but his heart was frightened and lonely. In repose his face sometimes took on a curious
expression, a look of deep and impotent anger. He often thought
he would have welcomed death.

Tukoji Rao was fire and Akka Sahib was air. Not long after
she came to Dewas, one of her two Kolhapur maidservants
brought her a story that the other had been sleeping with
Tukoji Rao. She beat the girl and accused her husband. He
denied it. She ran to her apartments and barred the door against
him. He could not persuade her that he was innocent, which
he was, and she exploded into hysteria. She bore him a son but
the crises of nerves became a pattern. In 1916, bewildered and
destroyed, he sent her home to the Kolhapur she had never
wanted to leave. By doing so he affronted a great family that
now turned against him. The Kolhapur spies who had always
watched Dewas now became *agents provocateurs* as well. Darling was long gone, Forster did what he could for a little while
as a stop-gap private secretary, the decline began. Tukoji Rao
started to build a new palace, but after ten years, still unfinished,
it began to disintegrate. Piece by piece he sold his three hundred
thousand dollars' worth of jewels, four-foot ropes of pearls,
emeralds as big as marbles, but by 1921 he was begging for
money from the usurers of Indore. The spies reported everything back to Kolhapur with glee.

Part of the trouble was with the British officials. One or two of
the Agent's subordinates after Darling were at worst bullies
and at best boors. Tukoji Rao had admitted to the Agent at

Indore right at the beginning, "If I am treated badly my blood gets up and I begin to play tricks." They treated Tukoji Rao badly and he began to play tricks. The old intellectual energy turned to listlessness. He spent a fortune he could not afford celebrating the marriage of his son Vikramsinha Rao, called Vikky, in 1926, and another welcoming the birth of a son to his favorite concubine. He maintained an expensive intelligence network in Kolhapur and elsewhere. To the official British, who had so admired him once for his early promise and his loyalty in the First World War, he was now intransigent. At the end of 1927 came the disaster. In a strange repetition of his own experiences, Tukoji Rao had kept Vikky and his new wife apart. Unable to stand the tension of separation and perhaps inflamed by agents from vengeful Kolhapur, Vikky drove over the border into Indore one night and sought the Agent's protection, accusing his father of attempting to poison him. Tukoji Rao collapsed in utter despair. The Agent managed an accommodation of sorts between the two, but there was no recovery for Tukoji Rao.

By 1933 the state of Dewas Senior was bankrupt. Peremptorily the government of India required Tukoji Rao to appoint a British expert to run his affairs. He did not answer. At the end of that year he announced a pilgrimage to an island at the very tip of India, a most holy place, site of a temple dedicated to Siva, the destroyer. It seemed logical. With his morganatic family and a few followers he drove south. Reaching Pondicherry, he turned and sought sanctuary from the French, who owned it. There were saddening rumors that he had sent the last of his jewels ahead as part of a deceitful plan. They could not have been numerous in any case, for he died destitute in Pondicherry four years later, thin as an ascetic and with eyes filled with pain and perhaps a touch of madness—or genius. His ashes were consigned to the sea and his obituaries maligned him. And his son later became, by a painful irony, Maharajah of Kolhapur. He is thus, today, the true and only heir of Shivaji, lord of all the Marathas.

7

The Tiger Freak

BY HUMAN RECKONING the elephant Hiragaj was over a hundred years old and even his mahout, who knew every inch of his dry gray hide and every cranny of his sagacious brain, could be no more precise than that. Hiragaj had served three maharajahs during his century; he was the doyen of all the elephants of Gwalior, for he was a beast of royal burden, and now he was to carry the heir to the British Empire in procession to the Gwalior palace. So on this February morning of 1922 he knelt, forelegs outstretched and hind legs folded under him, a gaudy painted mountain with a gold howdah perched on his back like a toboggan on a summit, with such majesty that the cavalry troopers, courtiers and palace servants milling in the station yard seemed merely his acolytes. His tusks were plugged and double-strapped with gold. Gold paint caked his legs, bright vermilion dye ringed his clouded eyes, gold tassels swung from the dark crimson silk covering his wrinkled flanks, and on his broad forehead, plastered with fresh gold dust, gleamed a huge fleur-de-lys. His Royal Highness the Prince of Wales was coming to

Gwalior, as his father and grandfather had before him, to shoot tigers for a few days. Gwalior was to tigers what Scotland was to grouse. The Maharajah Sir Madhav Rao Sindia of Gwalior, though not the finest shot of his day, was unquestionably the greatest tiger impresario of all time. If all the tigers over whose demise the Maharajah of Gwalior had presided could have been laid end to end, growling heads to black-barred tails, they would have stretched for two and a half miles.

Gwalior's imperial visitor this morning was the most important he had ever entertained, the most generally popular prince since Henry V to stand heir to the British Crown and all its far-flung territories. The maharajah had dressed accordingly in shimmering pale-mauve silk with a simple belt of pearls to mark the occasion, bringing his cannon and elephants and soldiers, horse and foot, to do proper homage to the young Prince whose vassal, if all went well, he would one day be. Prince Edward Albert Christian George Andrew Patrick David of Wales, familiarly known as David and more formally, later, as Edward VIII, King-Emperor, was in the middle of an eight-month tour of the Orient that was also to carry him to Japan, the Philippines and Borneo. In India he traveled more than eleven thousand miles hither and thither across the subcontinent, and in all that distance the only mailing address he needed was "Prince of Wales's Camp, India."

In the main, India remained a mystery to the Prince of Wales. In later years the one thing he could recall clearly was the smell, a compound of heavy blossoms, sour butter cooking in the pot, baked earth, spices, the smoke of cow dung, farmyards and massed human bodies. He found it pervasive and, on the whole, fragrant. He thought the princes' way of life "feudal and sometimes barbarous," but they gave him hospitality and sport "such as I imagined existed only in books." Three special trains had been placed at his disposal, one solely for his polo ponies, horses and carriages. He had also traveled by battle cruiser, aboard camels, in numerous automobiles and one palanquin, on several elephants, and once, propelled by his lanky twenty-two-year-old cousin Lieutenant the Lord Louis Mountbatten of the

Royal Navy, in a wheelbarrow. Lord Louis was a member of his entourage, and twenty-five years later became the Viceroy who liquidated the British raj forever.

The Prince had landed at Bombay on November 17, 1921, knowing little more of this gem of his inheritance than most Englishmen. He remembered great-grandmother Victoria's red-plush and white-marble Durbar Room at Osborne, the portrait of little prince Dhuleep Singh in the corridor next to the ferocious mustaches of Indian heroes, and the turbaned orderlies pushing her wheelchair in the feeble sun. He remembered that one of them had stepped on a cherished toy drum. Of the massive muted surge of tens of millions toward freedom he could know little. Standing on the quay at Bombay he delivered the usual formal speech. "I want to grasp your difficulties and to understand your aspirations," he said, then finished on the spur of the moment with "I want to know you and I want you to know me." There was little hope of that, for wherever he rode in British India the police lined the streets shoulder to shoulder, facing the crowds. Mahatma Gandhi had called for demonstrations along His Royal Highness' path; some had blazed into violence and the British were apprehensive. The Prince did not care for severe police measures and said so to his father. The King-Emperor wrote back sympathetically, deploring the radical changes that in his view were ruining the best hopes of "the natives," but comforting his heir with "The princes are all loyal, and if there was real trouble they would at once come to the assistance of the government with all their troops, which is quite a different situation to what it was before the Mutiny in 1857." Indeed, when he entered the Native States the Prince found that not a breath of Mahatma Gandhi's influence had preceded him.* This February morning the Prince would be arriving at Gwalior on the light railway which had been among

---

* Numbers of Mr. Gandhi's adherents in the proletarian Congress Party passed through the autocracy of Gwalior, stopping only to change trains. It was a favorite diversion of the Maharajah of Gwalior to pass among them on the platform of his railroad station, snatching away the little white caps they wore as a mark of party membership.

the maharajah's improvements to his state and which continued
to be one of his simple passions. He satisfied it by driving the
locomotive himself whenever at large.

It was still decently early when the train puffed into the
Gwalior station. The maharajah stood on the platform beaming
like the risen sun. He was the most engaging of hosts, eager as a
puppy to please and jaunty at the thought of the pleasure he
would give. His black patent-leather boots were the only somber
thing about him, for all above was pastel as far as the pink boat-
shaped hat peculiar to his noble Maratha line, which gave him
the air of a slightly bellicose Dresden shepherdess. The Prince of
Wales stepped down lightly toward this joyous figure while
artillery boomed the royal salute. He was wearing a white sun
helmet spiked with silver, and the dark tunic and tight overall
trousers and insignia of a colonel of the Welsh Guards. He was
the image of youthful elegance, slim, as divinely handsome as
the popular songs made him out to be. He was twenty-eight and
a demigod. Sindia bowed, with the dignity befitting a Maratha
prince but low enough to show grace, and bounced upright full
of vigor. Together the two stepped toward Hiragaj, who gave no
sign of the honor about to be bestowed on him, climbed the
ladder leaning on those massive ribs and settled themselves in their
golden howdah. The officers of the Prince's suite paired off with
noblemen of Gwalior's court and dispersed to the eighteen inferior elephants ranged in a semicircle beyond Hiragaj. Six of
the beasts were crusted with silver paint and bore silver howdahs,
and since most of the rest were daubed pale-blue, the effect was
to reduce the monsters to shapes seen through early morning
mist. Trumpets clarioned, the great forelegs heaved and the
howdahs rocked toward heaven. Two squadrons of Gwalior
Lancers jingled into position, and the procession scrambled into
order with Hiragaj in the lead and the other elephants two by
two behind. Sweeter than the stable fragrance of the elephants
and stronger than the odor of excited crowds, there rose from
the route the piquant sharpness of damp earth, for in a time of
drought the whole road had been drenched with water from

The Princes

H. H. Sir Bhupinder Singh of Patiala, statesman and Casanova, in review order.

H. H. Sir Krishnaraja Wadyar of Mysore, who annually approached divinity.

H. H. Sir Fateh Singh of Udaipur, arbiter of Rajput chivalry, in hunting kit.

H. H. Sir Pratap Singh of Jodhpur, cavalryman in the old style, ready to kill Germans for his King-Emperor.

The runaway lovers united. Jitendra of Cooch Behar and Indira of Baroda at their wedding.

Akbar the Great Mogul,
the most powerful man in the world.

H. H. the Begum of Bhopal—unliberated.

H. H. the Begum of Bhopal—liberated.

H. H. Man Singh of Jaipur, prince of polo players.

*The exiled Maharajah
Dhuleep Singh of Punjab,
who lost the Koh-i-noor
to Queen Victoria
and called her a thief,
but not to her face.*

H. H. Sir Jai Singh of Alwar bringing a little glamour to London before he was deposed for depravity.

H. E. H. Sir Osman Ali,
Nizam of Hyderabad,
who lost eight million dollars'
worth of bank notes
to his palace rats.

The Nizam of Hyderabad, still one of
the world's richest men, in retirement.

H. H. Sir Hari Singh of Kashmir, better
known as "Mr. A" in a scandalous
blackmail case.

The Maharajah Jagatjit Singh of Kapurthala takes his morning constitutional.

H. H. the Maharajah of Kapurthala (FAR RIGHT) is excused a foot fault

Their Pastimes

THE LONDON EVENING NEWS

*Ranji saves England! The Jam Sahib of
Nawanagar at play.*

*The Maharajah of Patiala, the Prince of Wales and Captain Metcalfe after
a morning at the pigs.*

THE PRESS ASSOCIATION LTD.

THE PRESS ASSOCIATION LTD.

The crack Camel Corps of Bikaner under the eyes of H. H. Sir Ganga Singh and H. R. H. the Prince of Wales.

The boys of Tyndale-Biscoe's school make a visitor welcome to Kashmir.

LEO COOPER LTD.

LEFT: *H. H. Sir Pratap Sinha of Baroda in full durbar. He later spent $10,000,000 in six weeks in America.* RIGHT: *Celebrating the birth of a son and heir to Akbar the Mogul Emperor. Akbar built a city to mark the occasion.*

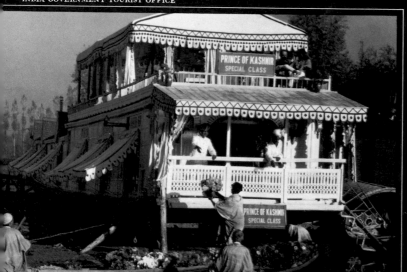

Kashmir morning on a houseboat at Srinagar.

Hiragaj, senior elephant of Gwalior, with the Prince of Wales and the Maharajah Sindia aboard. The elephant is in his second century of service.

The Palaces

ABOVE: *Inside the City Palace, Jaipur, with the maharajah's apartments above.*
MIDDLE: *The Lake Palace, Udaipur, now a hotel for American nabobs.*
BOTTOM: *Festival time at the City Palace, Mysore.*

hundreds of goatskin bags so that none in that glittering parade should be discommoded by dust.

It was a brief progress. The old town of Gwalior lay less than a mile and a half from the new town of Lashkar (The Camp), so named when a warlike ancestor of the maharajah first pitched his tents there in 1809. Now Lashkar boasted buildings of some permanence, not least of them three palaces belonging to the house of Sindia. Lurching solemnly along to the boom of vast kettledrums and the braying of barbaric trumpets, the parade soon came to the chief of these, a sprawling white cliff-side of marble looking, in size and configuration, startlingly like the Place Vendôme in Paris. Wealth and dominion spoke from every line of its Italian Doric style, the inspiration of Sir Michael Filose, a gentleman in the maharajah's service, and it rose from a surf of crimson bougainvillaea like an ice floe from a sea of flame. Hiragaj subsided in front of its columns, prince and maharajah descended by ladder, and the latter ushered his guest into the finest durbar hall in India, the carpet of which was said to be the largest in the world. It was like stepping into a petrified waterfall: glass mirrors covered walls and ceilings, glass curved up into dimness in banisters, rails and newels; fountains of clear water sprang from crystal spigots, and facet glinted against facet, an icy blue-white, in constellations of glass chandeliers. The candelabra and even some pieces of furniture gleamed with the same brittle and ghostly translucence. All else was gold and yellow velvet, and the darker, glowing skins of the best of the eight hundred tigers slain by the maharajah himself.

That afternoon was given over to formalities. First came a review of the maharajah's army, represented by five thousand men of all arms and by the maharajah's two children, George (aged six) and Mary (aged eight), named in duty after the King-Emperor and his consort, who had graciously become their godparents. These two had been outfitted in privates' field-service khaki tunics, breeches, puttees and boots, and hung about with canteens, knapsacks, pouches, belts and bandoliers thoughtfully reduced in size. They shouldered miniature rifles and marched at the head of a regiment of infantry as valiantly and rhythmically as short legs would allow, Mary with a fat black pigtail wagging from her regimental turban and George with a face twisted into a mask by the urgency of holding the step. Then, this pomp and circumstance having disappeared into the dust, the royal party moved to the gate of the new park presented that day to his people by Sir Madhav Rao. He had christened it "King George Park" after the Prince's father and in further token of his loyalty, which no one had ever thought to question. The park had formed part of the gardens of two of his palaces, a sprawl of lawns, shrubberies, meadows, copses, hillocks, enclosures and pleasances so vast that tigers had been in the habit of strolling through it, mistaking it for an extension of their wild territories, and leopards had felt at home enough to breed there. Public now, it contained a temple for Hindus and another for Sikhs, a mosque for the minority of Muslims, a house for the even more *outré* members of the Theosophical Society, sports fields, a menagerie, and a few pavilions where the poor might purchase refreshments. The Prince of Wales opened the gate to this elysium with a gold key and declared himself pleased at the outcome of the maharajah's exertions. All that remained was a banquet that evening and then he could get down to the real business of the visit. But even the banquet was unusual, for the maharajah served liqueurs, cigars and candy by means of a silver electric locomotive hauling freight cars that bore their luxurious cargo around the table with a lingering stop before each guest.

By eight-thirty the following morning Sir Madhav Rao was sitting on the steps of his palace impatient for the Prince's return from a fast gallop on the polo ground. He had prepared everything. It had not been too difficult, for not only was Gwalior more blessed than other states in the profusion of its tigers, it was not necessary to camp far afield to come upon them. A short drive from the palace was enough. The cavalcade was able to get away before noon, with the maharajah leading at the wheel of a ponderous open Renault. Ten miles away the tiger grounds waited. It was a distinguished location, honored two years before by the aged but vitriolic Clemenceau, to whom three tigers, perhaps in deference to his nickname, had loyally sacrificed themselves.*

By one o'clock all was in order, though an owl had hooted and flown across the approach of the royal party, an omen well understood by the locals to signify a death in the vicinity. It was later learned that a madwoman had been killed by a nearby tiger. The Prince had been told nothing of this lamentable proof of the prescience of owls and he stood in expectation with loaded rifle on a rocky ledge selected by the maharajah as a point of vantage and execution. Two hundred feet below him lay the floor of a dry ravine, part of a mile-long rift some two hundred yards wide. Scrub and stunted teak trees covered the cliffs on either side, but the dusty verdure of the valley bottom was broken by patches of bald rock and bare red earth.

The system of hunting had been refined into an exact science and the maharajah himself had written the book, *A Guide to Tiger Shooting*. A day or two before the shoot, tigers would be located by shikaris and kept under surveillance; any tendency to wander too far abroad would be checked by providing suitable prey—a goat or even a water buffalo. On the day itself the area would be staked out by two lines of "stops," peasants or

---

* Perhaps the most famous of all Gwalior trophies, however, was that acquired by Lord Curzon. In 1908, three years after his tenure as Viceroy had ended, he fell in love with the gorgeous, red-haired Mrs. Elinor Glyn, who was starring in London in the stage version of her own amorous best-seller *Three Weeks* with its climactic scene on a rug, thus occasioning the immortal

> Would you like to sin
> With Elinor Glyn
> On a tiger skin?
> Or would you prefer
> To err with her
> On some other fur?

Finding himself in competition for Mrs. Glyn's luscious favors with a fellow tribune, the saturnine Alfred, Lord Milner, Curzon played his trump by sending her his Gwalior tiger skin. The same thought, unfortunately, had already occurred to Milner. It is a matter of historical record, however, that the Gwalior specimen proved the more seductive.

soldiers whose duty it was to keep the tiger moving between them toward the guns. The other end of the two lines was blocked by a crowd of beaters moving toward the guns and driving the tigers before them. That was the principle. The practice, as the Prince was soon to see, was as near-perfect as Gwalior could make it. The shikaris had reported two or three tigers in the valley, and he could hear the beaters calling and occasionally loosing off an ancient shotgun. Without warning there came a golden flash under the cliffs. The Prince fired and missed, and the tigress galloped into cover. When she emerged a few minutes later the Prince was more alert. He hit her in the kidneys and she shuddered, leapt and vanished. The maharajah dashed along the top of the cliff in pursuit, caught sight of her, fired and missed. Officers went into the valley on elephants; one of them spotted her at last while lunch was being prepared and shot her. She died wedged between two rocks. She was a reasonable trophy, eight feet three inches in length, but no one could pretend that she had offered the best of sport.

Next day was better. The royal party left their cars at the luncheon tent and walked up a bridle path toward the killing ground. Scattered along the track were porcupine quills, which the Prince and his staff began to pick up, a diversion so pleasant that the Prince ordered the quills collected, for a purpose lost to history. Presently they came to a ravine bigger than the previous day's, rocky and jungle-covered. On the far slope the maharajah had had a tower built of stone, and to this citadel he now conducted his guest. It was quiet in the valley, save for the brief bustle of a couple of peafowl flying into deeper cover. On the floor of the rift, directly below the tower, there was a clearing twenty yards wide, like a fire break. Without warning, but deliberately, two great tigers pushed suddenly out of the brush into the clearing, standing with heads and shoulders exposed about a hundred and thirty yards from the tower. The Prince of Wales brought up his .400 express double-barrel rifle by J. Purdey and Sons of London and killed the one nearer him outright. It was a female. The male bolted and everything was still again, though the beat could be heard far off in the direction from which the tigers had come. Twenty minutes later a crackle of shots rattled along the edge of the cliff. A big tiger was pounding down the valley. "He gave a good show as he ran," an onlooker reported, "with shots and bangs going off right and left. It was a great sight as all the sportsmen stood high up on the ravine firing at the tiger as he rushed along a couple of hundred feet below." Everyone who could opened up, and the beast was hit repeatedly over a distance of several hundred yards before it careered into thick scrub just above the stone tower. When it emerged the Prince hit it again with a grazing shot. He had as little effect on a third tiger that appeared shortly afterward. All three animals were accorded to the Prince on the principle that he had either killed them or put in first shot, though the most ardent royalist might judge that on these grounds his claim to two of the tigers was at least debatable.

His Royal Highness gave orders that special care be taken of the corpses by the Naturalist to the Shoots, a former curator of the Bombay Natural History Society, and his squad of skinners attached to the entourage. Haste was of some importance, since the hot sun would soon make the hair fall from the pelt. The skinners' method was to spread-eagle the animal on its back with its legs roped to trees, cutting down the belly from the chin to the end of the tail. They would split open the pads and scrape clean the insides, pluck the whiskers and set them aside, and finally and most carefully cut around the mouth and eyes. The skull they boiled. The Prince was anxious to have the lucky bones from his tigers, the small sickle-shaped floating clavicles about three inches long much in demand as scarf pins. They were souvenirs of particular virtue because it was self-evident that they could not have been removed from anything but a dead tiger.

However, the Prince could hardly have known about the value of the tiger's other products. Claws and teeth made talismans to repel witches, the fat was a comfort to the rheumatic, gallstones dried up watering of the eyes, the whiskers would tickle love into life within the most inaccessible breast, the brain mixed with smooth oil removed pimples, half a pound of flesh would render any man impervious to snakebite, and fat from the kidneys if rubbed on the penis would make a man close to immortal.

Two afternoons at the tigers satisfied what little blood lust raced through the elegant veins of Prince Edward. He turned to horses, next day riding at the race track in four events and getting a third and a fourth place. Dispatched with all due pomp, he left Gwalior with his suite in the late cool of February 12 headed for Delhi* and the more somber duties in British India, leaving the maharajah plump and shining with satisfaction and already thinking about his next guest.

Sir Madhav Rao's hospitality continued to pour forth in a Niagara of bounty, and before long he had begun arrangements for the visit of a personage who, though less Olympian than the Prince of Wales, was still a figure of some eminence. His Excellency the Viceroy, the Earl of Reading, had been born plain Rufus Daniel Isaacs and was the first Jew ever to fill in succession the offices of Attorney-General, Lord Chief Justice, Ambassador to the United States, Viceroy of India and later Foreign Secretary. He had begun his career as a ship's boy in a full-rigged iron merchantman, had been hammered on the stock exchange and would be the first commoner to be elevated to a marquisate since the Duke of Wellington.† Few things were

---

* Where his cousin Mountbatten met with a romance worthy of a fairy prince. Two days after their arrival he sat out the fifth dance of a Delhi ball and proposed marriage to a girl who had made her intentions fairly clear by borrowing a hundred pounds for a one-way ticket to India and wangling an invitation to stay with the Viceroy. She was beautiful, vivacious, intelligent and charming. He was handsome, lively, intelligent and charming. The only criticism of this heavenly arrangement came from the Viceroy's lady, who wrote to the girl's aunt: "I hoped she would have cared for someone older, with more of a career before him."

† Lord Reading retired as Viceroy in 1926. It was customary for the King to mark such an event by raising the nobleman one step in the peerage or by embracing him into the Order of the Garter. Lord Reading would have preferred the latter, but when he was called to Windsor to learn the King's pleasure, it became clear that this foremost of all the orders of chivalry was restricted to those of the Christian faith. The new marquess was not too downcast, however, because he had found that there were two advantages to being a private citizen again: he would once more be able to eat curries made from canned powder instead of the loathsome ones his Indian cooks had concocted from fresh spices in his palaces, and he could carry cash for shopping, a luxury not permitted Viceroys, who might spend years of rule

more foreign to Lord Reading's early life style than blasting away at birds and beasts with firearms, but when he learned of his appointment to India he had taken care to practice a little, and eventually acquired a taste for the sport. By the time he entered his second year in India he was lusting for a Gwalior tiger.

April weather was hot in Gwalior, but preferable to the steady oppression of Delhi, so the Viceroy was glad to accept the Maharajah of Gwalior's invitation to a hunting vacation at his summer capital of Shivpuri during that month in 1923. Shivpuri lay seventy-five miles south of Gwalior city, thirteen hundred feet up on a wooded plateau favored by an occasional breeze. It was necessary for Lord Reading's party to change trains at Gwalior, where the maharajah awaited them with his usual animation in the cab and in the guise of an engineer. Sir Madhav Rao propelled the locomotive all the way to Shivpuri without serious mishap, crying in moments of seeming peril, "No danger, Sindia drives!" The real engineer fell off en route and cut his head.

Shivpuri had once been a cantonment for a small British garrison, but twenty-seven years before, the maharajah had converted its three barrack blocks into a summer palace. The Viceroy and his lady discovered that the heat was less well tempered than they had expected, for the sun beat back from tessellated pavements and through trellised verandahs and into stuffy bedrooms, so there was much coming and going with pillows and peignoirs in the early mornings by those driven outside overnight to seek a breath of air. In spite of such native discomforts, however, Shivpuri was a superb place for sport. It stood in a thousand square miles of preserved jungles and the maharajah's shikar staff had been given to understand that the object of the Viceroy's visit was to shoot as many tigers there as they could supply.

To this end they had selected some twenty locations within

---

without setting eyes or fingers on such a demeaning thing as a piece of ready money.

a radius of thirty miles of Shivpuri, each one an easy drive. The maharajah welcomed the viceregal party to his sylvan seat with a bombardment of japes. It being All Fools' Day, everyone but the Viceroy and Lady Reading was awakened with a cup of tea in which salt had been substituted for sugar. The boiled breakfast eggs turned out to be made of china, cushions squeaked when sat upon, lights suddenly went out, and the delicate wafers served with the sherbet disclosed a lining of blotting paper. Sir Madhav Rao even went so far as to confide to Lady Reading that his senior wife, the maharani, was unwell and would welcome telegrams of sympathy. These frolics gave the maharajah such evident pleasure that no one could take offense.

In more serious activities the maharajah's best efforts seemed at first to be shadowed by bad luck. His chief shikari had sent fifteen elephants by road to Shivpuri from Gwalior. Marching at night, they had taken a week to cover the seventy-five miles, and one of them, a big tusker borrowed from a Gwalior nobleman, had caused a tragedy. In the darkness he had scented a tiger crossing the road ahead and stopped with such a ponderous lurch that his drowsing mahout had been tipped over. He landed under the elephant's feet and was squashed. Knowing that such a calamity could have deranged the tusker somewhat, the shikari gave orders that he was not to be employed during the Viceroy's shoot, at least until his habitual calm returned. Early in the visit the shikari noticed the delinquent animal standing ready to take part in the beat and rebuked the new mahout but was told that the beast was his former happy self again. The shikari had settled the Viceroy and the maharajah in a shooting tower and went off to supervise the rest of the arrangements, but hearing shots, walked back for orders. Shouting that a couple of tigers had been wounded, the maharajah told him to go and finish them.

The nearest elephant available for this delicate mission was the mourning bull. The shikari called to the mahout to make the beast kneel and the mahout obediently jabbed him with his ankus. The elephant threw up his trunk, trumpeted in fury and lumbered toward the shikari, knocking down His Highness' physician on the way, as well as a medical orderly who was holding a medicine chest. One elephantine foot instantly pressed the life out of the orderly and, the shikari later reported, "the crushing of the medicine bottles was heard all over the place." Encouraged, the elephant headed for one of Gwalior's most distinguished generals, saw him dodge behind a tree, knocked it down and pinned him immovably. The Viceroy's military secretary, an English colonel, had been snapping pictures of his lord and master in the tower and was astonished when the elephant rampaged into his viewfinder. The colonel fled while the bull paused to trample his camera and his sun helmet; reprieved, the colonel fell over a tree stump and luckily out of the elephant's line of vision. The beast swung around on a couple of gaping servants. They ran unwittingly straight toward one of the wounded tigers, which emitted a murderous growl. The elephant stopped at once, turned with the precision and speed of a dancer and rapidly made for home. There, later that evening, he was shot with an expenditure of eighty-four bullets from the Snider rifles of the local police.

The elephant had left a scene of some confusion. The medical orderly's grotesque posture made it evident that he was quite dead; the doctor was unconscious from a clout on the head; the general was groaning under his tree; and the colonel was gone. He was discovered high in a tree, but when encouraged to descend, found it physically impossible owing to the tightness of his breeches and the stiffness of his boots, and had to be lowered by rope. How he had climbed so high with such disabilities was never explained. The maharajah was less than pleased by these events, though the Viceroy had found some amusement in the plight of his military secretary.

The mishaps were overshadowed, in any case, near the end of the Viceroy's visit. It was known all over Gwalior that a monster of a tiger was prowling the Valley of Ker Kho, but none of the maharajah's shikaris had felt able to promise delivery of him before the Viceroy's guns. The tiger's habit was to kill and devour the buffaloes left out as bait and then disappear without leaving a trail; he kept to hard ground or springy turf, leaping over dusty paths that would take pug marks. Just before

Lord Reading was due to leave Gwalior, however, some villagers caught sight of the tiger swimming a river and hastily reported to the maharajah's chief shikari, who rushed his master and the eminent guest to the river, where a hide had been built in a tree. Lord Reading declined to climb up into the hide, protesting that being perched so high in the air would make him giddy and put him off his shot. The maharajah and his shikari agreed that, all things considered, it might be better if His Excellency kept his feet on the ground.

Leaving the two noblemen standing facing the valley, which began on the other side of the river, the shikari walked quietly along the bank for about a hundred yards, parallel with the valley mouth. Suddenly he caught sight of the tiger, a great bright ochre animal, sauntering down the valley to the river. He froze, looked away, coughed and casually dropped his handkerchief, hoping to give the tiger the impression that he had not noticed it fifty yards away. The ruse worked. The tiger sat down to think. Still with his head averted, the shikari gently strolled farther away from the guns. As intended, the tiger slid away in the opposite direction, toward the guns, and stepped into the water. He headed diagonally toward the Viceroy, only the top of his head and muzzle exposed and making a V in the water. He was a strong swimmer. The shikari shouted and ran back toward the guns.

Lord Reading had watched the tiger's casual approach to the bank but had waited until the beast was well immersed before drawing a bead. He missed with both barrels of his express rifle. Still calm, he reloaded and tried again. The heavy bullets smashed columns of water on either side of the glaring golden eyes. As good manners dictated, the maharajah held his fire. Reckoning safety now more important than protocol, he brought up his rifle and took very careful aim just above the shiny black muzzle. There was a click. He had forgotten to load. A mite discomfited, the maharajah groped in his pocket for a cartridge, found a long metal cylinder and rammed it into the breach, where it jammed. He had seized a whistle. The Viceroy was beginning to shed a little of the imperial aplomb and was also having difficulty reloading. The tiger was swimming powerfully on as if nothing could prevent his enjoyment of a truly royal snack.

The shikari burst through the bushes and took in the situation. A professional, he instantly leveled his rifle at the tiger, which, perhaps sensing a change in the rules of the game, turned in the water with an easy swing and headed back for the valley. By now the maharajah had relieved himself of his whistle and the Viceroy had successfully reloaded. The shikari, using what authority he could muster, asked them to be kind enough to refrain from firing until the tiger had emerged completely from the water. Lord Reading was to fire first. The tiger reached the shallows and was gathering himself for a leap onto the bank when His Excellency pulled the trigger. His shot struck in the left hindquarters but had no visible effect. The tiger charged up the valley with undiminished vigor, encountered a group of beaters, and swiped one of them to the ground in agony.

The shikari sensed a troublesome afternoon. He suggested that the maharajah take his guest back to camp, which the maharajah did. The shikari then sent for a herd of buffaloes in the hope of stampeding the wounded tiger into the open. Numbers of sullen buffaloes were soon assembled and prodded into the bush, but the tiger showed himself and they left again at a gallop. When an elephant was brought up, the tiger broke cover in earnest, pounded away up the valley and chewed the head off a wandering beater. More huntsmen had arrived from the camp, so the shikari spaced them out along the high sides of the narrowing valley and cautiously moved into it himself. The tiger had turned off into a cleft in the valley side full of big boulders and darkness. When fired at from above, he replied with vigorous snarls.

The shikari decided that there was nothing for it but to offer himself as bait. The light was beginning to fade as he crawled over the boulders as stealthily as he could until he judged he was in position. He stood up and shouted. Instantaneously the tiger bunched his tremendous muscles and charged, more than five hundred pounds of malevolence and pain. The shikari shot him through the head with a soft-nosed bullet. The Viceroy was delighted to have the trophy; even his brief view of it had distinguished it as a massive prize. As indeed, when lugged back to camp, it proved to be, for it was announced that the animal measured eleven feet five and a half inches, only one inch shorter than the world record. This was held by a former Viceroy, Lord Hardinge, who had achieved it with the maharajah's help in a nearby location nine years before.

Alas, Lord Reading was not allowed to rest on his laurels. When the good news was brought to England, the ignorant politely applauded but the experts growled. By any standards, Lord Reading's tiger was a giant. It was common knowledge that a ten-foot tiger weighing four hundred and forty pounds was an excellent specimen; Lord Reading's was nearly a foot and a half longer and one hundred and fifty pounds heavier. The first note of discord sounded in *The Field*, a periodical given over to country matters of the most abstruse kind, when four months later a Mr. Dunbar-Brander pointed out that His Highness the Maharajah of Gwalior had presided over the dispatch of fourteen hundred tigers but only those killed by Viceroys had managed to extend over eleven feet when defunct. The correspondent could not restrain his curiosity about the methods of measurement. Reply came three months later from one of the Viceroy's aides-de-camp. He repudiated Mr. Dunbar-Brander's mild insinuations and explained rather plaintively that the three men who had done the measuring had not been strong enough to roll the brute onto his back among the boulders so as to measure it, as was proper, between pegs driven into the ground at muzzle and tip of tail. So Lord Reading's tiger had been measured perforce "round the curves." Mr. Dunbar-Brander had been made privy to the contents of the letter and was able to answer it in the same issue, this time pointing out the uncomfortable fact that whereas tiger skins usually stretched about a foot between the jungle and the taxidermist's, Lord Hardinge's record tiger from Gwalior had actually shrunk by the time it arrived in London. The correspondence became irreverent. One gentleman proposed the reclassification of vice-regal tigers as *Felis tigris superbus,* and another claimed to have found a steel tape measure in Gwalior that measured only eleven inches to the foot.

If the innuendoes caused the maharajah pain, he gave no sign of it. He had his critics, who said he was one man in public and another in private. For his own part the maharajah felt that he was answerable only to himself and his King-Emperor and to the code of honor of his Maratha race. But a few British officials went so far as to think him "unreliable." More considered him a shrewd politician and applauded his usefulness, but deplored his bullying way with subordinates or those he thought his inferiors. He had once humiliated the young Maharajah of Datia by purposely making him drunk while he was his guest at dinner, a shameful breach of hospitality. A neighbor, the Maharajah of Datia revenged himself by thereafter keeping a number of female tigers caged near his boundary with Gwalior. When in heat, they attracted excellent male tigers from Gwalior's carefully tended jungles. The aggrieved prince could then cheerfully riddle the lustful beasts from his side of the river.

Sir Madhav Rao Sindia was the ninth of his line to rule in Gwalior, and though his house was of humble origin, it had long shone in splendor. Geographically Gwalior was the principal fragment left from the empire that Shivaji, sweeping down from the dragon's back of the Western Ghats, had wrung from the Moguls in central India.

The most obvious symbol of Gwalior's pre-eminence was the mighty fort squatting atop the Shepherd's Hill, the ridge of basalt that dominated the maharajah's chief city. The fort had a long and dreadful history. There the Moguls had poisoned prisoners no longer useful by administering the juice of poppies mixed with poisonous flowers; Rajput women had annihilated themselves by fire behind its walls and many an assault party had hurtled screaming in defeat down its smooth black bastions. More than once the British had held the fort and returned it to Sindia.* In Sir Madhav Rao's time it was no more than a relic, though grim and historic enough for that.

Sir Madhav Rao was a modern man; though the fierce memories of his warrior ancestors could fire his blood, his inclination was more to the future than the past. Inventive but untrained, he loved tinkering with toys and gadgets and was happiest groping in the silent guts of his automobiles. But his passion was the jungle and killing tigers, which, as another devotee put it, was "like young love and champagne and poetry and getting religion and getting elected, all rolled into one."

Sometimes the inventiveness and the passion conjoined in a single scheme: in 1916 it occurred to the maharajah to attempt the introduction of lions into Gwalior and sent to East Africa for three pairs. Though the First World War was raging there as elsewhere, he encountered no difficulty, for he had friends and part of his army in East Africa, often closer to lions than they were to the Germans. To get acclimatized, the lions were kept in a walled compound in a lonely part of the Gwalior jungle for four years, during which time they increased and multiplied and did not seem unduly distressed by the incensed tigers roaring all around them. The maharajah released the first pair of lions in August 1920. They vanished. The second pair wandered disconsolately around the outside of the walls until they were shooed away; within a day the male had succumbed to an outraged tiger. Three more pairs left in turn, only the last being heard from at once. This couple took to stealing cattle from the villagers scattered in the jungle, and when the villagers countered by piling lion-proof hedges around their cattle, the lions ate the villagers instead and had to be shot. The rest wandered wild for some time but were eventually dispatched one

---

* One of the more spectacular successes at the Gwalior fort was its capture one broiling night in August 1780 by Captain Popham, who had bribed some local brigands to point out to him where its forbidding rock could be scaled. The ingenious captain cut up some army blankets, stuffed the pieces with cotton and wrapped them around his soldiers' boots. This brilliant ruse brought Captain Popham wide fame at the time, so he was doubly surprised when, twenty-five years later, by then a general and full of honors, bureaucracy caught up with him and deducted the cost of the blankets from his pay.

by one by an assortment of maharajahs, one of whom by good fortune was Sir Madhav Rao Sindia of Gwalior himself.

The maharajah was distinguished by great personal bravery: once, when he was tent-pegging at Hurlingham outside London, his horse bolted and he jumped off, pulling its head down as he was dragged along just in time to prevent it from thundering into the crowd of very fashionable and fragile ladies. A defective howdah once tipped him on top of a wounded tiger; the maharajah pursued it into the jungle and was gone so long that his followers began to fear for his safety, but he walked into camp out of the night with the tiger's skin on his back. His valor was accompanied by intense loyalty. During the First World War he bought a hospital ship, the *Loyalty*, and a convalescent home in Nairobi, sent a battalion of infantry to East Africa and another to the Suez Canal and Palestine, as well as transportation units to Flanders, Gallipoli, Salonica and Mesopotamia. The cost of all this was over eleven and a half million dollars. When the Afghan War came in 1919, Gwalior Lancers, infantry and service troops marched toward the Khyber. It was not so much the intrinsic worth of these gifts to their cause that pleased the British as the thought behind them; the expense was hardly crippling to a man who once found ten million dollars hidden under his back stairs. The British honored Sir Madhav Rao with their sincere friendship, with an addition of two guns to his existing salute of nineteen, with orders of chivalry, with the honorary rank of lieutenant general in their army, and with one doctorate of laws each from Oxford and Cambridge.

Sir Madhav Rao's Gwalior was a model state, secure in its finances, prudent in its economic planning and progressive in its social programs. Its administration of justice was at least as even-handed as that of British India, for the court officers were instructed that when they sat in judgment "they should consider themselves in a sanctuary, free from all outside influence and responsible to none but to the God Almighty and that no hint or direction even from the Ruler should disturb their equanimity." Such malefactors as felt the weight of that equanimity received interesting therapy in clean, peaceful jails, where they were employed in chicken farming, painting and polishing carriage bodies, weaving cane screens to shade ladies keeping purdah and, perhaps more for instruction than for economy, in tailoring and mending the uniforms of the police.

Indigenous industries were encouraged. Sandalwood essence, and combs made of the same wood which oiled the hair automatically, rose water, medicated soot for lining the eyes, ivory bangles and lacquered bric-a-brac were shipped all over India. Experimental farms increased the yield of the great variety of crops growing in Gwalior's well-irrigated soil and improved the blood and weight of Gwalior's cattle. The state's hospitals were well staffed and liberally equipped, and its schools were already well established and numerous, providing a scheme of education that reached a peak in the Victorian College at Lashkar. There was even that indispensable adjunct to an increasingly technological state, a lunatic asylum.

Sir Madhav Rao Sindia left many monuments, some of a funerary kind. His mother's death had so desolated him that he built a pavilion for her in which he placed her likeness, life-size and of pure glistening marble. This cold revenant was attended, as in life, by a retinue of women who bathed and arrayed it in jewels, fine garments and perfumes, bringing food as usual while a band played occasional airs. An electric fan alleviated excessive heat and a couch was brought for comfort when the sun was at its height. Sometimes the maharajah would entertain his mother's old friends nearby. The effect was the opposite of morbid; indeed the maharajah visibly relaxed in his mother's chaste company, and the devotion accorded by prince and servants alike to the stone matriarch carried an air of dignified cheerfulness. One perceptive lady visitor, far from finding the maharajah's arrangements curious, thought they demonstrated "the high sanity of his faith." As she put it: "He has visualized the lasting things of memory, and this with no sacrifice of dignity or regret."

In 1925 the maharajah set forth to pay his duties once more to the King-Emperor. He did not reach London. In Paris a carbuncle on his neck swelled so painfully that doctors had to be summoned. They could do nothing. The maharajah's body was burned with Hindu rites in the mortuary grandeur of the cemetery of Père Lachaise near the tombs of Rossini, Chopin, La Fontaine and Oscar Wilde, and its ashes were carried home to Gwalior by a faithful and grieving shikari. Sir Madhav Rao was memorialized by his loyal people with a mausoleum at Shivpuri, his old hunting grounds, erected on a site he had designated in his will, facing his mother's pavilion. This *chhatri* was six and a half years in the building and cost over half a million dollars, but when finished, it was a monument, the partial said, second only to the Taj Mahal. Unlike that calm symbol of Mogul taste, the maharajah's mausoleum was thick with the ornamental stone-work for which Gwalior was famous. A pillared hall of audience led to the sanctum from which rose one great bullet-shaped dome ringed at its base by smaller domes and cupolas, all capped with spikes like war helmets. Inlay and mosaic of agate, jasper, carnelian and lapis lazuli winked and glowed from the dead white of marble cut into traceries, creepers and singing birds picked out, inevitably, with gold. Silver doors and electric chandeliers shone against the marble so exquisitely and exhaustively worked that it seemed to have lost all weight. The effect was, as the maharajah's spirit had been, exuberant.

Sir Madhav Rao was succeeded by the little son who had marched so valiantly before the Prince of Wales. George Jivaji Rao Sindia was then aged nine, so a Council of Regency was appointed under the presidency of his father's senior wife, a sprightly woman not more than three feet tall but of great intelligence and charm. The boy maharajah's seminal years were disturbed only once by the lightning that plays about princely heads. His father had been dead three years when the British Resident announced that the twelve-year-old George would vacate his Lashkar palace, where a palace clique (headed, it was hinted, by one of the maharanis) "had deliberately set out to debauch the boy ruler" and take up residence for his "physical and moral wellbeing" in the brooding citadel of Gwalior atop the Shepherd's Hill until he was old enough to enter one of the princes' colleges run by the British. In the event, George never went to college; a succession of British tutors succeeded in shaping him into a model of an English public school boy with a proper love for hockey, tennis and sports generally, and his mother reinforced their efforts for his moral development by cooking all his food herself to obviate the possibility of poison. He assumed full powers in the state in 1936 when he reached his majority, and five years later married a princess from Nepal. He busied himself with race horses and finance, and when the political earthquake came in 1947, with constitutional reforms. He retained his father's interest in the Gwalior jungles but never tried to attain Sir Madhav Rao's eminence as a master of tigers.

When Gwalior became absorbed into the new India, its game preserves, no longer protected by the maharajah's shikaris, enjoyed an open season during which any villager was free to slaughter whatever he wished. The jungles grew still. At the end of a decade of anarchy, sixty-one square miles of forest near Shivpuri were turned into a government park. Poaching was stopped and once more the chestnut chinkara gazelles flirted through the teak brakes, and tigers sauntered down the rock gulleys toward the rank scent of forest pig.

The age when Sir Madhav Rao had given eight tigers to a Viceroy in a single day, nineteen to another during a longer stay, and three tigers and a leopard to his twelve-year-old daughter in a single electric beat, had gone forever. Instead there was a lodge with a thousand-candlepower arc lamp beamed onto a clearing where the tigers would be lured to a kill; when they began to eat, the lamp's power was gradually increased. Marshal Tito came there as a guest of the government of India, and declining to shoot, announced that he would prefer to use a movie camera if any tigers appeared. Gwalior's shikaris had not lost their art. As a reward for his humanity, Tito got four tigers in a single shot.

8

❖❰❖❰❰❖❰❰❖❰❰❖❰❰❖❰❰❖❰❰❖

The Big Spenders

THE LAND OF Baroda bred excesses. Its hot and humid climate, held by many the worst in India, forced men into a state of unnaturally saintly endurance or alternatively drove their livers to erupt in bouts of rage. The Maharajah Khande Rao, Gaekwar of Baroda, whose term lasted from 1856 to 1870, was the capricious sort. Everything his fancy settled on he had to have at once. One day it was diamonds, big ones. Another day it was religion: he collected a holy man sitting in a trance on a dunghill, shipped him to the palace and surrounded him with other sadhus for study, but to no avail, for the holy man did not respond even when a pistol was fired by his ear. Khande Rao once accumulated sixty thousand pigeons of all breeds, had his priests conduct a marriage ceremony over a pair of them, and gave a vast banquet with fireworks afterward. He lost interest when a palace cat carried off the bridegroom, and turned to organizing a battle between five hundred nightingales.

Some of Khande Rao's diversions were more vigorous. Baroda was always famous for its arena where, echoing imperial Rome, beasts and men were matched. It was three hundred yards long and two hundred yards wide, and was enclosed by twenty-foot walls washed a staring candy pink. At its western end a grandstand sheltered the ruler and his invisible ladies, while the populace clambered atop the walls or festooned convenient trees. There were always a couple of bull elephants crazy with musth, a condition of the rutting season which could be induced artificially by a diet of butter and sugar for three months. A solitary bull might be teased by men with spears and firecrackers, waving red veils, or by a horseman with a lance. There might be a fight between two rhinoceroses, one painted black for identification, the other red. Rams and buffaloes were always available, charging themselves silly. But the only event that sometimes concluded in death was the wrestling, for in Baroda men fought with claws of sharpened horn lashed to their fists. Intoxicated with liquid opium and hemp, they became oblivious to pain; a loser might literally be torn to strips before he was carried off. The winner could be certain of money from the maharajah, and perhaps a rope of pearls and a silk coat of honor. On a single day Khande Rao might distribute twenty thousand dollars' worth of such trifles.

His own jewels were more serious. In 1867 he paid four hundred thousand dollars for the Star of the South, the first diamond of any size and repute to be taken from the newly developed Brazilian mines.* Closter of Amsterdam had cut it from nearly 262 carats to 128½ and had revealed within it an exquisite pink fire. When the stone arrived in Baroda, Khande Rao accorded it a triumphal parade graced by a saddled and bridled giraffe. He then placed it in a necklace with a lesser stone of only 76½ carats, the English Dresden, a pear-shaped diamond of such purity that when the Koh-i-noor was tested beside it, it made the Koh-i-noor seem slightly yellow. It had cost Khande Rao two hundred thousand dollars. He had paid another hundred and seventy-five thousand dollars for the Akbar Shah, a tear-drop

---

* It was also at the time the largest diamond found by a woman. She was an African slave. Her reward was her freedom and a pension for life.

diamond of 70 carats thought to have been one of the eyes of a peacock on the Peacock Throne of the Moguls.

When these acquisitions strained Khande Rao's treasury, he simply issued a proclamation. "His Highness has seen with regret that corruption has found its way into various departments of his administration," it read, "but he hopes that this state of things will forthwith come to an end. He counsels all those officials who have allowed themselves to be corrupted to bring into the royal treasury the sums received in this way for the last ten years. His Highness, considering this restitution as making honorable amends, will forget the past." Even ministers the maharajah had not suspected contributed: in two weeks nearly a million and a half dollars had been regurgitated. Khande Rao swung between wealth and bankruptcy, between excessive kindness and extraordinary cruelty. He was quirkish.

Khande Rao looked like the last of the Mohicans, for his head was shaven save for a lock of hair at the nape. In the morning he would not open his eyes until he knew that the commander in chief, his favorite minister, was standing by the bed to give an auspicious start to the day. Court manners directed that his belches and farts be greeted with enthusiastic applause, but no one might sneeze in his presence, for that was so evil an augury that all business must be suspended for the day. When the maharajah yawned, all present must snap their fingers to discourage flies. The British viewed Khande Rao's idiosyncrasies with detachment, accounting him a competent ruler on the whole, perhaps because of the large white marble statue of Queen Victoria he was astute enough to provide for the beautification of Bombay. In any case, in all his excesses he was surpassed by his brother, who lived in jail.

After seven years behind bars the brother succeeded to the throne as the Maharajah Mulhar Rao, Gaekwar of Baroda. His first act was to place his deceased predecessor's favorite, the commander in chief, in irons and on a regimen of salt water and pepper, which pickled him in fifteen days. Finding the treasury at low ebb, Mulhar Rao farmed out the taxes: what had been customary oppression in Khande Rao's time now became flagrant. Eager to get rich while still in favor, the courtiers flogged the last rupee out of the most remote peasant. Baroda's tribunals swiftly became so corrupt that justice spoke only from gold. The wives and daughters of respectable men were seized in open day in the street and sent, as a contemporary euphemism put it, "into domestic slavery in the Gaekwar's palace." Lands and personal property were confiscated without warning or cause, and their owners left to slow starvation. The more truculent were bound, roped to the hind leg of a trotting elephant and dragged through the streets, a particularly unpleasant form of execution which ended, if the victim had not succumbed to the perambulation, with his being revived with a drink of water. His head was then placed on a stone and the elephant stepped on it. Such horrors could not long be hidden. At the beginning of 1873 the wrong man saw them.

The British Resident, Colonel Sir Robert Phayre, was a soldier of thirty-four years' service, a fussy man of clockwork habits, an aide-de-camp to the Queen. He was a veteran of the First Afghan War, the Mutiny and the invasion of Ethiopia. He was a Bible thumper and a pamphleteer, and he was as suspicious as a spinster. He quickly reported Mulhar Rao for gross misgovernment, and His Highness was advised by the Viceroy to mend his ways. On November 9, 1874, Colonel Phayre got up as usual, made his toilet and went for a short ride. Returning at seven-thirty, as was his habit, he walked straight into his dressing room where his customary glass of pink grapefruit juice was waiting by the washstand. He took a couple of sips. It tasted a little odd and the colonel put it down. He began his correspondence, but after half an hour the strange taste had not left his mouth and he felt a slight nausea. Annoyed, he threw the contents of the glass into the garden below his window. Some brown sediment was left in the bottom of the glass. A thought came. At once the colonel dashed off a wire, in clear, to his superiors in Poona: BOLD ATTEMPT TO POISON ME THIS DAY HAS BEEN PROVIDENTIALLY FRUSTRATED. MORE BY NEXT POST. A second thought. He ordered a servant to scrape up the remains of the drink he had thrown into the garden and sent it, with the sediment from the glass, to be analyzed by two English doctors.

The gears of British justice ground into high and His Highness Mulhar Rao, Gaekwar of Baroda, was charged on four counts of instigating and bribing servants at the British Residency to spy on Colonel Phayre and poison him. The Gaekwar was to be tried, in short, for attempted murder by a specially constituted commission. Wisely, the maharajah hired the best lawyer he could find, Mr. William Ballantine, who was formidable enough to have frightened even the Prince of Wales when there was a prospect of His Royal Highness' being examined by him.* He was the first British advocate to accept a brief in India, and his fees, in days when not all lawyers were wealthy, was a staggering fifty thousand dollars. Ballantine gave value for the money, however. He soon made it clear that the decision to try Mulhar Rao had been a disastrous mistake.

Ballantine was welcomed by a large sector of Baroda's native society with music and flowers and an address which read in part: "May pure justice be dealt to our prince in a pure and undefiled way! In that case we shall sing merry songs expressive of your great glory. Then will your praise be sung everywhere." Sightseeing before the trial, Ballantine was oppressed by the appearance of the city. It was very dirty and joyless. "I never saw a smile upon a countenance or heard a sound of gaiety," he wrote. "The men we met scowled at us, and certainly the impression made upon me was that the Europeans were most thoroughly hated."

Though the British had no legal right whatever to try a native prince on a criminal matter in his own territories, they

---

* In 1870 the Prince of Wales had been summoned to give witness in a divorce hearing brought by an acquaintance, Sir Charles Mordaunt, against his twenty-one-year-old wife on grounds of adultery with two of the Prince's friends. The Prince himself had visited the lady and had written her letters. Ballantine appeared for Mordaunt and tactfully declined to cross-examine His Royal Highness, who was greatly relieved. Ballantine's reputation for brilliance was enhanced and he had the pleasure of dining with the Prince at the Garrick Club at a later date.

pressed the charges at the personal wish of Queen Victoria. The result was that they seemed to the Indian public to be intent on making a martyr of the maharajah. The commission assembled in the dry heat of February 25, 1875. The Chief Justice of India, Sir Richard Couch, presided; its members were the Chief Commissioner of Mysore and a Commissioner of the Punjab, both English, the maharajahs of Gwalior and Jaipur, and the Indian Prime Minister of Gwalior, one of the most famous administrators in India. The prosecutor was the Advocate-General of Bombay. Ballantine was not overwhelmed.

He showed first that a week before the alleged poison attempt, Mulhar Rao had politely petitioned the government for the removal of Colonel Phayre, deploring the colonel's unwarranted slights and indiscretions but not questioning the colonel's conscientious motives. The petition had not been answered. This might have seemed to indicate a good reason for the maharajah's taking more drastic action. But Ballantine then asked the commission to note that Colonel Phayre had declined a request from the governor of Bombay for his resignation. The colonel had in fact been sacked by the Viceroy three weeks after the poison incident, and before the trial, on the grounds "that he had thoroughly misunderstood the spirit of the instructions both of the Government of India and the Government of Bombay and that the duty of Resident could no longer be entrusted to him with any reasonable prospect of a satisfactory result." It was revealed that Mulhar Rao knew before the day of the so-called attempted murder that the colonel's dismissal was at least likely. Thus Ballantine established an absence of any pressing motive.

He next destroyed the more technical evidence about the attempt proper. The doctors who had analyzed the brown sediment had informed Colonel Phayre that it contained common white arsenic and some fine silicious matter that seemed under the microscope to be powdered glass. Phayre had hastily inquired of them by letter "whether in your opinion the silicious matter can possibly be powdered diamond. Previous to the receipt of your letter I had received secret and confidential communication that the poison administered to me did consist of common arsenic, finely powdered diamond dust and copper." It took a good deal of pressure to make the colonel reveal the source of this secret communication. The source was Mulhar Rao's bitterest enemy, a man who knew Colonel Phayre's habits, who had complete access to Phayre's dressing room, and who had been there on the morning in question. The implication was clear —at least to Ballantine—that there had been a plot to fabricate evidence injurious to the maharajah. Ballantine then demonstrated that evidence supporting the prosecution's case had been obtained by illegal means, the least of which was intimidation. None of Ballantine's arguments made much impression on the English members of the commission. Much of the evidence they merely ignored. The Indian members were convinced that there was absolutely no case against Mulhar Rao. The trial ended without any hint of what the commission's decision might be.

Ballantine, who was nobody's fool, always distrusted the doctors' evidence and believed that whether Phayre lived or died had been immaterial. In his opinion Mulhar Rao's enemies wanted to use Phayre to bring down the maharajah and so arranged the whole thing as provocation. The eminent counsel drove to his ship through a mass of well-wishers, gratified by a parchment testimonial signed by fifteen hundred of Bombay's most prominent citizens thanking him for his exertions "on behalf of the oppressed prince." Colonel Phayre went on to the command of a division, published a number of broadsides with such titles as *The Bible versus Corrupt Christianity* and *Monasticism Unveiled*, and died a full general.

Within a month of the trial's end the government of India acted. It brushed aside the whole business of Mulhar Rao's guilt or innocence of the poison charges, though admitting that the commissioners had been divided, and announced in a formal proclamation: "Incorrigible misrule is of itself a sufficient disqualification for sovereign power. Her Majesty's Government have willingly accepted the opportunity of recognizing in a conspicuous case the paramount obligation which lies upon them of protecting the people of India from oppression." In reality, it seemed a conspicuous case of an alien government protecting the people of Baroda from an evil which at least they knew, and certainly preferred, to the evil they did not know. But that was the end of Mulhar Rao. He was a rascal, but he had not had justice.

There was now a problem of succession. In deposing Mulhar Rao, the British also excluded his descendants from the throne. His predecessor's widow had to search about for a suitable male child for adoption. The family tree of the Gaekwars was kept, like those of other Hindu princes, in the town of Nasik on the holy Godavari River, a place second only to Benares in sanctity. Some thirteen hundred groups of Brahmin priests congregated at Nasik, one of which guarded the Baroda dynasty's antecedents. Much study produced a farmer with four sons, of whom the second, a boy of twelve, was chosen by the widow, adopted and placed on the vacant throne in that same year of 1875. Unable to read or write, familiar only with the soil and the mud puddles of a remote village, Sayaji Rao, the new maharajah, was assigned a tutor, a hard-driving Englishman from the Bombay Civil Service. The little boy missed his father very much and would wave to him from the roof of the palace when no one was looking. In confirmation of the child's importance, the Prince of Wales himself came to Baroda on a state visit at the end of 1875. Sayaji Rao was, a member of the royal suite noted, "a boy such as one may see all over the place" and his soft, mild eyes were sad. But he could salute the Prince of Wales with cannon of solid gold weighing two hundred and eighty pounds apiece and it took twenty-four men to lift the howdah in which they rode together—also of pure gold—onto the elephant's back.*

The plain, mournful little boy was the second-richest prince in India, ruler of two and a half million in a land the size of Massachusetts that was known, for its fields of millet, maize and

---

* The elephant used for this task was the strongest available; it was specially fed with nutritious sugar cane and rewarded with a pint of sherry on duty days. The whole equipage, elephant and howdah together, was worth a million dollars.

opium poppies, its canebrakes and golden orchards, as the garden of Gujerat. His jewels were barely inferior to the fabulous collection at Hyderabad, and his palaces were as vast and numerous as any. Surrounded by dedicated and rather humorless Englishmen, he was so molded that with these advantages he became a model among great princes.

Sayaji Rao's youth was spent in a harness of Victorian rectitude so confining that even when he was released into manhood there were muscles he never used. So far as was known, he was the only prince of his time of whom it could be said with certainty that he never kept a mistress. Even the two dancing girls who performed rather primly of an evening in the durbar hall were a mother and daughter of exemplary private habits. Sayaji Rao married first a princess of Travancore who died after giving him a son, then the daughter of a Maratha nobleman from Dewas. She was beautiful and strong and they lived happily together for half a century.

During that time Sayaji Rao and his maharani brought Baroda out of the Middle Ages. The maharajah's person was far from majestic. His head was inelegantly round and his belly inclined to the same shape, though he drank only one glass of water half an hour after each meal and dieted himself on Karlsbad water and minced chicken. He had a double chin and a pudgy nose and a rather dull complexion. His hands and feet were small and shapely, and his clear voice was pleasant. His manner was always mild, though sometimes distracted as if by a hidden grief. His brain was one of the most powerful in India. It never rested; he read Plato in Greek and moved easily with Jeremy Bentham and Herbert Spencer. Alice's adventures, the Mad Hatter and the White Rabbit so enchanted him that he had the story translated into Marathi. His thoughts tumbled over themselves, so that he spoke in rapid bursts like a woodpecker hammering.

Intellectually the maharani was his equal. Her book *The Position of Women in Indian Life* was hailed by the socialist Ramsay MacDonald as "an extraordinary revelation of the educated eastern mind of the present day" and recommended as a guide to professions and occupations for Englishwomen. For years the maharani pounded at the barriers of purdah; in 1927 she presided over the first All-India Women's Conference. This disposition made Baroda the most modern and sophisticated of states. She was the finest shot of her sex in India, passionate for tigers, and once while eating an alfresco lunch, casually brought down a couple of herons without getting up from the table. She was fond of gardening and kept ten acres beside the palace for her groves of oranges, mangoes, limes and stranger fruits.

The style of life at the Lakshmi Vilas palace, Lakshmi being the goddess of wealth, tended toward English affluence. The building itself was a sprawling Indo-Saracenic mass of white stone, cypress-green marble and carved cedar much highlighted with gold or mosaics of brilliant birds. Most of the furnishings in the more public apartments were comfortably Anglo-Saxon, and the senior staff was only a little more cosmopolitan. The cook was French but the major-domo was an archetypal faithful English retainer. A couple of the chauffeurs were Italian, because their cars were, but the master of the stables was a whip-cord Irish sergeant major. The maharajah's valet was English, and so were the personal maids of the maharani and her daughter as well as the maharani's lady-in-waiting. The maharajah employed Englishmen to run his army, his police force, his hospitals and his colleges, and in later years there was even a professor of comparative religion.*

The maharajah's table linen was specially woven in Belfast, and when a new dinner service was needed he merely melted down one of several stored in the vaults and sent the bullion to London, where Bond Street craftsmen fashioned something a little more modern. What an English guest described as "the usual kinds of drinks" were offered—whiskey or hock with seltzer at breakfast, champagne and port in the evening. Dinner might be accompanied by selections from a small string orchestra conducted by the maharajah's French bandmaster, composer of

---

* For a while the maharajah had an American phase, culminating in a Director of Commerce who thus predated in some ways the labors of the Ford Foundation. He was inspired to buy the streetcar system of Bombay—track, horses and cars—and for a while Baroda's traffic snarled to a halt.

a Baroda national anthem not unlike the "Marseillaise." On high days there would be something more stirring, "Blue Bonnets over the Border" or "Bonnie Dundee" from the clamoring bagpipes of the Baroda Highlanders in their kilts and bizarre pink tights. At Christmas, following the turtle soup and the cannonball pudding blue with brandy flames, there was certain to be a rendering of some favorite ballad like "Little Boy Blue" by a bosomy contralto booming beside the Bechstein among the potted palms.

Outside, too, the habits of the West overlaid intrinsic India. The cricket ground, watered and rolled daily, was the greenest and smoothest on the subcontinent. Beside the asphalt tennis courts, where a dozen ball boys skipped about in green-and-gold uniforms, stood tree-shaded tables with iced lemonade and cigarettes, as in an English garden. The flowers might be more garish but the swans that queened it in the fountain pools were as disdainful as any that floated on the Thames. And yet there was a difference. Although the maharajah in his brown velvet knickerbocker suit and worsted stockings might take a walk like any rural duke, six men in scarlet livery followed with a sedan chair just in case. The carriages crunching up the gravel drives carried smart footmen perched in back, but they were silver affairs ornate as ice cream carts, and yoked white bullocks pulled them. The garden parties, all chiffon and flowered hats and uniforms and bijou sandwiches, were enlivened by snake charmers, magicians, and the specialty of Baroda, a troupe of performing parrots. An ingenious Muslim had trained a couple of dozen of the little green birds in acrobatics; they rode minute bicycles, practiced short-range archery and, climactically, loaded and fired a cannon, which always caused a flutter.

The unexpected was never very far away in Baroda, but the tenor of life was even and progressive. The first high school was founded in 1881 and soon education was compulsory and free throughout the state, for the first time in any part of India. Baroda's library system, the best in the East, reached every village, for the maharajah believed that "The people must rise superior to their circumstances and realize that more knowledge is their greatest need, their greatest want. Libraries will not then appear a luxury, but a necessity of existence." The speech might have come from the lips of Andrew Carnegie. Democracy began for the maharajah at the village level; his aim was to revitalize the *panchayats*, the village councils that his predecessors' wantonness and a certain climatic apathy had vitiated. He did not wholly achieve it. But he built a science institute, an art school, one of the best picture galleries in the country and a museum of catholic range.*

As he grew older, Sayaji Rao became deeply occupied with religion. In 1933 he attended the second World Parliament of Religions in Chicago, a gathering of a hundred sects from eleven great creeds. In a long and moving address he said: "God is at work. He is a democratic king and asks our help. He recognizes no hierarchy but that of service. Democracy means also the emergence of the common man, the demand of the backward peoples for a place in the sun." He concluded: "There is no God higher than the truth, no beauty without harmony. Our economic and political problems are ethical and spiritual problems." This was the spring from which Sayaji Rao's charity welled. He was the only prince in India to concern himself with the lot of the untouchables, an attitude that endangered his own caste standing. He himself had suffered the lash of social and racial prejudice: the club in the British cantonment was exclusively white and Sayaji Rao made the superbly disdainful gesture of buying it a new pavilion. Sayaji Rao clothed and fed the untouchables, built hostels and provided more than two hundred schools for them. Perhaps most important of all, he financed the education of the first great outcaste leader, the tortured and brilliant Bhimrao Ramji Ambedkar. Sent to Columbia with the maharajah's money, Ambedkar studied anthropology, economics and law, but back home in India could not even rent a room. He wrote, entered politics and fought bitterly

---

* A stuffed buffalo calf with two heads and six legs vied as the prime exhibit with a recumbent Eve in marble in the grand staircase. Also very popular was a life-size plaster likeness of Professor Eugene Sandow, the world's strongest man, which unaccountably tickled giggles out of both sexes.

for the abolition of caste, and because of him Mahatma Gandhi took up the plight of the untouchables and became their champion.

Good works flowed from Sayaji Rao and his wife in a river of beneficence. In their views of the duty of sovereignty and in their style of public life they were modern and Western. Yet in religion and in some of their social practices they were traditionalists in the old Hindu pattern. The tension between ancient and new produced, among other things, a generation gap as wide as the Ganges. Two sons, though expensively educated in England and full of promise, drank themselves into oblivion. There was also a problem, less tragic, with their daughter Indira, a raving beauty. Wherever she went hearts shattered like eggshells. One of the many belonged to a minor canon of Chester Cathedral, a muscular young man devoted to cold baths and good fellowship who spent a year as the maharajah's guest and wrote long letters to his mother from which it was clear (from references to the exquisite figure beneath Indira's silken sari and the sweetness of her disposition) that he nourished secular as well as spiritual passions. His cause was forlorn. The trouble was that the princess' own heart remained entire. She reached the age of sixteen without commitment, which to her parents, hampered by their Hindu traditions, meant that she was permanently on the shelf. Without much hope they invited themselves and Indira to Dewas Senior, where there was an eligible young Maratha maharajah, but Tukoji Rao had lost his mind over the wayward princess of Kolhapur. The prince of Dewas Junior, however, was so smitten with Indira that he joined her in the train back to Baroda, his eyes idiotic with love, having brought no more baggage than a hastily borrowed handkerchief. Though kind, Indira offered him no encouragement. Depressed, her parents took her to London for the coronation of King George V, where she did more damage.

Also present for the ceremonies and the brilliant social season of 1911 was Sir Madhav Rao Sindia, the burly, blustering Maharajah of Gwalior, tiger hunter. Though he was sixteen years older than Indira, he agreed to accept her as his second wife.

Much relieved, Indira's parents announced the engagement. Worn down at last, Indira endured the congratulations of a celebratory garden party at Ranelagh beside the Thames. She even cheered up a little while shopping for her trousseau, but before boarding the boat train with her parents, secretly dispatched a letter to her fiancé sweetly but firmly calling the whole thing off. The fact was that she was finally in love, with a young man who was the scion of a noble but rather unfortunately controversial family.

The ruling house of Cooch Behar in Bengal had the gifts of good looks and high style. But the father of Indira's inamorato, the Maharajah of Cooch Behar, had married a daughter of the saintly Keshub Chunder Sen, a leader of the Brahmo Samaj, a unitarian movement believing in one God and reconciling some Hindu with some Christian teachings. The Maharajah of Cooch Behar had naturally been converted to the Brahmo faith, which meant that as far as Indira's parents were concerned, all the Cooch Behars, however ethical and elegant, were dangerous heretics. Both the Barodas and the Cooch Behars had been great favorites at the Edwardian court and knew the grand hotels of Europe at least as well as the streets of Calcutta. The sons of both families were at Eton or Harrow* and their daughters, including Indira, had been school chums at Eastbourne. The second son of the Cooch Behars was the personable and poetic Jitendra, eight years Indira's senior and her love. When both families attended the Imperial Durbar at Delhi later in 1911, Jitendra and Indira were hardly ever apart. They rode in the mornings and fox-trotted at night in the silk-hung marquees of the Cooch Behar camp, but the prohibitions remained. After that, they met whenever their families came in contact in Bombay or Delhi, at a hill station or abroad. Soft notes passed, and sighs, but nothing more serious than a dinner party or a dance or a few stolen minutes on a bridle path was possible. After two years the young lovers grew desperate.

---

* Rajendra of Cooch Behar was the first princely heir to be educated wholly in England, first at Mr. Carter's preparatory school at Farnborough, then at Eton and Oxford.

Both maharajahs owned establishments in Bombay; at the beginning of 1913 both were staying there *en famille* preparing for the usual pilgrimage to Europe. Though forbidden to meet, by some means Jitendra and Indira found occasion to plan an elopement. Jitendra was ingenuous enough to put the schedule on paper. The note was intercepted and a special guard was promptly mounted in front of the iron gates of the Baroda home. Relations between Indira and her parents were by now limited to frustrated silences and she was accompanied everywhere by a guardian lady of the court. The Baroda entourage made its way as planned to St. Moritz and settled into the Suvretta Hotel. They were not alone. Unknown to them, room 121 was already occupied by two servants of the court of Cooch Behar, and Jitendra himself was installed in another hotel within striking distance. By now Indira had adopted Western dress and spent a good deal of time at the dressmaker's. One day a box arrived for Indira from room 121. When opened, it was found to contain some rather seductive lingerie. Questioned, Indira supposed airily that her friends just wanted her to have some underclothes for her travels. It began to look as if an elopement was again being arranged.

Then the tension broke. After two years on the throne, Jitendra's elder brother was dying in England. Jitendra, now heir to Cooch Behar, went to be beside him. Indira's parents gave in at last and let her go too. She married Jitendra with Brahmo rites in the Buckingham Palace Hotel and in a civil ceremony at a convenient registry office. A few days later the brother died and Indira became Maharani of Cooch Behar, but the elevation was not enough to heal the breach with her parents. Jitendra and Indira had five children and much happiness and after some years even became reconciled with the Barodas. Their chief home was a mansion with a strong Victorian Gothic air near Calcutta called Woodlands, but they spent enough time abroad for Indira to become well known in London and, according to a social note, "in hunting circles in the shires." After eight years of marriage Jitendra died. At twenty-nine Indira became regent for her little son, the present maharajah.

By the time uremia ended her father Sayaji Rao's long and beneficial reign in 1939, all his sons had died. His successor was his grandson Pratap Sinha, a thirty-one-year-old hedonist with a fair claim to be the last of the big spenders. Pratap Sinha inherited the Lakshmi Vilas palace and a couple of others in Baroda, a number of mansions as far apart as New Delhi and the heather lands of Surrey, some of the rash profligacy of his distant predecessors, cotton gins, textile mills, chemical plants and salt factories, a sword worth twelve hundred thousand dollars and an assortment of jewelry valued at around fifteen million dollars. A conservative guess at his total worth was three hundred million dollars. The sun, it seemed, was shining on the Maharajah Pratap Sinha, lord of Baroda. He liked that.

Moon-faced, portly and cheerful, the maharajah exuded well-being wherever a race horse galloped and the internationally unemployed gathered. Such locations were mostly in Europe, and there the expatriate maharajah spent much of his time. His way of life was a little curtailed by the Second World War, which His Highness spent as a gentleman pig farmer in Hampshire, but he survived in good-enough financial shape to claim the first Rolls-Royce to come off the line after the war. In 1943 he had married a considerable social asset. No one had ever heard of the state she came from, but very soon the name and appearance of Seta Devi were embossed on every mind. Both she and the maharajah were already married when they met at the race track: she merely announced her instant conversion to Islam, which automatically dissolved her marriage to her Hindu husband, then embraced Hinduism once more; the maharajah, who had married a princess of Kolhapur in 1929, simply chose to ignore the bigamy law his grandfather had introduced. Seta Devi was —and is—voluptuously beautiful, and fully accustomed to the luxurious life. They were, in short, a very well suited couple. During the war they acquired a racing stable at Newmarket; as soon as the hostilities were over they began to improve it. In one four-day burst the maharajah spent nearly three hundred thousand dollars on bloodstock and later set a world record by paying nearly fifty-two thousand dollars for a yearling colt.

Though the money poured out, Pratap Sinha bought wisely, for
the worth of his string at its peak reached a quarter of a billion
dollars. In 1948 his horse My Babu crowned his efforts by winning the Derby. His Highness had recently been in Baroda
dealing with some political difficulties and would have missed
the race had he not been able to excuse himself on grounds of ill
health. The maharajah's resumption of the grand old princely
life immediately after the war ended coincided with a cataclysmic change in India. There were those who gazed sourly on
the maharajah's generous and wandering way of life.

In the spring of 1947 he arrived in New York for the first
time in ten years. Interviewed aboard the *Queen Elizabeth*, he
confessed to some fears for the safety of his infant son (later
known as "Princey") from kidnappers but was reassured all the
way to the Waldorf by the solid presence of Lieutenant Peter
Pfeiffer and three more of New York's finest. Greater dangers
loomed. The following year Pratap Sinha was accused of having
got rid of ten million dollars during that six-week visit to the
land of opportunity. The voice of protest came from the government of Baroda which was by now, of course, no longer the
private property of the Gaekwars but a part of the Republic of
India. What made the voice particularly damaging was its ac-
cusation that the ten million had come from the state treasury.
His Highness got the word aboard ship to England but greeted
his lady quite calmly at Southampton and quietly loaded his
baggage as usual into the three trucks provided. He flew to
Baroda in his luxurious Douglas C-47, with a brief pause in Paris,
and matters were soon straightened out. It was true that he had
been in the habit of taking a few interest-free loans from the
state treasury, but he would be paying back the ten million by
installments out of his yearly income of about eight million. Save
for a wage strike by his two hundred and fifty servants, all was
well with the world once more. Or so it seemed.

The restrictions placed on his style by the new proletarian
government of India irked Pratap Sinha's aristocratic sensibilities.
He spoke a word here and there among friends and relatives who
shared his interests. The result was the Union of Princes, formed

in December 1950, one year before the date fixed for India's
first general election, ostensibly to discuss religious matters and
marital alliances as between equals. The Indian government,
then in the hands of the Congress Party, was not deceived. It was
obvious that the Union of Princes might well dispense large
sums to opposition parties of the right. Accordingly, the President of India wrote a two-page letter to the maharajah charging
him with conduct harmful to the national interest and general
irresponsibility, and giving him a month to think of some ex-
cuses. His Highness was reminded that five million dollars remained outstanding against his name in the books of the treasury
of Baroda. No answer being forthcoming, on April 14, 1951, the
government stripped away all Pratap Sinha's titles and privileges
(including immunity from arrest and customs duties and a
twenty-one-gun salute) and stopped payment of his yearly pension of five hundred and fifty thousand dollars. His son Fateh
Sinha assumed his office at a lower rate of pay—two hundred
and ten thousand dollars a year.

Clearly, there is something about hereditary nobility that
clings tighter than the shirt of Nessus. Pratap Sinha still expected
to be addressed by his lost title, though he and Seta Devi were
now properly plain Mr. and Mrs. It was a small thing, after all.
Their visits to India grew less frequent, though Pratap Sinha
went there in 1951 at the government's request to transfer forty-
one million dollars' worth of property to his son the maharajah.
They were not left actually destitute, because in addition to
Pratap Sinha's thoroughbreds and a variety of holdings there
were some liquifiable assets. The nature and extent of these
were unknown, but some convincing theories were abroad.

Some of the jewelry that had been in Baroda before the war
was now elsewhere. It had never been easy to know exactly
which pieces belonged to the state and which to the family of
Gaekwars, but by the time Pratap Sinha's marriage to Seta Devi
was dissolved in 1956 a few things were becoming clearer. There
had been a necklace of huge pearls, value two and a half million
dollars, present whereabouts unknown. There had been a necklace of famous colored diamonds, value about two million, now

strangely dispersed; the Empress Eugénie,* the pink Brazilian Star of the South and the clear English Dresden had passed to three eminent gentlemen of Bombay; and the canary-yellow Moon of Baroda was absorbed into the Treasure Chest Collection of the Meyer Jewelry Company of Detroit. There had been four carpets made of a ground of pearls studded with turquoises, rubies, emeralds and diamonds, value not known, intended as a canopy for the Tomb of the Prophet in Medina but never dispatched. There was an earring composed of the three finest pearls in the world, value not known. There was a great black pearl, value not known. Only two things were known for certain: there were gaps in the inventory, and no blue stones were missing. There never had been any blue stones in the Baroda treasury, for they were held inauspicious by the Gaekwars. Seta Devi, however, felt herself immune from such augury, for at Ascot in 1969 she was inviting guests to touch the 30-carat sapphire on her right hand for luck.

Pratap Sinha, so far as could be observed, had not shown much concern at the news of these discrepancies in the inventory. In any case, his troubles were ended the summer of 1968, when he died in a London hospital. Fortunately his style at least could be perpetuated, and his former lady bent all her efforts to doing so. Despite the demotion of her former husband and the dissolution of their marriage, Seta Devi struggled on as Her Highness the Maharani of Baroda, in confidential moments of nostalgia recalling the good old days when she was even referred to as royalty and saluted with a hundred and one guns, which, if the truth were known, were distinctions never granted any prince by the British or their more left-wing successors. Still, in her early forties, the handsomest of women, Seta Devi continued to be welcome in the columns of the *New York Times*, which was always careful to accord her proper awe and her erstwhile

---

* Originally owned by Potemkin, favorite of Catherine the Great, the 51-carat oval had been a gift from Napoleon III to his bride. When France fell to the Prussians in 1870 it was wrapped in newspaper with her other jewels and smuggled out of the Tuileries by the empress and her American dentist, who then made for the Hôtel du Casino in Deauville and by chance found sanctuary and a Channel passage in an obliging Englishman's yacht.

titles. Like an exotic migrant fowl she swooped into Claridge's as June blossomed, with her own sheets from Saks Fifth Avenue just to be on the safe side, a hundred pairs of shoes and a thousand saris. The list of guests come to nibble on smoked trout or sip some of Baron de Rothschild's good Bordeaux in her box at Ascot (cost twelve hundred and sixty dollars for the four days) read like the roll call for the last trump of the world's chivalry and wealth. In Monte Carlo later in the summer, or in St. Moritz or New York, or at home in her Paris apartment, she managed never to lapse from the grand style. She no longer smoked thirty-dollar cigars in a ruby holder or flew from New York to London just to make a few phone calls, but the fruit on her table came from Fauchon and the wine from Fortnum and Mason, and her Rolls-Royce still sported the armorial bearings of Baroda on its creamy doors. All in all, between looking after the race horses, rearranging the Louis XVI furniture and worrying about the dinner parties six weeks in advance, her life remained a full one. Moreover, there was comfort in the constant presence of her son, born in 1945, suavest and most elegant of young men, who bore the name Sayaji Rao in memory of his illustrious great-grandfather but who had become famous as plain "Princey." Some skeptics may have thought him a playboy, but his mother was always quick to testify that he worked a full eight-hour day in her behalf and never got up later than three in the afternoon. She had absolute confidence in his color sense and he was never too proud to run a little errand. He in green velvet or very open shirts and the tightest of pants, she in glittering sari and four strands of enormous pearls that recalled the splendors of a vanished Baroda, they became a popular-enough part of the international scene for *Esquire* magazine to accord them in January 1970, as one of the "Fun Couples" of the preceding year, a minor Dubious Achievement Award.

9

The Erection Center

IT WAS WHISPERED of the Maharajah Jagatjit Singh of Kapurthala in the Punjab that at the age of nineteen he had difficulty in copulating. The problem was that he weighed nearly two hundred and seventy pounds, most of it fat and much of it deposited around his middle. The best efforts of the sprightly young ladies employed to teach him the arts of love were set at naught by his intractable physique, though experts were imported from as far afield as Lucknow, long noted by authorities as "the center of fun and frolic," and though professional dancers of surpassing beauty adopted complicated poses sanctified by centuries of Hindu art. Exactly why the problem should have seemed so difficult to surmount in a land of such prolonged amatory experience never became clear, but the court of Kapurthala was greatly exercised by it. Then a middle-aged lady of some expertise made a proposal. If, she suggested, the chief hindrance was the princely belly, let the keeper of the elephants be consulted. The officer was summoned. Under close questioning he gave a totally erroneous account of the way in which elephants reproduce, maintaining that nature had made them too awkward to do so without the help of man. Ramps were therefore built for them in the woods, he said, on which the female could recline on her back and more easily support the great weight of the male. Hope was reborn. The chief engineer of the state was ordered to produce such a contraption within a week, though not of course in the woods. An inclined bed of wood and steel, with a spring mattress, was ready on schedule. After a few last-minute touches from the middle-aged lady who had inspired this stroke, prince and court found relief at last. The maharajah was able to leave for his honeymoon, and his savior retired with a pension for life.

The pursuit of Venus was not always so complicated in the Sikh states of the Punjab. For one thing, the Maharajah of Kapurthala soon lost most of his weight, so much in fact that in his more mature years he was known throughout Europe as a rather slender man, clean-shaven but for a mustache, whose most striking feature was the hotness of his gaze. Some thought him like a Medici in appearance, and all found him the most charming and cultivated of men, ladies particularly so. His state was not large—only half the size of Rhode Island—and his revenue not excessive, but he was able to conduct his affairs with a degree of style. His palace in Kapurthala, if not an exact replica of Versailles, showed enough similarities to startle the visitor at first sight, since in the distance there glowed the snowy flanks of the Himalayas. Within, according to the wife of a visiting Viceroy, it was "one mass of gold with nymphs disporting themselves on vaulted ceilings and innumerable Sèvres ornaments and vases and objets d'art." Nymphs were one of the maharajah's major pleasures, whether he was in Kapurthala or in Paris, where he owned one of the few houses within the Bois de Boulogne. He outraged King Edward VII's sense of propriety by occupying a neighboring suite in the same hotel in Biarritz as the King with a lady not his wife. She was a Spanish dancer by the name of Anita Delgrado. They later married and she bore him a son, but he was autumnal and she vernal and she waltzed away, having divorced him, with a son by an older wife, and danced thereafter for amusement only in the Ritz Hotel in Paris.*

Another of His Highness' loves, a tall ivory-skinned French girl, first impressed him in a pink silk pajama suit in a couturier's in Nice. Their romance bloomed over tea at the Hôtel Negresco and she accepted his invitation to Kapurthala, though engaged to an American gentleman resident in Paris. Welcomed with a full guard of honor and the state band trumpeting the "Marseillaise," she found the palace's Louis XIV drawing room comfortably like home and took up occupancy of the west wing for a year or so, officially as His Highness' adviser. She could stroll in the exhilarating air of Kapurthala through gardens laid out like those around a French château, enjoy the cuisine (tempered with Evian water) of cooks trained in Paris, flaunt a tiara of rubies and strings of pearls borrowed from the treasury, and cruise the Sutlej in an English launch all seasoned mahogany and solid polished brass. But her story too ended less than happily for the maharajah. Sometime later he sent her in Paris a rope of superb pearls as a birthday present and was understandably chastened when she accepted them as a wedding gift and joined with hers the thanks of her new husband.

Jagatjit Singh's emeralds were judged the finest in India and he also owned the world's largest topaz, four inches of amber fire worn as a belt buckle, and a noteworthy ornament for his turban made of three thousand diamonds and pearls. These accessories became well known in many cities, for His Highness was an avid traveler in South and North America, North Africa and Asia, and liked to wear them at such formal occasions as English coronations and dynastic marriages like that of Signorina Edda Mussolini to Count Ciano. His journeyings were arranged by Messrs. Thomas Cook and the business of his state by British officials, so Jagatjit Singh's life and reign were unblemished by

---

* The Maharani Anita seems to have been flirtatious. The Nizam of Hyderabad wooed her nightly with jewels hidden in her dinner napkin during a visit with her husband. She spent an afternoon viewing the interior of the Nizam's harem at his invitation and to the maharajah's annoyance.

anything untoward. Twice he represented the native princes at sessions of the League of Nations. When in 1947 death ended his sixty-nine-year reign, he was seventy-four; he left behind the sweetest of memories and an official record of quiet distinction. He was, however, unable to pass the state of Kapurthala on to his heir, because by then it had become one of the territories of the new India.

Paramjit Singh, the heir apparent, was in at least one respect a chip off the old block. Choosing not to sit around in Kapurthala, he began that broadening of the mind which travel brings with extended trips to Europe. There he was captivated by a young lady who was playing the piano for the cabaret in one of the better restaurants. He translated her as his mistress to a cottage in the grounds of the Kapurthala palace, where she gained a certain amount of control over his movements. His first wife, a princess from one of the hill states near Simla, had born him three daughters, after which relations between them had become distant. Paramjit Singh's father, the maharajah, grew uneasy at this prospect of the termination of his line and began to insist on a second marriage in spite of the seductive pianist's objections. Backed by the full weight of the government of Kapurthala, the maharajah sent a mission into the hills where, he felt, good breeding stock might be found.

The Chief Justice of Kapurthala, the court physician, a lady doctor and some confidential secretaries of discretion, attended by guards, factotums and cooks to the number of about a hundred, set up camp in the mountains and proclaimed their purpose by beat of drum. Their terms of reference were particular. The girl must be of medium height, slim and well-proportioned, and under the age of seventeen. She must have blood brothers (as proof of her potential for bearing a boy), a pedigree of gentle ancestry extending for not less than ten generations, and good general health uncomplicated by venereal disease. Candidates must have no objection to being medically examined or to marrying the heir apparent if selected. The fortunate parents would be well rewarded. Girls with the necessary qualifications were more common than might have appeared. They were processed very thoroughly, first in an oral interview by the Marriage Committee under the presidency of the Chief Justice, then alone by the private secretary to the maharajah's senior wife, then by the lady doctor and finally by the court physician. Most thorough of all was the private secretary, who had something of a reputation as a lady-killer. His manipulations with a tape measure caused complaints to the committee. When interrogated, the private secretary maintained that he was merely carrying out the maharani's personal instructions and could not therefore accept the committee's right to question his discretion, ignoring the fact that the committee had been uneasy about his intentions, not his discretion.

The lucky girl who finally emerged from these investigations was taken into the palace and prepared for her marriage. Thereupon the prospective bridegroom's pianist announced her departure and the prospective bridegroom fell into a swoon. However, she soon proved amenable to a financial offer, stipulating only that her lover's visits to his new wife be regulated to one trip a month between the hours of seven and eight in the evening. Some months passed after the marriage before Paramjit Singh could bring himself to take advantage of the schedule. But since the marriage had still not been consummated and Paramjit Singh had no heir as yet, reasons of state at last made it imperative that he undertake the first of his nuptial visits. Bathed, perfumed, bejeweled and anointed, the palms of her hands and the soles of her feet stained vermilion, the bride waited in the palace among the attendants and observers proper to the occasion. Paramjit Singh arrived rather gloomily on the dot of seven accompanied by his valet with a pair of silk pajamas. Priests sang and the prince departed five minutes before the deadline of eight, looking, a bystander reported, "rather tired and pensive." Duty done, he left for a European vacation with his European friend, and in due course his wife bore a son. The child eventually succeeded his father but by then, of course, there was no state of Kapurthala to rule, and he was in any case fully devoted to his career as a colonel in the army of India.

Though vital to its ruling family, the dynastic problems of

Kapurthala were of relatively small concern to the government of India. Kapurthala was only one of fourteen major and twenty-two minor principalities in the Punjab, and only the strong personality of the Maharajah Jagatjit Singh brought it to the fore. Kapurthala was overshadowed by the Sikh states of Nabha, Jhind and Patiala, whose rulers, as well as those of Kapurthala, claimed descent from a Rajput prince, and beyond him from the moon herself. While Kapurthala was in part a creation of Ranjit Singh, Lion of the Punjab, and had sided with his kingdom against the British, Patiala and its neighbors, all three situated on the side of the Sutlej River farthest from that rapacious old genius, had first sought and then repaid British protection, particularly at the time of the Mutiny. Patiala, a powdery hot land, was bigger than Connecticut by a thousand square miles. Flat as an ironing board, Patiala's dim horizons spread to the south-west with the Sutlej's flow, but at its other extreme the state's border ran up to where the Himalayas began their climb. It was a powerful state, influential and impressive, and no better figure-head could have been found for it than the seventh prince of the Patiala line, the archetype of the oriental potentate both in public and in the privacy of his harem.

His Highness the Maharajah Sir Bhupinder Singh of Patiala was a fraction under six feet six inches tall and weighed two hundred and eighty pounds, most of it bone and muscle. Stiff with pomade, his mustache swept upward like the horns of a bull above full, sensuous lips, and a dense black beard neatly rolled in the Sikh fashion over a cord fastened beneath his turban of apricot or crocus-yellow, scarlet or somber jet. His face was a heavy oval, and from it his inky eyes glowed in an arrogant, un-winking stare. He carried his menacing bulk with such ramrod erectness when mounted on one of his massive chargers that he seemed forever to be posing for an equestrian statue very much larger than life. In his gleaming thigh-length boots, white buck-skins and long red tunic crusted with gold, he would pace the lines of his magnificent troops—two regiments of Patiala Lancers; four of incomparable Sikh infantry—seeming at the very least imperial.

The maharajah lived in a pink palace a quarter of a mile long with rose-red roofs sprawling over eleven acres. White peacocks screamed among its pinnacles, ruby-eyed, and an Afghan staghound might answer from the driveway or a tiger rage from its chains beyond the lotus pools. There were thirty-five hundred domestics of various kinds in the maharajah's service and they fed him well. He swallowed fifty pounds of food a day, though he professed to eat only one meal. Three whole chickens might disappear as a teatime snack, but after dinner he left his guests to their dessert and addressed himself seriously with his fingers to an immense gold platter of rice and meats and sugary confections, inexhaustably refilled. His fleet of cars was managed by an Englishman trained by Rolls-Royce to look after twenty-seven of the firm's products as well as ninety-three various also-rans. There were five hundred horses for the maharajah's personal use, dozens of champion gun dogs and some saluki coursers in his kennels; hundreds of suits from Savile Row in his closets; some three hundred and fifty women behind the walls of his harem. It was believed that the maharajah spent 60 percent of the entire income of the state on himself, for, as a contemporary historian delicately put it, as yet the administration had "not developed along constitutional lines." From his accession in 1909 to his death in 1938 the Maharajah Bhupinder Singh *was* Patiala, *was* perhaps the Sikh nation, and even, for many in Europe, *was* India.

He was not easily denied. When he wished to stay in London, the Savoy Hotel surrendered to him every one of the thirty-five suites on its fifth floor and kept them fragrant with fresh roses daily. He had his own kitchen up there, a new elevator in scarlet and gold lacquer, bodyguards sleeping across the thresholds and twenty chauffeurs waiting in the yard. The Savoy chef, not the most obsequious of men, would send him a douceur of a Patiala elephant carved out of ice and bearing the day's choicest pineapples from Covent Garden. He never arrived with fewer than two hundred pieces of baggage, some of them steel safes for his jewels, and when he left, his crocodile of limousines was often followed by four or five trucks stuffed with guns, rifles, saddlery and cricket gear, and maybe half a dozen polo ponies.

Bhupinder Singh loved polo and made the Patiala team, the Tigers, the terror of India in their black-and-orange shirts. His weight prevented him from reaching the top flight himself, but he compensated by riding after pig. The more fanatical devotees of pigsticking professed to see in the sport a means of resolving racial differences in times of political unrest and evolution in that it gave white man and Indian a sport in common. They claimed with Lord Baden-Powell (as famous a sticker of pigs as he was a Boy Scout) that it added to the attractions of polo and racing "a taste of the brutal and most primitive of hunts—namely, the pursuit, with a good weapon in your hand, of an enemy whom you want to kill." Pigstickers recognized that the kill was their whole object, though their bible was perhaps sublimating a little when its author, a military man, avowed: "I do not think a boar does feel his death much. There are seldom long miles of sobbing wind and fate ever pressing behind him. His is probably a sudden wakening from sleep, a sharp run at full speed, and then a last hard fight with blood at fever heat, and the red light dancing before his eyes. When the blood is hot, experience shows there is little pain from wounds."

Whatever its sentiments when thus faced with a steely death, the Indian wild boar was a formidable adversary. Weighing as much as three hundred pounds, hard with muscle, and standing as tall as three feet at the shoulder, it could open horse or man with a single slash of its eight-inch sickle tusks.* Riders were divided into "heats" of four or five horsemen; the pigs were beaten out of the scrub and the first heat would spur after the most likely boar. A rider's object was to get "first spear" whether the thrust was lethal or not, so the short chase was always at a breakneck gallop, often over treacherous country filled with potholes. The preferred spear tip was a flat oval four

---

* These were prized as souvenirs. They were used as labels for decanters or as handles for walking sticks and umbrellas. Two large ones made an attractive frame for a photograph or handles for a silver cup or, more ingeniously, when fitted with a silver hinge and clasp, an unusual dog collar.

inches long, ribbed at each side with a blood channel. The purpose of the channels was to provide evidence of a "first spear," since blood and fat remained in them. The first spear might hit while the pig was in full flight, but more often when he sensed a rider pulling close, the pig would jink away and stop dead, facing the horseman. He would then charge, hard. The rider was expected to force his horse fast at the pig, make his point in the shoulder, and if possible leap the pig at the same moment. Very few men could finish a pig with this one thrust. If the rider could not continue, others might then attack, one at a time. Since spears went the wrong way and the pigs were agile and very powerful, numbers of Englishmen and more than one young Indian prince died proving their manhood during a morning's pigsticking.

In 1922, at a hog-hunters' morning in Patiala, the Prince of Wales's heat killed five pigs, two of which fell to His Royal Highness himself, for he was a gifted and fearless horseman. The Maharajah Bhupinder Singh's heat drew a blank, which at least was tactful. It had not been the smoothest of operations, for as a lady spectator reported: "An old tusker gave my elephant one of the best on the trunk. It then knocked over a man and rather hurt his leg. Later on another pig knocked another man off his horse. I thought the man was dead, but he had come round by the time the car had been fetched." The day ended happily for all with the Prince of Wales's five pigs laid out in attitudes of extinction on the bloodied steps of the palace for a souvenir photograph with prince and maharajah in the pose of conquerors. After that there was dinner off the new silver service Bhupinder Singh had imported from London in honor of the visit, at a cost of one hundred and fifty thousand dollars.

Bhupinder Singh's relationship with the British establishment in Delhi and London was cordial if not too intimate. He did all the right things during the First World War, foursquare with the British, and after it he stoutly maintained, to a nodding of old-school heads, that the Soviets had completed a plan of campaign to loot India. He himself had much to lose, including a five-million-dollar pearl necklace and the Sancy diamond. On of-

ficial occasions, decked in emeralds each one of which would
have overflowed a dessert spoon, he was a superb and comforting sight: if this was India, what power could challenge the
British Empire? He attended the Imperial War Conference in
London and the League of Nations in Geneva, and was first
(and subsequently) Chancellor of the Chamber of Princes in
New Delhi. During the 1920s he was very popular in Simla,
summer capital of the government of India, much of which had
once belonged to Patiala. He still owned property there, houses
called Oakover and Rookwood and The Cedars, all stockbroker
stucco among the Himalayan pines. In the fall of 1924 he appeared at the Viceroy's Chinese Ball at Simla, the fantasy of the
year,* in the gold and steel of a samurai, gigantic against the
scarlet orange and bright blue of the gala decorations, and irresistible. Otherwise decorous young ladies admitted to a tremor
or two, for Bhupinder Singh burned with an animal heat that
could not be resisted. It was his downfall. The paragon of the
ballroom, the parade ground and the conference chamber was
a womanizer with one of the most rapacious sexual appetites
ever satisfied.

As a young man the Maharajah Bhupinder Singh had equipped
his private quarters with the usual accessories. There was a pool
where great blocks of ice floated in the torrid summer, bringing
the temperature down some fifty degrees to a pleasant sixty and
affording lodgment for serving girls with whiskey and tidbits.
There were frescoes exhibiting the catalog of Indian erotic expertise, and hammocks to lend an extraphysical or ethereal dimension
to the maharajah's labors. But with time such simple pleasures
palled and gratification became a business. The harem was highly
organized; within it were beauty salons, perfumiers, jewelers,
hairdressers, dressmakers. And doctors, English, French and

* The Viceroy's lady had arranged it all. After dinner a dragon with auto
headlamps for eyes disgorged Simla's pretty dancing teacher, who performed
a little oriental number. Next came a rickshaw towed by two unmarried
ladies of the viceregal court and occupied by Miss Megan Lloyd George,
daughter of the former Prime Minister, with presents of a parasol and a fan
for Their Excellencies. The supper tables were decorated with Chinese
birds' nests made of chocolate.

Indian, capable of undertaking plastic surgery (such as the re-shaping of breasts in accordance with the eddyings of His High-ness' taste) and gynecological works, to which the maharajah lent his authority by attending in person. A deep study of de-odorants, lotions, philters and douches was encouraged, less for the ladies' ease than for the maharajah's pleasure. After all, he needed what support he could get, for there were three hundred and fifty women behind those adamantine walls. Inevitably there was recourse to aphrodisiacs. His Highness' Indian doctors tried combinations of gold and pearl, spices, silver, iron and herbs. They made some headway with a concoction of carrots (perhaps because of the fitting shape) mixed with the brains of that lascivious bird the sparrow. At last the Frenchmen were consulted. They recommended an infernal machine containing radium, guaranteed "to increase the spermatogenic power and capacity of the testicles and to stimulate the erection center." But the loss of spermatogenic power was not what ailed Bhu-pinder Singh. It was boredom and utter selfishness.

His Highness acknowledged no superior but the British, and that reluctantly. He was one of the last princes to exercise abso-lute power within the state and he did so absolutely. He even raided across the border into the lands of his cousin the Maha-rajah of Nabha for a fair-haired, blue-eyed girl he had noticed while hunting. When the matter came to issue, Nabha lost. Bhupinder Singh showed no mercy to those who opposed him and used his prerogatives to satisfy his appetites. At last, in 1930, he was subjected to a sort of trial by a tribunal that had no legality, on charges that ranged from murder through abduction, false imprisonment and forced labor to "immoral overtures" to an Englishwoman. The investigation was made by a committee appointed by the Indian States' People's Conference, a body thoroughly unsympathetic to Bhupinder Singh and his peers. But the committee's findings, published as the *Indictment of Patiala*, made fairly convincing and thoroughly disturbing read-ing. The document was a bewildering jumble of statements, but even if its accusations were on the imaginative side, there could be no doubt that the administration of Patiala was a faint but grim shadow of the tyranny then spreading across Europe. It was noted that Bhupinder Singh had found something to talk about with Signor Mussolini in Rome and Herr Hitler and General Göring in Berlin.

The maharajah never deigned to answer the charges and the government of India took no action against him, but there was a cooling. He did not live to see the eclipse of his state. In March 1938 he lay dying in Patiala as innumerable pigeons moaned in the red apertures of his titanic palace, and through the tropical foliage of the garden half a dozen tall Sikh footmen pushed the perambulators containing that week's crop of babies. His dead body was bathed by his gurus according to the Sikh custom, dressed in its familiar scarlet coat hung with decorations and jewels, and seated for the last time on the throne of Patiala. When all had filed before it in final homage it was carried to its pyre through the city, where more than a million people had come to watch it pass. Bhupinder Singh's last offspring was born nine months later, give or take a couple of days. It was a son.

10

※《◆《◆《◆《◆《◆《◆《◆《◆

The Enchanted Vale

IT WAS IMPOSSIBLE to be unhappy in Kashmir, unless you happened to be a native of the place. It was a land slightly crazed with beauty and altitude, five thousand feet clear of the dun heat of the northern Indian plains. Kashmir was an emerald dish, a Shangri la, set in interlocking series of Himalayan ranges, the dreamland at the back of every man's mind. Except for a brief cruel winter, the seasons painted it with a shifting glow of color, in spring a blue mist of harebells, clumps of violets and counterpanes of crocuses. The roof of every house sprouted new grass, dotted with the deep mauve of irises or the scarlet of tulips. Kingfishers flashed, bolts of blue light, along the sedges by the river. Sometimes an eagle might ride the mountain breezes, quartering the high cobalt and catching the light in his swing toward the sun.

All fruits and flowers that grew in England reached perfection in Kashmir. The lawns of the Residency garden at Srinagar would not have disgraced a bishop; its currants, raspberries, strawberries, gooseberries, plums, pears, cherries and peaches grew so plump that they burst at a bite. In early morning and at sunset the Residency swam in a mist of perfume. The great varieties of the Edwardian heyday of the rose flourished there— General Jacqueminot, Carmine Pillar, Maréchal Neil, Mrs. W. J. Grant, Dorothy Perkins—and banks of columbine, pinks, gladioli, poppies, fuchsias, sweet william, dahlias, hollyhocks and opalescent delphiniums from Mr. Luther Burbank, the famous plant breeder of California. The effect was of an unending afternoon fragrant with tea and cucumber, the whisper of a silk skirt brushing a croquet hoop or the far *ping* of a tennis ball driven not too unkindly by a sporting vicar, while now and then a mulberry plopped through the branches, a reminder of fecundity.

The Residency itself was a transplant, the rambling half-timbered pile of some wealthy squire in a fat county. At a discreet distance the trim gabled houses of the English colony squatted in degree—each, as its occupant never doubted, a castle. The British enclave ran along one bank of the Jhelum River, which bisected the city of Srinagar, summer capital of Kashmir. It contained its own little stores, a bank, the church and the cozy parsonage, and of course The Club. In the 1920s, purple generals could be seen at its bar lamenting the rigors of peace, but there were polo and cricket grounds for the younger chaps, and tennis courts and croquet lawns for the ladies. Once a week there was a dance. Between the buildings and the river, along the bank, stretched a pleasant walk suitable for morning and evening strolls and such casual assignations as were possible. The British denizens of Kashmir seemed somehow more eccentric than their colleagues in the plains below, the thin clear air breeding perhaps a finer madness. Residents and their assistants had a tendency to ignore cables from the far-off government, or mislay their code books, or even to disappear for long periods among mountain outposts on the roof of the world on missions that had to do with bears or horned sheep or rare botanical specimens. Outlandish visitors appeared in the middle of Srinagar bringing tales of magic fastnesses beyond the skyline of snow and knowing nothing of the world's great affairs during the past year or more.

The British colony at Srinagar included a detachment of the

Church Missionary Society engaged in teaching and medical work. One of these was a remarkable servant of empire and the Lord by the name of Cecil Tyndale-Biscoe, whose first claim to fame had come as coxswain of a victorious Cambridge eight. It conditioned his whole approach to life, so it was not inapt when the doyen of Cambridge oarsmen Steve Fairbairn wrote of him in *The Times:* "I have often said of rowing 'As you meet your stretcher so you will meet your God.' That cox, Tyndale-Biscoe, met his stretcher perfectly." A small round man, Canon Tyndale-Biscoe was a teacher before he was a shepherd of souls. His mission, as he saw it, was to transform the male youths of the Happy Valley, whom he called in their crude state of nature "bipeds," into what he regarded as the highest form of human development, always printed in capitals: MEN. He saw himself dragging them out of their original sin* by forceful and ingenious methods, the chief of which was swimming instruction. Until Tyndale-Biscoe's arrival, no high-caste Hindu in Kashmir had ever swum; it was a caste matter so stringent that a Brahmin seeing his brother drowning must send for a coolie to effect the rescue. For the Brahmin boys at Tyndale-Biscoe's school, however, things were different: the fees of those students who did not learn to swim were raised every term. The penalty was strong enough to break the tradition. The good canon was wise in the ways of Kashmir: his record books listed not only a father's salary but also his probable income from bribes; boys were assessed on such virtues as "freedom from dirty tricks" (blowing the nose without a handkerchief) and there was a column in the report sheet for "Color of Heart." According to Tyndale-Biscoe, there were eighteen shades between white and black. Though he rode roughshod over many customs he

---

* Some of the sin was fairly original by Western standards but not so original as the canon's exorcism was by Eastern standards. Catching a boy with one of the numerous volumes of sexual instruction, voluptuously illustrated, that were accessible to aspiring Indian youth, he made him eat a section of it, arguing that since he had filled his mind with the filth, he could not object to filling his belly with it too. Swallowing paper defiled a Brahmin, but Tyndale-Biscoe reinforced his logic with a cane laid close to hand, and prevailed.

did not understand, his motives were pure and his energy cyclonic, and under the brusqueness there were deep wells of kindness. He followed his vocation for some sixty years in Srinagar, fighting physical and spiritual oppression daily, and at the end there was no doubt what shade must be entered for Cecil Tyndale-Biscoe under "Color of Heart."

Most of the canon's lay compatriots were less concerned with good works. A few were so remote from salvation that they lived with ladies not their wives. The majority were retired people, soldiers or civil servants, or habitual vacationers leading a lotus life in a tiny settlement of wooden chalets at Gulmarg, forty miles and four thousand feet higher up the valley, or in the houseboats that were a unique feature of life in Kashmir. The houseboat had been invented by a peregrinating Englishman of means whose passion it was to shoot the duck that abounded in Kashmir. Conceiving it as a means of living on the job, as it were, the Englishman constructed a floating palace culminating in a combined clock tower and dovecote. His imitators were less ambitious, but even the most modest of houseboats contained at least twenty-odd feet of lace-curtained living room stuffed with easy chairs, sofa, desk, a bookcase stocked with Gothic or French novels beside the fireplace, and prints of Scottish braesides planted with stags or faithful Highlanders. There would be a dining room and a couple of bedrooms, each with its bath. And there would be another boat for the kitchen and the servants, who actually lived in a third. The houseboats lay moored in clusters on the river or in the adjacent canals or backwaters of the exquisite Dal Lake of Srinagar. They had names like *Skylark, Royal George, Butterfly* and *Cutty Sark* if occupied by the British, but some, lurking in backwaters, remained anonymous, for they were houseboats of ill repute.

With such amenities it was impossible to be unhappy in Kashmir unless, of course, you were a native. The state was twice the size of Ohio and was comprised, as its first ruler had put it, of one-third mountains, one-third water and one-third fiefdoms. The valley, which was its artery, with Srinagar as the heart, was only a little bigger than Rhode Island, or one fortieth part of the whole. The inhabitants of this Vale of Kashmir, the real Kashmiris, were the Irish of India. A mere whisper could fill their imaginations with prodigies of epic story. They lied out of a kind of esthetic. They were absolutely untrustworthy and absolutely enchanting, craven without being ashamed and indomitably whimsical. The rest of the people of Kashmir said, always with a smile, that they could "see the air." The people of the Vale had been forcibly converted to Islam and confined to it by a succession of Afghan and Mogul overlords. Most of the rest of the state's inhabitants were Muslims, too, but differed radically from the Kashmiris in other respects: to the south they were tough Rajput stock, and in the north and east they were even tougher hill men steeled by the hardship of the mountains. Most of the time there was food enough, but there was little more. To keep out the winter wind the Kashmiris wore loose-woven woolen shawls and carried little containers of burning charcoal under them for warmth. Because of this they were prey to a peculiar form of skin cancer. The women sang quivering ballads comparing the red core of the tulip with the heart of a lover. The men sang:

> "We have been slaves,
> We have poured out our sweat;
> There is no one but God to redress our wrongs,
> But we shall rise!"

They were ruled, these Muslims, by a Hindu maharajah under the influence of a coterie of Brahmins acknowledged as easily the cleverest in India.

The origin of this situation lay with the incomparable Ranjit Singh. The Lion of the Punjab had come up there in 1819 to make it part of his Sikh kingdom, installing as his governor one Gulab Singh, a minor local chief in his service who had won his esteem and the title of Rajah of the province of Jammu. When Ranjit Singh's death and the anarchy following it were exploited by the British, Gulab Singh was able to buy Kashmir. The Sikhs had been unable to pay their war indemnity to the British, who therefore offered the state to the resident proprietor of Jammu for three and three-quarter million dollars, thus gaining a staunch friend and breaking off a major portion of the old Punjab. As Maharajah of Jammu and Kashmir, Gulab Singh thereafter paid a yearly tribute to the British that included half a dozen Kashmir shawls, which came in handy as wedding gifts from Queen Victoria to the ladies of her court. Gulab Singh was accused of flaying his prisoners alive, but in general he was considered a mild and friendly prince, warlike when necessary and astute always. His successors followed his propitiatory policy toward the British, having little choice. His son welcomed the first Prince of Wales to visit India at the winter capital of Jammu to the south. His grandson entertained the third, also near there,* in February 1922, with the added attraction of a company of lamas come to dance for His Royal Highness. The monks had been traveling through the mountains with handcarts full of gongs, masks and eight-foot trumpets since the previous October. All the preparations had been long: it had taken an entire year for the master carvers of Srinagar to create furniture fit for the royal bottom, but the Prince was only able to stay for twenty-seven hours.

Gulab Singh's grandson had grown accustomed to the vagaries of the British, having occupied the throne, with a couple of lacunae, for thirty-seven years. Long before, his grandfather had complained about the excessive amounts of saffron and other treasures the first travelers had carried off. The Maharajah Pertab Singh, though something of a religious recluse, retained enough political astuteness to forestall all attempts by the British to buy land in Kashmir. He and his Brahmins saw to it that whatever the British built in the way of vacation cottages lapsed to the state in twenty years. They were equally adamant about the

---

* Where the Prince almost lost his life. After dinner His Royal Highness mounted an elephant for a ride around the tented camp in the dark. A strangely dancing figure stopped him almost at once. His Royal Highness was irked. "What does the bloody fool want?" he inquired. The bloody fool was an Indian police officer warning the heir to the throne that he was about to ride smack into a high-voltage cable strung just high enough for an elephant to amble underneath it.

sanctity of the cow, their punishment for killing one in Kashmir being imprisonment for life. Their application of the bovine laws was insidious and persistent; a respectable English mail order house whose catalog offered bull's eyes, a cannonball candy much favored by English schoolchildren, was severely questioned, and an English official discovered with a contraband jar of meat extract for his convalescent wife was hauled off to the Resident's court.

Almost the only deficiency in the quality of life in Kashmir was the absence of beef. Happily, there was a substitute in the multitudes of game birds available. Snipe zigzagged across the rice paddies, and partridges drummed over the mustard fields, but the climax came in the fall when the duck and geese flighted in from Siberia and settled in their tens of thousands among the lily pads and waxen blooms of Kashmir's lakes. The hunters crouched in barrels sunk at the water's edge, haunted by brilliant dragonflies, and merely waited for the black cloud to swirl over them in a battering of wings. A devoted gun would claim five or six thousand mallard and teal in a season; the record stood at ten thousand. The most lamentable shot could hardly fail, though one morning Lord Reading fired off a hundred viceregal shells for a credit of two birds. One, he explained with saving whimsy, had already been wounded and had merely dropped dead at his feet, while the other had expired of concussion. Lord Reading's host, the Maharajah Pertab Singh, took no part in these activities, being forbidden by his religion to destroy life.

The Maharajah Pertab Singh's preoccupation with his soul tended to overshadow some of the most practical aspects of rule. Throughout his reign his Brahmin priest was more powerful than his prime minister, with the result that from time to time Kashmir's affairs deteriorated so far as to warrant the maharajah's removal from direct participation in them until a British official had righted his ship of state. It was not unknown for taxes to be extracted by means of thumbscrews. The basic fault was not that the regime was excessively oppressive, however, but that it was not competent to deal with the state's peculiar problems, of which the chief at the time was the turbulence of its borders, soluble only by large military expenditures. Pertab Singh had only been on the throne for six years when, in 1891, the first bankruptcy occurred: the state held monopolies on the sale of all fruit, birch bark, tobacco, hides, saffron, violets, silk and water chestnuts, exacted customs dues on the quantities of opium and hemp derivatives passing through, and taxed everything, even prostitution and grave digging, yet could not keep the wolf from the door. Three decades later there was a difficulty of another kind. The Brahmin oligarchy considered the Muslim peasants no better than serfs and treated them as such, but nationalism was abroad, the knives came out, religious heat blazed, and only British troops could restore the maharajah's authority.

Despite the flaws of the maharajah's government, somehow it was always patched together. Pertab Singh himself enjoyed a great measure of personal popularity. He was so small as to be almost dwarfish and wore a gigantic *Arabian Nights* turban that only emphasized it. His smile was ready and ingenuous, he was frugal except for what trappings his rank required, and his devoutness commanded respect. The chief criticism leveled against him was his habit of withdrawing either into a series of ritual observances or behind the veil that opium drew, though there were those who believed that he used the latter device as much to alleviate painful or boring interviews as for esoteric pleasure. If the crowd's acclaim was any standard, he was liked by his people, for they swarmed wherever he appeared.

Every summer Pertab Singh, returning to Srinagar from his winter capital at Jammu, would be welcomed by a popular demonstration of great warmth. The ceremonial route into Srinagar's hodgepodge of varistoried wooden buildings was always by the Jhelum River. Any guests expected in Srinagar would be met by the maharajah above the city in his long galley rowed by sixty oarsmen in scarlet and gold, to glide in stately fashion between the thousands perched along the waterfront like seabirds on a cliff. Canon Tyndale-Biscoe could always be relied on to think up some jape to impress a visiting Viceroy. Once he threw a steel hawser from rooftop to rooftop across the river, hung a bamboo framework from it and there suspended enough boys, somewhat contorted in red, white and blue, to spell out WELCOME. As the flashing oars drew near, the canon blew his whistle, the greeting disintegrated and the boys plopped from a great height into the river, so astonishing the Viceroy that he raised his cocked hat to them. For another Viceroy, Tyndale-Biscoe hung a white sheet fifteen yards long from the upper balcony of his school, cut in it seventy slits and inserted in them seventy boys' heads to spell the inevitable WELCOME, and arranged below it the whole flotilla of the school's boats, fully manned. At the whistle their crews capsized the boats, demonstrating once more the value of swimming. Impressed, the Viceroy floated on in majesty to the palace, where a final banner trumpeted: GOD BLESS THE VICEROY, GOD HELP LADY READING.

The maharajah's loyalty to the King-Emperor had once been briefly in question, when he was incorrectly suspected, at the time of his temporary deposition in 1889, of a flirtation with Russia. But his services in the First World War, when sixty thousand of his troops fought more valiantly than most, wiped out that memory. What confirmed his devotion in every mind was his addiction to cricket, that national testing place of the heart's nobility. He attracted first-rate players to Kashmir and patronized the game in person, toddling onto the field in gold slippers and always managing to score a respectable number of runs, which on his birthdays, by some alchemy of sportsmanship, invariably equaled his age. It was believed that the maharajah, whose hooded eyes were deceptively bleary, was unaware that his batting average was a compliant fabrication of bowlers and umpires. But in a moment of truth the prince explained to a sympathetic official at the Residency that while of course he was quite useless at the game, he felt compelled to pursue it because he gave amusement to so many people by going along with the transparent but harmless fraud. By such subtleties Pertab Singh endeared himself to everyone who knew his enchanted valley. When his ashes were committed to the Ganges at Hardwar, so many marigolds from mourning hands accompanied them that the river was transmuted from bank to bank into a bright, immortal yellow.

He left no heir of his own blood and was succeeded by a nephew whose pseudonym was for a time better known to the world than his real name. While heir apparent, more sinned against than sinning, Hari Singh became protagonist of the notorious "Mr. A case." It was an event tailor-made for the gutter press—a foreign prince being protected by official anonymity, a supposed seductress and a conspiracy to blackmail for an enormous sum, all spiced with hints of oriental lewdness.

In reality, Prince Hari Singh was very much the martyr. When the First World War ended, Hari Singh had yet to make the grand European tour that had become the final flourish in the full education of the Indian prince. During the summer of 1918 he met a Captain Charles Arthur, a British officer convalescing in Kashmir after war service in Mesopotamia. Mrs. Arthur was with the gallant captain, and the two of them reveled in Hari Singh's limitless hospitality and trust. In Kashmir everything seemed not only possible, it seemed right. No doubt the prince's travel plans were discussed and dreams were dreamed. Where Mrs. Arthur's fancy lay will never be known, for she soon faded from the picture. Captain Arthur, however, had conceived some very ambitious plans. He so insinuated himself into Hari Singh's affection that the prince claimed him for his sole aide-de-camp on the tour, though he was not in the government of India's employment. The British knew that Arthur's service record was unprepossessing. The Resident in Kashmir objected, the Political Department of the government of India objected, but at the prince's insistence the Viceroy agreed to the appointment. It was disastrous, for Captain Arthur's dreams were of money, lots of it, and all available from Hari Singh's innocent pocket.

Wide-eyed and eager, Hari Singh arrived in London in 1919. He was a moon-faced young man of twenty-four, retiring and very nervous, and absolutely gullible. London was swinging to a frantic, searching beat. A madness was still in the air, bred of the war and relief at its completion, and the fear that there might be no meaning, after all, that would justify the slaughter; failing answers, there was jazz with the lights low and smoky, champagne and gin fizzes, dancing till dawn, and sex. Hari Singh approached the heady scene with all the anticipation of a spaniel quivering on its first day out with the guns. Captain Arthur made all ready for his initiation. He booked adjoining boxes at the Albert Hall for the Victory Ball celebrating the first anniversary of the Armistice. Bejeweled, scented and impressionable, Hari Singh walked into his box with his Indian secretary, and fell fatefully in love. She was on the other side of the pillar, blond and slim, full-breasted and vivacious. Since fancy dress was optional, she was costumed rather revealingly as a grasshopper. Her name was Maude.

Mrs. Maude Robinson was an experienced lady of advanced tastes without, as a contemporary newspaper might have put it, any visible means of support. She lived in an expensive apartment in Belgravia and was dressed by the best fashion houses, but her husband, a bookmaker, was currently bankrupt for the second time and her own company—Grasshopper Pills—not infrequently showed a deficit. Mrs. Robinson was aware of Hari Singh's attention, as her pretty companion, Lillyan Bevan, was of the secretary's. Nothing more than glances was exchanged that evening, but the next day Captain Arthur was able to introduce the ladies to the prince at his hotel. Early in December Mrs. Robinson climaxed a series of assignations by joining the grateful prince in his bed. At approximately the same moment her friend gave similar pleasure to the secretary. Captain Arthur's fish was hooked. Hauling him in was another matter.

Crude and sly, Captain Arthur was a leech with no other drive than to fasten onto a victim and suck him dry of money, love, and everything else of use. For an officer and a gentleman he cultivated strange acquaintances. He knew Mrs. Robinson and he knew Montagu Noel Newton, a burly middle-aged petty criminal with a prison record for fraud. Mrs. Robinson and Newton were intimates. Newton had a friend more sinister still, an attorney's clerk called William Cooper Hobbs, a part-time usurer with a little beard and pince-nez and a powerful and dominating criminal mind—a tiny, vicious man who professed to know every loophole in the law. With the addition of Mrs.

Robinson's rather occasional husband, an unwitting pawn, the circle of conspiracy was complete. The plan was simple: Newton, in the guise of injured husband, was to discover Mrs. Robinson in bed with her paramour. Arthur would then suggest to Hari Singh that the husband be bought off before he instituted embarrassing divorce proceedings. Naturally, that would be expensive. The snag was that the loving couple could somehow never be found in the right place at the right time. It is possible that by then Mrs. Robinson had conceived a genuine affection for the prince, who certainly was likable and very ready to return such feelings, and so hesitated to betray him.

Enthralled, the prince suggested Christmas in Paris. The two ladies accordingly arrived at the Hotel Brighton in the Rue de Rivoli on December 20, 1919. The next day the happy pairs were reunited. Captain Arthur was expected on December 23, so for the sake of propriety and convenience, Hari Singh moved the ladies to a two-bedroom suite in the Hôtel St. James et d'Albany, where Newton visited them on December 22 to reconnoiter.

The lovers celebrated Christmas nonstop and only got back to the St. James et d'Albany at six o'clock in the morning of December 26. Two hours later the door of Mrs. Robinson's bedroom crashed open. Newton stood there, big and angry. "Now I've got you!" he shouted. Mrs. Robinson rushed at him, crying, if the evidence is to be believed, "My brute of a husband!" and began flailing him with sharp fingernails. Hari Singh, kind-hearted to the last, tried to pull her back with "Maudie, Maudie! After all he *is* your husband." Then he sought the sanctuary of the Hotel Brighton and helpful Captain Charles Arthur, who pointed to the delicacy of the prince's position: his uncle the maharajah was none too fond of him and might see a chance to appoint a different heir, the priests would deplore such unclean behavior, and the Indian government would certainly question his moral fitness to succeed. The best course, doubtless, would be to purchase the husband's silence. That, in his view, would cost money—say, around a million and a half dollars. The prince had three million in his account in Kashmir and additional funds in London. There and then he signed one check for three quarters of a million cashable immediately in London, and a second for the same amount to be honored as soon as more money arrived from Kashmir. It was decided that Arthur should convey the checks and the ladies to London by the night boat train. As soon as Hari Singh had promised Maude his continuing help and sadly waved them good-bye, they were joined in their compartment by Montagu Noel Newton. Mrs. Robinson was not told how much had been extorted, or even that Arthur had the checks. The time had come for the next move, the double cross.

In London, Newton and Arthur hurried to Hobbs's seedy lodgings off Piccadilly to confer. They decided to announce takings of only one hundred and twenty-five thousand dollars, to be shared between all six partners in the action—their three good selves, Mr. Robinson and Maude and Lillyan. After lunch Hobbs deposited Hari Singh's first check for three quarters of a million dollars in the name of C. Robinson at a branch of a well-known bank. The real Robinson patronized a different branch of the same bank. Hobbs and Newton then broke the news to Robinson, who knew nothing thus far, that his wife had been enjoying a dubious relationship in Paris with "a black fellow." "A nigger," they added, to make things clear. Presumably as a precaution, they offered Robinson compensation and he accepted it. Hobbs, Newton and Arthur first pocketed two hundred thousand dollars apiece, then split the supposed prize of a quarter of a million dollars with their accomplices. Arthur got twenty-five thousand dollars, the rest twenty thousand each. Arthur then took the final step in the plot. He hired a reputable attorney in Hari Singh's behalf, which was vital if he was to retain his appearance of probity, and told him that the prince had been surprised in bed with a lady and had bought her husband's silence through a lawyer called Hobbs.

The attorney at once visited Hobbs in his law office crying blackmail. Hobbs tore up a piece of paper, pretending it was the second check, and the attorney left. He could not offer Captain Arthur much more comfort for his master but the captain was not unduly disheartened, for he had the second check in his pocket. Everything seemed to have gone extremely well—except that Hari Singh was alternating between heartbreak and terror in Paris, and Maude Robinson in London was growing alarmed and distressed because she had heard no word from him. There had originally been a plan to rendezvous in Nice on St. Valentine's Day. Maude and Lillyan arrived on schedule, but there was no sign of Hari Singh and his secretary. A mysterious foreigner delivered a note: it ordered them to leave Nice. Disconsolately they hung around Monte Carlo for a few days, then went home. Maude Robinson suffered a nervous breakdown and spent the next three months in a nursing home. The prince, writing off his losses, as he thought, and still not suspecting Captain Arthur, was on his way back to Kashmir, where spring was in the air. But the Valley had lost some of its enchantment. People noticed that the prince, formerly so gay at garden parties, so open in his kindness, lacked some of his wonted bounce. He had lost money, but he had also lost his love. He had hoped to bring back Maude Robinson to Srinagar as his concubine and she had seemed willing.

There followed a curious interval. Arthur was no longer close to the prince but still within his orbit, and still hoped to find a safe way to cash the second check. Newton, of similar mind, joined him in Calcutta. The prince, however, was in religious seclusion following the death of his wife. Since there was no other person they could approach to discover whether the check would be honored, Newton sold his piece of the business to Arthur and withdrew. With his blind bloodsucker's instinct Arthur went up to Kashmir in September 1922, accompanied by two charming Viennese ladies whom he introduced as his new wife and sister-in-law. Since Hari Singh was not available, the gambit failed.

The ladies sailed for England at the end of the year, by chance on the same ship as the wife of the British Resident at Srinagar. The sister-in-law and the Resident's wife grew so friendly during the passage that the sister-in-law could not hold back the revelation that neither she nor the supposed wife had any legal relationship to Captain Arthur. Arthur followed them to England in the summer. He was broke. When Hobbs predictably refused to loan him money, Arthur devised a revenge of sorts. He sought out Mr. Robinson, told him that the sum he should have shared in was three quarters, not one quarter, of a million dollars, and gave him the address of the branch of his bank where Hobbs had originally deposited the money in his name. Robinson was crazed at the thought of losing this fortune. He sued the bank for negligence in not recognizing a forgery of his signature.

The case was heard on November 19, 1924, in that monumental Gothic reminder of Victorian probity, the Law Courts, with Lord Justice Darling, a noted wit, presiding. The bank was represented by Sir John Simon, a former Attorney-General and Home Secretary, and a cold and merciless counsel. By this time various sections of the establishment had risen like a flock of disturbed pigeons because the name of an Indian prince was on the check. The Secretary of State for India conveyed to the judge the need for absolute discretion, and the judge, bowing to reasons of state, ordained that the prince be referred to only as "Mr. A" and Captain Arthur only as "the Aide-de-Camp." Lured by this mystery like sharks to a bloody slick, the public turned its full attention to the trial, which had its vivid moments. It transpired that the vile Newton had given the viler Hobbs a silver matchbox engraved by the noted silversmiths Messrs. Longman and Strong i'th'arm with the outline of a safety razor. This curious souvenir was a reference to the prince's request to Mrs. Robinson that she shave all her body hair in accordance with the custom of his country. It would have been unthinkable to refer to such a matter in open court, so the razor was referred to as "the instrument." To the popular press that expression could have only one connotation—abortion. In order to correct that impression the court was forced to abandon circumlocution, but by then the press had had a couple of profitable days out of it. Mr. A's identity remained secret, which was just as well, for Sir John Simon had referred to him anonymously as "a poor, green, shivering abject wretch." Secure in all the righteousness of the law and the bank his client, Sir John had been no kinder to Mrs. Robinson. Fumbling to deny her part in the conspiracy, she said she had hoped for "a brilliant future" with Hari Singh. "To go to the East and live as a kept mistress," Sir John asked in his precise, dead voice, "is that the brilliant future you are talking about?" There were unshed tears and a wasted life in Maude Robinson's reply. "Well," she whispered, "some of these people can give a little more happiness than the white ones."

Of course Robinson lost his case against the bank. Hobbs had inevitably been dragged into the civil action. He was arrested before the verdict was known and the fat was in the fire, because the charge against Hobbs was a criminal one, which meant a trial at the Old Bailey, where polite fictions like "Mr. A" were ruthlessly blown away. Whatever fears of exposure Hari Singh had had for so long, far off in Srinagar, were also blown away when the news broke. The British reaction in Kashmir, as well as all over England, was shame that a young man entrusted to the care of an Englishman should have been so misused. Even the Secretary of State for India was moved to Olympian pity for the prince, who, he wrote, "paid so much and got so little for it —not even privacy for a squalid amour." What no one considered at the time was that for the principals at least the amour had not perhaps been very squalid.

Hari Singh succeeded to his uncle's throne three months after Hobbs had been sentenced to two years in prison, and the chapter was closed.* His spirits rose somewhat and he enjoyed the perquisites of rank and wealth, including a salute of twenty-one guns, until the reckoning came to Shangri-la in 1947. Hari Singh had been more liberal than his predecessor, less priest-ridden and more competent. But he was a Hindu in a land of Muslims, and forces more powerful than politics were rumbling through his mountains. When independence came he had the

---

* Except that he was sometimes held up to his peers as an example. One Political Officer, fearing a similar scandal involving a married lady and the prince he was advising, asked His Highness one day whether he was familiar with the case of Mr. A. The prince acknowledged that he was. "I should not have mentioned the matter," the official was able to murmur, "had I not begun to discern a danger of Your Highness becoming Mr. B."

choice, in principle at least, of acceding to Muslim Pakistan or Hindu India. He prevaricated. The fall was turning the plane trees of the Vale red and gold, and the leaves of the willows fluttered silver and sere in the cooling breeze, and still the maharajah would not decide. He had been selling mineral rights as fast as he could, he had made inquiries about buying a jet plane with a range of a thousand miles (though he hated flying), and because the roads into the Happy Valley passed through Pakistan, he had tried to get a new one pushed through the passes into the new India.

At the end of October 1947, a convoy of country buses growled up one of the roads. They flew the sickle banner of Islam and they were packed with Pathan tribesmen whose lust for raiding and loot had in the past been suppressed by the British. With the British troops gone it was open season in Kashmir. On their way, casually, the Pathans killed a mother superior and a few stray English,* and blew up the power station. They reached Gulmarg and began to threaten Srinagar. Forced to act at last, the maharajah acceded to India. The Indian government commandeered every plane within reach to fly troops into Srinagar. The tribesmen had been distracted by the glorious chance to loot and were driven out after they had rampaged through Gulmarg and taken what they could. And Kashmir, the place of peace, the home of that strange reality beyond the commonplace reality, thereafter became the first battleground between India and Pakistan. By then the Maharajah Hari Singh had died, and innocence with him.

---

* The small British colony of retired soldiers and officials still in Srinagar had been offered transportation and escorts of Gurkhas to safety. When they discovered that the same provisions could not be applied to their dogs, they elected to stay.

11

The Man Who Was a Goddess

IN THE FAR-OFF DAYS of darkness, strange, capricious gods ranged across southern India in conflict and dalliance. Over the soft and secret land of the Hindus hung the minatory presence of a personage with the head of a buffalo bull and the propensities of a tyrant who, through excessive generosity on the part of the great god Siva, his creator, had been promised immunity from attack by any man. Such was the depravity of this beast Maheshashur that at last Siva's wife, the beautiful and motherly Parvati, determined to subdue him, Siva himself (since he was male) being helpless. Assuming her other aspects as Kali and Durga, destroyers and avengers both, Parvati fought nine days and nights until the monster Maheshashur was subdued, surviving only as the name, compressed by usage into Mysore, of a great state and city.

All this was long ago, thousands of years before the West was born; and human memory being frail, there are other versions of this epic struggle. In these, Parvati's victory over the minotaur was more easily won and she then turned upon two inferior demons currently infesting the area. These two, Chandi and Mandi, were also dispatched in short order and Parvati took their names for her own, becoming Chamundi and taking up her residence atop a hill a couple of miles outside the city of Mysore. There she remains, all of solid silver blackened by the centuries, two feet high, her ten arms indicating her all-embracing maternal love, the object of the devotions of successive maharajahs of Mysore and the fountain of their near-divinity.

To the house of Wadyar, princes of Mysore, the story of their patroness Chamundi was of course far more complex and spiritually meaningful than the vulgar legend disclosed. To His Highness Sir Krishnaraja Wadyar Bahadur IV (1884–1940), devout and beloved ornament of his line, the goddess was not only the source of all good things but the guardian of his throne, his destiny and his princely soul. Her grace and power touched him, passed through him and showered benefits on his people, so it was vital that he should pay her homage, particularly in the climactic festival of Dasara, which he and his line celebrated yearly in October, the autumnal equinox. For nine days, corresponding to the nine days of Chamundi's battle with various evils, the Maharajah of Mysore approached godhead.

For the maharajah, Dasara was a time of intense contemplation and purification. He meditated on the nature of Parvati in all her forms, searching for the infinitely complicated truths lying beneath the legends, and pondering the symbolic processes that made the brute forces of human desire into the buffalo-headed Maheshashur, or the male principle of Siva into a stone phallus. He saw Parvati first as a guardian warding off misfortune and disease, then as an ocean-born divinity bestowing wealth and prosperity, and finally as the source of all enlightenment, patroness of learning and the arts. Deep in his palace, fasting, he worshiped the image of his goddess daily and absorbed from her, gradually, the aura of divinity.

For nine days he stayed unshaven and unwashed and his clothes were untended, for during this transformation no human hand might touch him. Each day of the nine he would emerge from his oratory to be shriven and blessed by the priests, and especially by the high priest of Chamundi, second in the land only to the maharajah himself and accustomed to be borne on men's shoulders in luxurious state wearing robes of apricot silk and a gold crown and accompanied by a bodyguard of cavalry. Each day of the nine had its own observances. On the first the maharajah assumed his throne, called the Lion's Seat, first bowing to it in reverence and circling it three times, and blessed the sword of state. Another day was reserved to the consecration of all books, another to all the tools used for work, another to weapons of war, another to animals and all kinds of transportation, which in later days included Rolls-Royce cars smothered in flowers like floats in a carnival of roses.

Such were the maharajah's religious duties, public and private, and they were rigorous. But Dasara was also a time of joy, and every evening the maharajah held a great durbar, visible to his people though he might not leave the precincts of his palace. This huge building in the middle of the city, put up in 1897 when Sir Krishnaraja was eleven years old, was outlined with tens of thousands of lights trailing roof edges and abutments, balconies, domes and towers so that it looked like a monstrous battleship riding at anchor in the night. The durbar hall itself, one of the biggest in India, was open on one side to a courtyard. Its focus was the lion throne embossed with gold and silver animals, shaded by a canopy of strung pearls and raised upon a flight of shallow golden steps. A curtained balcony ran behind the throne for the convenience of the secluded ladies of the household, while for those not keeping purdah there were pairs of opera boxes at each side of the hall.* In the center of the courtyard was a wooden stage, and overlooking all stretched a second balcony with tiers of chairs for special guests. Behind the throne stood sixty or seventy priests from Chamundi's temple, some in the vivid blue-green of particular holiness, others

---

* When ambassador to India, John Kenneth Galbraith enjoyed the spectacle from one of these in the company of some of the maharajah's kinswomen. He was bold enough to remark on the beauty of a necklace one of the princesses was wearing, a string of about fifty medium-size rubies and diamonds. "It's just an old piece from the south," the lady said. It was worth, the eminent economist judged, about half a million dollars.

in orange or crimson, all chanting from time to time the rhyth-
mic names and titles of the maharajah in sighing, gentle waves
of sound. Sweet fumes of sandalwood drifted everywhere, min-
gling with the fresher scent of roses when favored guests were
sprinkled with attar from long-necked silver jars.

Every night there were entertainments. Pairs of wrestlers
would leap with a bunching of oiled muscles onto the stage, or
a troop of Mysore cavalry would clink and jingle through the
gyrations of a musical ride. Small girls danced for their prince
with more innocence than grace, or their older sisters swirled in
red and gold through the hectic, rapturous ballets of the south.
The maharajah's famous white pony might appear, prancing on
its hind legs to the music of the green-coated palace band. And
always at the climax came His Highness' elephant pressing
through the crowd to the foot of the golden steps, where he
would lift his trunk in salute and then with one hurricane puff
blow out a cloud of rose petals that flickered and wafted over
all in a flurry of pink and red. So for eight days and nights the
Maharajah Krishnaraja and his people celebrated the power and
glory of their goddess. The ninth night, in the days of the
British raj, was reserved to that paramount power. On this night
the British Resident drove in coach-and-four to the city palace
and took his seat on the maharajah's right, and then, in a ceremony unique in India, the British living in Mysore passed bowing before His Highness. No Indians were present during these
proceedings. Paradoxically, it was in part a reminder of what
the Wadyars owed the British, for their throne itself had been
rescued by the British from a lumber room into which a usurper,
destroyed by them, had thrown it.

On the tenth night Dasara ended in a blaze of splendor. For
the nine nights preceding the maharajah had sat in attitudes of
piety immured in his palace. Now he descended in the late afternoon for the last act of purification and revelation. His elephant
was clad in gold and armored with a gold plate on his forehead
embossed with jewels. Camels headed the procession, then came
Mysore infantry in red and green, then squadrons of cavalry in
dark blue picked out in gold, silver and steel. The maharajah's

standard-bearers swarmed around him with silken banners furled, tasseled umbrellas, white yaks' tails, peacock-feather fans, and poles with symbolic disks of flashing gold. The chief nobles sat in a high juggernaut cart painted, gilded and pillared, hauled by an elephant with her calf trotting bewildered beside her. Drums and trumpets rumbling and braying, the procession snaked through the palace gates northward toward Chamundi Hill. It stopped briefly at a shrine where the bough of an ancient sacred tree was kept so that the maharajah might do his reverence and prick its bark to discover the omens for the coming year. Then, as the sun was beginning to redden the clouds, the long parade wound into the racecourse for the final act.

Chamundi's Hill was darkening to indigo as the maharajah climbed down from his gold howdah and disappeared from view in a crowd of priests. They shaved him, bathed him with ceremony and gave him food. Throwing shadows like men on stilts, the soldiers of Mysore marched to their review positions in the stadium and waited, silent and still. The sun sank and all was utter darkness. There was a hush over the thousands massed there, as though the great amphitheater were empty in the warm black night. Then an immense flood of light swept over everything, picking out the ranks of troops and glittering on their weapons, and into it on a black charger as into a lake of shimmering fire came riding Krishnaraja, Maharajah of Mysore and scion of the moon. To the north, atop her ridge of rock, silver Chamundi the bountiful emerged in her gala robes and garlands of jasmine and was brought to a dark lake in the hollow below her temple. Soft lights circled the water and clustered around her vessel. It carried a shrine of gold protected by the carved wings of swans at prow and stern. The bird boat glided, obscurely gleaming, around the small shores of the lake, and silently returned. Dasara was over.

Dasara was by no means the sole religious duty of Sir Krishnaraja, who was known as the most devout of princes. He never ate with Europeans and it was said that he bathed after meeting them. He was a man of medium size with an expression invariably calm and a deportment of quiet and dignified grace. For many years he believed his faith prevented him from traveling overseas, for the crossing of the black water was the equivalent of mortal sin. However, after four decades of rule he ventured to Europe, where the rooms in his London hotel included a temple and a special kitchen. Three years later, in the summer of 1939, His Highness sallied forth again with a retinue of more than fifty and a train of six hundred and fifty pieces of baggage. Appropriately enough his first call was upon Pope Pius XII. Suites had been reserved at Rome's Grand Hotel, where the corridors were wide enough to accommodate the servants sleeping as usual outside their masters' doors. The maharajah's party included ten musicians, a troupe of dancers and four eminent Indian singers; when the maharajah was received in private audience by the Pope at Castel Gandolfo these entertainers accompanied him, at least as far as the reception hall, where they made themselves comfortable on the cold marble floor. Emerging with the maharajah from Gandolfo's bowels, Pope Pius was greeted with pontifical hymns and a selection of Mysore airs, of which he was gracious enough to remark that they were "a precious gift brought from the cultural treasure of a people eminent in the history of humanity." His Highness presented His Holiness with a crucifix of ivory mounted on silver and encrusted with gems, and received in return His Holiness' head on a gold papal medal.

The orthodoxy and depth of Sir Krishnaraja's beliefs and the piety of his daily life made him of all Indian princes the ideal of a Hindu king. Yet his Hinduism did not make him intolerant of other faiths: when opening a mosque in 1927, he said, "It has been a real sorrow to me to see lately in different parts of India great clashes over the externals of religion showing, if they show nothing else, a tendency to pursue the shadow rather than the substance." His Prime Minister was a Muslim, a friend of his since boyhood, a prim thin-lipped sort with steel-rimmed spectacles and a tendency to peer under carpets to see what might have been swept under them, but one of the keenest and most adept administrators in India. Between them, Hindu maharajah and Muslim minister made Mysore a model state. They governed through two constitutional assemblies in which women had the vote, made primary education compulsory and medical treatment freely available, established India's first birth control clinic in the maternity hospital at Bangalore, founded a university and technical colleges, set up a co-operative land bank, taught the deaf, dumb and blind to spin and weave, erected the first hydroelectric power plant in India, provided a yearly grant for the encouragement of authors, and financed everything through reasonable taxation and a broad-based industry that included the deepest mine in the world and the export of sandalwood essence to the perfumeries of France and ten thousand tons of granite a year to England. They kept the maharajah's stable of sacred horses as a reminder of the ancient Vedic days when equine sacrifices were required. But they abolished the debased temple virgins, the devadasis, through whom God was supposed to speak, long before it was done in those parts of British India surrounding Mysore, where the maidens, through the long corruption of religion, continued to lose more than their sanctity.

Though Sir Krishnaraja's roots were buried deep and true in the distant past, he was able to assimilate much of the West. In his neat semi-European suits he looked and acted the part of the contemporary maharajah, but always in moderation. At Ootacamund, that transplanted English village nestling in the gorse-covered downs of the Nilgiri Hills on the southern boundary of Mysore, he became a country gentleman. He maintained a gabled manor house there called Fern Hill, gave garden parties and hunt breakfasts on its lawns and rode like any red-faced squire behind Ootacamund's pack of expatriate foxhounds. Invitations to his musical evenings were prized; Sir Krishnaraja was an accomplished violinist and music was his chief delight. He kept a string quartet in Mysore for chamber music. Sometimes he would arrange an evening of Eastern and Western music in various modes, each little concert in its own room in the palace appropriately decorated to embellish Bach or a raga from Bombay.

Vigorous and penetrating of mind, Sir Krishnaraja was also an athlete of parts. He was formidable on the tennis courts and

self-assured enough to wipe the floor with the much younger
Prince of Wales at squash. Though not an avid shot, he kept his
jungles of bamboo, teak and walnut at the foot of the Nilgiris
full of tigers and gaur, the curious wild oxen of India, biggest
of the bovine kind, rising over six feet at the shoulder and
weighing a good two thousand pounds and credited by the jungle
dwellers with the nasty habit of taking stones in their nostrils
and expelling them at an intruder with the force of musket
balls. Sir Krishnaraja could offer his guests some of the best
big-game shooting in India. For the most important of all he had
a special treat, afforded nowhere else—the wild-elephant
roundup.

Few of the elephants so prevalent in the courts of the princes
were born in captivity. They had come from Burma, Siam or
Assam in the east or perhaps from Mysore in the south, where
their capture was a recent and brief innovation. It was abandoned as a business enterprise in 1900 because of the high
casualty rate among the captives. After that the maharajah
would resurrect the hunt only for an exceedingly important
person. Sir Krishnaraja's elephant forests lay some thirty-five
miles south of Mysore city and were reached by a road marked
by black milestones for most of its length, since elephants were
known to pull up white ones and play with them. When a suitable visitor was expected, the maharajah ordered the drive to
begin a week or two ahead of time, and a thousand men would
start beating the twenty or thirty square miles of jungle in which
a wild herd was roaming. Without arousing the elephants' sus-
picion, the beaters would gradually direct them into a moated
enclosure about a mile in circumference. Once inside they were
cossetted with rice shoots, sweet grasses and other fine fodder.

Within the larger area was a strongly built and camouflaged
corral so designed that the herd could be split up by way of
chutes and pens. As many tame elephants as could be assembled
then surrounded the wild herd and pressed it with much trumpeting and firing of guns into the corral, where individuals
could be roped and tethered. With a dozen six-ton elephants
screaming as they smashed at the log stockade, the *keddah* was

a stirring sight, and none-too-safe an occupation for the mahouts urging their tame elephants to hustle their wild brothers into a corner. A few days in shackles, with the prisoner guarded on each side by a tame elephant (who was said to soothe his charge with a flow of gurglings and moans), was usually enough to subdue a captive. A truck took him to the elephant stables in Mysore, four acres behind the palace, where in a few months he learned the twenty-seven words of command and was rewarded for good work with an extra ration of sugar cane. Sir Krishnaraja was a connoisseur and collector of elephants. One he owned, a former temple elephant called Padmanabhan which had killed six of its attendants, was the most famous beast in India until it ran its tusks through a seventh man and was shot. The maharajah bought a replacement from Siam whose only wickedness was to lift the roofs off peasants' houses and reach inside for the rice. Another of the maharajah's beasts starred in the movie *Elephant Boy*.

The era of the elephants, together with some other grandeur, died with Sir Krishnaraja in August 1940. The new maharajah was Sir Krishnaraja's nephew, an immense man of thirty-one who had been christened Jaya, for "Victory," because he had been born as the guns were booming for the end of the First World War. The Maharajah Jaya Chamaraja Wadyar followed his uncle's precepts by living without excess, though the fittings of his automobiles were still of ivory and gold. A man of intellectual distinction, the maharajah was welcomed by universities in England and America for his lectures on art and philosophy, as well as by the ladies of the Darien Community Association in Connecticut in the spring of 1961, where he spoke on a slightly more popular level. He said of his recent experiences of the United States in the Kennedy era, "I have seen a spiritual surge, a quest for values, something I did not expect and will never forget. It is as if Americans are anxious to do the right thing, an urge to justify their conduct. This appeals to me: for in my country, men attach great importance to the spirit. If I am ever exiled, America will be my second home." One of the prince's early acts of patronage was to offer the backing of the Maharajah of Mysore's Musical Foundation to Mr. Nicholas Medtner, a composer of rather limited appeal practicing in England, by arranging for the recording of every one of Mr. Medtner's works, which ranged from three concertos, through arabesques, dithyrambs, novelettes and fairy tales, to songs set to words by Nietzsche and Pushkin. It was the first occasion in the annals of music on which the entire creative output of a composer-pianist had been recorded in his own interpretation.

In private the Maharajah Jaya Chamaraja lived in much the same fashion as his uncle had, cultivating the arts, enjoying sport and honoring his god. In public he was one of the few maharajahs to retain under the new government of India some of his former power. He was first Governor of Mysore, then of Madras, and he served the democrats in Delhi well. He even served as chairman of the Indian Board of Wild Life, a good deal of which still prowled what had once been the Wadyar family preserves.

Early in 1971, when Mrs. Indira Gandhi, Prime Minister of India, was trying to strip the princes of the last of their privileges and perquisites guaranteed them by the Indian constitution, His Highness was still in office. The time came for the solemn ceremonies of Dasara beneath the Hill of Chamundi when the princes of Mysore became touched with divinity. The maharajah did not observe the ancient rituals of the Wadyars. Not, at least, in public.

12

Children of the Sun

DAWN SCOURED THE Hill of Chitor and the fort, crowning it with a raw and cruel light. Long and narrow as a man-of-war, and as deadly, the fort had so grown into the escarpment that it seemed a part of the rock, immutable and harsh. It was a place of sacrifice and the receptacle of the honor of India's chivalry. The Rajputs, and the Jats they ruled, were of Scythian origin and thus shared a common stock with the Jutes and Goths of northern Europe, as well as a buccaneering way of life and certain immortal longings. "The Rajput," wrote Colonel James Tod, their first and greatest historian, "worships his horse, his sword and the sun, and attends more to the martial song of the Bard than to the litany of the Brahmin."

The country of which Chitor was the heart was Rajasthan, south of the Punjab. Bigger than Arizona, it spread far into the Great Indian Desert on its western marches and southward into a greener but still-rocky land. In flat administrative terms it comprised twenty-one units supervised by an Agent to the Governor-General with his headquarters at Mount Abu, but in the roll call of their names—Jaipur, Bikaner, Jodhpur, Jaisulmer, Alwar and Udaipur—sounded the snarl of tigers and the clash of steel. The rulers of these states were great and haughty princes with some cause for pride, for their bastion of Chitor had never been occupied while a Rajput lived to fight. That was not to say that it had never been captured, for mere loss of life was not defeat to a Rajput, so long as honor had been upheld. Chitor had seen much blood and fire.

In the time between the last Hindu dynasty and the coming of the first Muslim invaders, the Rajputs ranged northern India fighting among themselves, establishing principalities clan by clan, and acquiring the five attributes of the Rajput prince—a fort, a palace, a temple, a lake and a garden. The first of them to do so belonged to the house of Udaipur, descended from the sun, with a genealogy five feet long, and displaying a rayed solar disk of gold on a circular fan of black ostrich feathers as a family device. The first prince of Udaipur to be recorded ruled in the region of Chitor in the eighth century and from that time forward his descendants were the arbiters of Rajput manners and morals. They were formidable men. An early historian wrote of one of them, "He exhibited at his death but the fragments of a warrior," having lost one eye in a squabble with a brother, an arm to a Muslim sultan and the use of a leg to a cannonball, and having received a total of eighty lesser wounds from sword and lance. What befell such princes and their Chitor fort affected every warrior of the Rajput race, whatever his clan. Where Chitor was concerned, therefore, death was invariably preferable to dishonor, and though the fortress might have withstood any direct assault, it fell on three separate occasions to besiegers because its defenders chose to die rather than endure a long investment.

Each time the manner of their end was a holocaust. It was a consummation ordained in the Rajput code, the rite of *johur*. Once the defenders had decided on a last desperate sally, the women put on their most brilliant clothes and descended to rock chambers hewn deep in the fort's interior, there to be consumed by fire. The men, clad in their saffron robes of glory, launched themselves down the savage hillside to fight until they were cut to pieces. The first *johur* was in 1303 when they were attacked by a Pathan emperor of Delhi who lusted after the prince's exquisite wife. When he climbed the hill, the Pathan found nothing but the ashes of thirteen thousand women. The second immolation came in 1535, when thirty-two thousand Rajput warriors died on the slopes. The third, when the Mogul Emperor Akbar came in person in 1567, saw the end of nine princesses among the women in the fire pits and the slaughter of eight thousand men. That was the last *johur*, for the young prince Udai Singh (who had not been in the siege) abandoned Chitor's blackened walls and built a new city of shining white, named Udaipur after him. So for four centuries Chitor has remained a grim, high charnel house of pride, swept by owls and peopled by the wind, and the fire-tempered symbol of an invincible spirit.

There was no grimness about the new city. The sun shone there on arcades, balconies and gilded minarets and glittering blue-tiled terraces. Fretted marble casements shaded by mango trees gave out onto the loveliest lake in India, where palaces and pleasure houses seemed to rise straight from the still water. The prince voyaged to them in a state barge, like a barbaric doge, but the ordinary traveler took his boat below the great walls of the prince's main palace, where the slim Rajput women in harsh vermilion, sky-blue, maroon, turquoise, pink, saffron or indigo filled their brass pots, and glided out until there was no sound but the clunk of oar in rowlock and the drip of the lifted blade. Like all else in Udaipur the walls reflected in the water were white; spraying above them was the green of the fruit trees in their courtyards. One of the island palaces, Jagmandir, had once sheltered Shah Jehan from the vengeance of his father, Jehangir the Mogul emperor, and later forty-two English women and children from the sabers of the mutineers of 1857. Eight elephants of stone, life-size, were ranked at its entrance, and above them grinned in bas relief the face of the sun, father of the Rajputs, its rays writhing in golden fire. Inside, its walls were bright with stylized cranes and antelopes and noble horsemen riding tigers down. Light coming from the lake rippled through carved window screens and played on ceilings and walls or on a great bedstead of glass and silver as if the chambers themselves lay fathom-deep in the castle of some lacustrine king. Another island, the Jagnivas, was the prince's summer palace,* and scattered about were other islands, other bournes. At the southern end of the lake there was a kind of pavilion overlooking a hillside that lay bare and silent until late afternoon. Then a couple of servants appeared on the terrace roof of the pavilion with huge baskets of corn; a horn blasted and through the scrub charged a gray-brown crescent of wild pig. Rushing and trampling after the shower of corn, they stirred up such a cloud of dust that soon they were obscured, though through it still came the scrape of sharp hoofs on stone and the tearing squeals of their greed. Farther up the hill was another terrace, overlooking some more distinguished hogs kept in a pit. These patrician pigs were fed on cakes of buttermilk and chopped sugar cane, which they accepted lethargically as only their due, for they had vanquished tigers in the arena.

From 1885 to 1930 the lord of these delights was one Sir Fateh Singh, a slim man, not too tall, with a pale eagle's face and a superb white beard cleft and swept up at each side like a Hapsburg's. He usually wore a curved sword, like all the males of Udaipur over the age of eleven, for Fateh Singh was conscious that he was keeper of a strict and proud tradition: alone among the Rajput states, Udaipur had never given a princess in marriage to the Moguls, nor had a ruling prince of Udaipur done homage before the Mogul throne. Sir Fateh Singh regarded the British in much the same light as his ancestors had the Moguls; if his predecessors had never traveled in humility to Delhi, neither would he. For years, by convenient bouts of fever or other devices, he managed to avoid having to abase himself before a Viceroy. Delicacy maintained the honor of both sides,

---

* In 1962 it was translated, reportedly at the suggestion of Mrs. Jacqueline Kennedy, into a luxury hotel complete with decoration by a lady from New Mexico, piped music, and a showplace bridal suite featuring a velvet swing with bells on.

but when the greatest durbar of all was announced for 1911, when the King-Emperor in person would be enthroned in Delhi, Sir Fateh Singh's pride became a problem perhaps too heavy for delicacy to solve. But by this time the British had grown as sensitive to Sir Fateh Singh's predicament as he was himself. They appointed him to the personal staff of King George V so that he could take his official position on the dais, thereby eliminating any necessity for him to join the procession of princes bowing below the steps. Suspicious to the last, Sir Fateh Singh appeared in Delhi but was prevented by a sudden adventitious return of his ill health from appearing at the more formal occasions. Presented with the greatest honor available, the rank of Grand Commander of the Order of the Star of India, he declared himself conscious of its worth, but in private swore fiercely that he could never wear the gorgeous sash and badge of the order because they made him look like a messenger in a government office, and he would be at no man's beck and call.

In the end, however, he had to bow to the twentieth century, for his traditional methods of government could not keep pace with the changing times. There was unrest among some of his people that he could not control, nor even understand, so the British gently took away his administrative authority and gave it to his son and heir, a cripple whom he disliked. When old Sir Fateh Singh died at the age of eighty-one, his son found a letter among the masses of hoarded papers; it was a demand from a journalist for the fees Sir Fateh Singh had promised him for a number of articles criticizing his son's abilities as a ruler. Despite such hindrance and his physical handicap, the son soon proved himself an excellent prince and a worthy custodian of the memories of Chitor.

Chiefly because he stayed much at home, Sir Fateh Singh could never boast the international reputation of other Rajput princes, and especially of his contemporary the bold Sir Pratap Singh of Jodhpur. Sir Pratap Singh first made his mark in London when he was presented to Queen Victoria in 1887. Laying his sword, which differed from others in that it was always sharp enough for use, at her feet, he took the little hand

extended for the customary kiss and put it across his eyes,
explaining later that it was to signify the surrender of a warrior's
greatest treasure—his sight. A couple of days later he set the
court atwitter again when, other princes having come prepared
with formal gifts called *nazar* for the Queen-Empress, he had
to improvise by giving her the diamond decoration from his
turban, which she wore thereafter as a pin. This ready gallantry
and a thirst for warlike service made Sir Pratap Singh of Jodhpur
above all his fellows the *chevalier sans peur et sans reproche* or,
as the more literate put it, the Bayard of India.

Born in the fort of Jodhpur in 1845, the third son of the
Maharajah Takhat Singh of that place, Sir Pratap Singh's early
signs of natural valor were hardened by a monstrous regimen.
As an infant he never crawled on hands and knees but dragged
himself about sitting upright. He learned to walk by hanging on
to toy horses and elephants, but his feet turned out at such an
angle that his father had his two big toes tied together to
straighten them. Because of a large childish paunch he was denied food and dosed with mercury, which was thought to have
retarded his teeth, so his gums were rubbed top and bottom
with coarse salt until they bled.

Pratap Singh had no sense of physical fear. At the age of five
he wrestled with a big monkey his friends had been teasing and
both fell grappling from a fifteen-foot wall. He was in bed for
a month. A playfellow maddened by his taunts gave him two
sword cuts on the arm. Questioned, he rolled up his sleeve,
flexing the arm so as to press the wounds closed, and said they
were scratches from a twig. Dared to jump from a high tree by
his small companions, he did so instantly. He broke both legs
and for the rest of his life walked with a peculiar, shuffling, rapid
limp. It was not much of a handicap, however, for he spent most
of his time on horseback. He took his first riding lesson at the
age of seven, choosing an instructor who used the whip without
discrimination on pupil and steed alike. By the time he was nine,
having been refused a shotgun, he had taught himself to kill
everything from partridge to leopard with a heavy double-
barreled rifle of his father's. At that age he tried to dispatch his

first leopard with his sword, but while drawing it, realized that
the beast was about to leap and brought up his rifle instead. The
leopard obligingly seized the barrel in its jaws and the boy blew
off the back of its head. In less bloodthirsty mood he and his
companions improved their co-ordination by throwing wild
pigs. They would select a year-old boar whose tusks had not
yet grown, incite it to charge, then cover its eyes with the right
hand to slow it down, turn it partly by tugging its left ear with
the left hand, seize its hind legs with the right hand, then the
forelegs with the left, and flip it onto its back. Such expertise
enabled Sir Pratap in later years to offer a courtesy to Sir Frederick Roberts, commander in chief in India. A pig speared in the
belly by the gallant little Sir Frederick had reciprocated by
ripping open the underparts of his horse and throwing him out
of the saddle. Sir Pratap hastily dismounted and took the boar
by the hind legs until Sir Frederick could collect himself and his
spear for the quietus.

Sir Frederick and Sir Pratap were to find that they had much
in common. The former had fought in the Mutiny and served a
total of forty-one years in India, gaining his fame by a spectacular march through the savage ravines of Afghanistan from Kabul
to Kandahar. The latter had not been allowed to join the British
in 1857 because, at twelve, he was judged too young to ac-
company the five thousand men of Jodhpur who went to their
aid, and twenty years later was prevented by affairs of state
from following Sir Frederick into the mountains. Sir Pratap's
first experience of large-scale action happened at home. A
brother, ill advised by ambitious men, seized a fortress some way
from Jodhpur and declared himself independent. Sir Pratap invested the fort with troops belonging to various loyal noblemen
with neither discipline nor common uniform. In order to distinguish them in the coming assault, Sir Pratap ordered all loin-
cloths to be dyed saffron. The brother spied this death-or-glory
color of Rajput honor and immediately surrendered.

Sir Pratap and Sir Frederick found themselves in company
and in complete agreement in March of 1889. Jodhpur had
raised two regiments of cavalry in answer to a request from the

government of India for imperial service troops—cavalry, foot or artillery for employment under British orders outside the state when needed in an imperial cause. The Jodhpur Lancers were to prove crack troops indeed. Their badge was a falcon above crossed lances, that bird being the incarnation of Jodhpur's patron goddess Mansa, and the troopers seemed to be hawks with their predatory faces and their Rajput pride. Sir Frederick looked them over and announced, "I can promise the princes, nobles and well-born Rajputs who take service in this cavalry that their high birth and the grand traditions of the Rajput race will be most carefully respected when the time comes for them to take their place in the field with the troops of the Queen-Empress of India!" They were christened "the Sardar Rissala"* after Sardar Singh, heir apparent of Jodhpur, who had been sold to Sir Pratap for a pound of salt to avert the evil eye because his father, the maharajah, Sir Pratap's brother, had lost all his previous children.

Sir Pratap took a regiment of the Sardar Rissala to China in the Queen's service to help squash the Boxer Rising in 1899. They camped at the end of the Great Wall between two regiments of Cossacks, whom they considered interesting but inferior. In their first action they charged an unfortunate rabble of Boxers, using only the blunt end of their lances until they were sure Sir Pratap had drawn first blood.

Sir Pratap once wrote: "Religiously, for a Rajput, war is an open door to heaven." The door opened widest for the Sardar Rissala in August 1914, when Sir Pratap hopped on his bowed legs onto the red dust polo ground outside his house waving a message and yelling, "I going knocking over one German, dying for my King-Emperor!" The Lancers sailed from Bombay with orders for Suez and the defense of the Canal but Sir Pratap refused to set foot in Egypt, where there were no Germans. The Rissala landed at last at Marseilles and headed north for Flanders. There Sir Pratap and Sir Frederick, now Field Marshal Lord

---

* Their memory is preserved by the last horsed regiment in the Indian army, the 61st Cavalry, an elegant, brave and highly effective body of men. Breakfast eggs are served in their pleasant mess in eggcups bearing the crest of the Sardar Rissala by a butler who fought at the relief of Chitral in 1895.

Roberts of Kandahar, met for the last time. The little field marshal had come to see his beloved Indian troops in the hour of their greatest testing, but the early cold of winter bit at him and he died in their midst of pneumonia. Sir Pratap kept the body company all the way to its state funeral in London.

The Jodhpur Lancers stayed on the battlefield, digging trenches, drilling and briefly fighting as infantry for over three years. Sir Pratap did his best. "Whenever I met the generals," he recorded, "I used to ask them when the cavalry charge will take place, and they always said it will come about soon." Sir Pratap had known Haig, the British commander, since he was a polo-playing captain in the 7th Hussars at Secunderabad and Delhi, and nagged him. "One day he told me frankly," Sir Pratap wrote, "that the time had not yet arrived for a charge, and that we should not hurry. Whoever of the two belligerents will make undue haste will suffer defeat. But when the time comes we will give the Jodhpur men a chance." The chance seemed to have arrived at daybreak on November 10, 1917, at a place called Cambrai. After three years of battles of attrition and hundreds of thousands of casualties, the British used tanks to break through the advanced trench lines but were stopped by a canal. The cavalry were brought up for the cataclysmic charge the generals had promised, but were also stopped by the canal, which was just as well, for beyond the canal the workmanlike machine guns of the German support line were waiting. Early in 1918 the Sardar Rissala and the rest of the Indian cavalry were shipped to General Allenby, who was about to drive the Turks from Palestine, and there they won their glory.

Early in July 1918, the Lancers were in the Jordan Valley, a pestilential trench rotten with dysentery, malaria and choking dust. On July 14 two squadrons charged at last. They broke the Turkish line, and Major Dalpat Singh with only his trumpet-major beside him galloped at a machine gun, killed all its gunners and captured the gun and the Turkish commander, thus winning the Military Cross. He was the cherished son of Sir Pratap Singh's oldest and closest friend. Allenby started a major advance at dawn on September 19. Sir Pratap, now seventy-four years old, stayed in the saddle for thirty hours, with a break of five, because mounting and dismounting at every halt were now too painful for his twisted legs. He was also shivering with fever. Before the advance was over he was summoned to Jodhpur to act as regent, the young maharajah having died suddenly. He missed the Sardar Rissala's greatest moment. On September 23 the cavalry of Jodhpur took the little town of Haifa at the charge, lancing any Turk bold enough to face them in the streets and rounding up seven hundred prisoners. Dalpat Singh was killed. Allenby telegraphed the news to Sir Pratap. When asked what to reply, Sir Pratap said, "I thinking you sending this: 'Dalpat Singh's great day has arrived.' " It is said that the Sardar Rissala was welcomed home to Jodhpur when peace came with the rather churlish question, "Why are you not dead?" They had won eighty-eight awards for valor, including a Military Cross for Sir Pratap's own son, but death and glory were inseparable in Sir Pratap's Rajput mind.

Sir Pratap's formal status was a curious one. For many years he was given the honors of the head of a state, though he was only briefly a ruling prince. He was three times regent of Jodhpur during the minorities of its maharajahs, and for a while Maharajah of Idar, a small state in the Bombay Presidency whose ruling house was of the same line as Jodhpur's. Yet he shone so with the qualities of a Rajput prince and was so much in the public eye that he became the archetype. He welcomed and guarded all three Princes of Wales on their Indian tours and could claim the friendship of Queen Victoria, Edward VII and George V, and at least acquaintance with the Prince who became Edward VIII. Sir Pratap attended Queen Victoria's Golden and Diamond jubilees, at the first introducing jodhpur breeches to London when he had to explain to a tailor how to cut them, his clothes having been lost en route in a shipwreck. For the Diamond Jubilee he brought the first Indian polo team to challenge the British on their own turf, but fractured an anklebone and had to keep on his boots for seventy-two hours for fear of missing his duties as a royal aide-de-camp. He rode beside the royal coach at King Edward VII's coronation with the maharajahs of Gwalior and Cooch Behar.

At home he was no less spectacular. Lord Curzon, who was not overly fond of him, perhaps because Sir Pratap had a natural talent for upstaging most people, made him honorary commandant of his creation, the Imperial Cadet Corps, conceived as a means of instilling into the sons of ruling Indian princes those English virtues they had not already absorbed at school. Sir Pratap invented its white uniform with sky-blue and gold facings and suggested that the annual vacation be abolished or that each cadet be placed for a similar period in the charge of an elderly gentleman with a taste for sports. "The result of this," Sir Pratap cheerfully affirmed, "will be that during the vacation the young man will have no chance for seeking luxury and ease." Luxury and ease were the devil's work, as Sir Pratap sought to convey to the young noblemen in his own school at Jodhpur. He would have them sleep on marble beds (he himself used the floor or a broad wooden plank slightly inclined toward the foot, where there was a platform for his dogs) and provided a leopard, securely muzzled and gloved, for them to wrestle with. It is recorded that during Sir Pratap's absences from Jodhpur attendance dropped to one.

In religion Sir Pratap was less severe. He had begun on the orthodox path, but in maturity he and his brother came under the influence of the great guru Swami Dayananda Saraswati, founder of the Arya Samaj. This was a reforming sect of great force and enlightenment which broke down caste restrictions and preached such innovations as the education of women. Sir Pratap had never shown much regard for the strictures of caste. In 1897 a young English officer died while his guest. Sir Pratap helped carry his body to the grave, though warned by the Brahmins that he was defiling himself irrevocably. The officer's father reported the story to *The Times*, whereupon Sir Henry Newbolt, one of England's more bellicose poets, became inspired to the extent of twenty verses, in the last two of which Sir Pratap answered a priest:

"My caste! Know thou there is a caste
Above my caste or thine;
Brahmin and Rajput are but dust
To that immortal line:

Wide as the world, free as the air,
Pure as the pool of death—
The caste of all Earth's noble hearts
Is the right soldier's faith."

Sir Pratap and his brother embraced the Arya Samaj with fervor, after one slight hesitation: like many Rajputs they were great carnivores, though not of course of beef. The swami was able to assure them that their meat-eating would not exclude them from his movement. In relief Sir Pratap commented: "In the history of the world there is not a single instance to show that any vegetarian community ever became brave or warlike."

Sir Pratap derived enough from his faith to be able to face his death as he had faced his life. One night in 1920 he was taken ill. He had himself dressed in his finest uniform and placed upright in a chair, where he sat, sword in hand, for his last battle. But his adversary did not arrive until two years later and then it was without his knowing it. He was cremated on September 9, 1922, close to the parade ground on the hillside below the fort of Jodhpur which he had made, in a way, a more modern version of Chitor.

Beside Sir Pratap Singh, the rulers of Jodhpur in his time seemed pale. However, he had a counterpart in everything but panache. This was the prince of a desert country far across the waste founded by a scion of the Jodhpur line, the sixth son of Jodhpur's own creator. Major General Sir Ganga Singh of Bikaner ruled the second largest state in Rajasthan, a domain of sterile dunes, in whose hollows dried pools of alkali glistened, and of thorny bushes sprouting grotesque pods that tasted, freakishly, of spinach. It was a land invented for the camel, or vice versa; such was its aridity and emptiness that the question was unimportant. It was surprising, therefore, traversing this wilderness where the bitter wells were four hundred feet deep and lined every inch with camel bone, to come upon a pink and glowing city edged with comfortable green. Five miles of walls kept out the marching dunes and ill-disposed foragers and guarded a sandstone palace in the Mogul style with a broad terrace two hundred yards long. Even here, amid this mighty architecture, the locust swarms of Bikaner pattered down in a hideous chitinous rain, or the sand hissed in on the malevolent wind of summer. Sir Ganga Singh did what he could to alleviate those natural disadvantages. He ran his state with benevolent despotism, and considering their surroundings, his people were well served. His main care was, of course, to find water. He brought it through a concrete canal from the Sutlej River and then dispersed it through smaller waterways until at least some part of his desert bloomed.

Sir Ganga Singh was not much inclined to smile, and his waxed, upswept mustache gave him a ponderousness that discouraged the light approach. He liked formality and appearance for appearance' sake, complaining once that a Viceroy's wife had eaten cheese off her knife, not seeing that she was more capable than most of understanding him, and readier. But he was a generous host and could offer two pleasures not available elsewhere. The first was the pursuit of the Indian bustard, an ungainly but wily bird. Lines of spotters mounted on camels were thrown out across the desert, and like so many beacons they would signal when a bustard settled in the dunes. The maharajah and his guests would drive toward it with all speed in an old and steadfast Buick tourer. Surprised, the bustard would lumber off the ground and the charioteers would shoot it.

More famous by far was the shooting of sand grouse, a highly organized affair. Beside an artificial lake nineteen miles outside Bikaner city lay a delightful country palace, the color of a flamingo's breast. Here the fortunate would assemble in the early morning under swirling, swooping flocks of the delicious little birds, so many tens of thousands that the whole sky was sibilant with their wings. For three or four days before the shoot, men were stationed at the lake and at all wells and ponds for miles around to drive the sand grouse away when they fluttered down to drink. By the time the guests were ready, the birds were frantic and no bombardment could keep them away from water. Using three guns and three loaders, the maharajah had shot as many as a thousand in a single morning, but the record for a day's sport stood at eleven thousand bagged by forty guns. Electric boats collected the corpses in becoming silence, then the grouse were plunged into boiling oil to remove both skin and feathers. They were counted the most delectable of India's gifts. It was not inapt when a wit remarked that Sir Ganga Singh was prince of Bikaner "by the grouse of God."

Sir Ganga became as familiar a figure in London as Sir Pratap Singh of Jodhpur, though on a different level. While Sir Pratap galloped about breathing fire and socking polo balls, Sir Ganga Singh became the stone-faced statesman. His counsel was heard at the Imperial War Conference in 1917 and again at Versailles in 1919, where he was painted by Sir William Orpen standing in the Hall of Mirrors behind President Woodrow Wilson and the victorious signatories of the peace treaty. He was wearing khaki and succeeded in appearing at once the proudest and by far the handsomest of that august but perhaps mistaken assembly.

Sir Ganga Singh's strongest inclination was toward military matters. Bikaner had its Lancers and its infantry, even its pack artillery, but its pride was a camel corps known fittingly as "the Ganga Rissala." The corps was formed in 1884 when Sir Ganga was four years old. When he grew to manhood he took it to China to fight the Boxers in the Queen's behalf. Its most famous encounter, however, took place in East Africa in 1903 when about half of it was sent against a thorny renegade called the Mad Mullah. The theme was classic—romantic hero versus crazy villain.

Doubts as to the Mad Mullah's sanity are difficult to resolve, in a historical perspective. The British suggested that he suffered from a disease caused by vitamin deficiency which periodically unhinged him. What is certain is that he was a fanatic nationalist, which, in those colonial days, was perhaps in itself enough to diagnose an unseated reason. The trouble was that the Mad Mullah's ability to gather about him hordes of dervishes as he wandered the desolate flats of Somaliland aroused in the British uncomfortable comparisons with the Mahdi and the shocking end of poor Gordon in Khartoum. Sadly, the camel corps's effect on this uncomfortable peregrinator was far from conclusive and it was shortly shipped back to Bikaner to more congenial duties of a ceremonial kind.*

Still, it had been a good try and nobody had been hurt. For many years the Bikaner Camel Corps remained the most graceful of military spectacles, mounted on pale camels of unusual distinction dressed with cowrie shells and fine needlework, and embodying that aura of romance mixed with efficiency which all such squadrons seemed to command in the public imagination. For the British, few crack troops were ever as crack as camel corps: some of that glamour invested also their commander in chief Sir Ganga Singh.

If Sir Ganga Singh of Bikaner was a desert Medici, there was a Rajput prince southward who bade fair to be a Borgia. He was not popular with his fellow rulers of Bikaner, Jodhpur and Jaipur, though he was a Rajput. By their standards he was something of a parvenu, being descended from an eighteenth-century splinter from the clan of Jaipur, and by any standards he was erratic. Wild tales whirled around the reputation of the Maharajah Sir Jai Singh of Alwar. They said he took babies from the women of his state and left them out as tiger bait, assuring the mothers that he would get the tiger before the tiger got the baby, for he was the surest shot in India. They said that when his guru died during his absence from the state, he sent orders to pickle him until he returned for one last act of devotion—or mockery. There was no fathoming Sir Jai Singh's whims. They said he killed any dog that crossed his path lest it defile him. They said he was a homosexual who chose his officers with sensual care and forced them later. They said many terrible

---

* Several campaigns were mounted against the Mad Mullah but none succeeded until the beginning of 1920, when a flight of DH-9 bombers managed at enormous cost to reduce his mud forts to the dust they had come from. Hounded about and stripped of his following, the Mullah nevertheless managed to die in his bed on November 23, 1920, of influenza.

things and all were possibly true, for the Maharajah of Alwar had a demoniac mind and did things in plain sight which De Sade might have envied. He had been playing polo at Mount Abu, headquarters of the British Agent for Rajasthan and one of the few places where a strolling tiger was a golf hazard. A pony's performance displeased Sir Jai Singh, so he poured gasoline over it and sent it up in flames. That capped it for the British.

Before he was deposed, however, Sir Jai Singh ruled Alwar for almost forty years. He regarded his domains, which consisted of series of dry jungly hills in area one-third the size of Vermont, as a game preserve. For years he resisted the building of a motor road from Delhi through Alwar to the other states of Rajasthan on the grounds that it would disturb his tigers. He cut strips through his forests for clear fields of fire, set up lines of scarecrows whom he called his "gentlemen," and then beat the area with a battalion of drilled and hardy Alwar infantry. He built himself a new palace in the midst of his preserve, and a straight new road to it which none but he might use. The palace interiors were papered with imitation tiger and leopard skin, and outside, under a powerful spotlight, stood a table. To entertain guests dining on the verandah he would lay a tied goat on the table below, and a leopard grown accustomed to the jest would obligingly come and kill it. There was no cowardice in Sir Jai Singh, but there was not much mercy either.

No one ever really knew the prince of Alwar. One sage civil servant called his ambience "sinister beyond description." People thought him "baffling" and "uncanny." All saw his elegance and feline beauty: he had a fine-drawn mask of a face and a trim, sinewy body; he would dress in a brocade of pink roses, in beige satin or in midnight-blue velvet, with caps and turbans the color of dying embers or winter pines, without much jewelry save his necklace of superb emeralds. He was never seen without gloves of chamois or silk because he could not touch leather: when he was expected to visit Viceregal Lodge in Simla, the furniture was reupholstered in cloth. On first acquaintance, perhaps even for longer, his charm was overwhelming and his conversation glittered and entranced. He captivated the Prime Minister in London, cultivated the Secretary of State and the Viceroy, spellbound the mighty and unwary with his talk of the transmigration of souls. The great men found the rumors of his evil way of life difficult to accept, so those British officials who knew the truth but were of inferior rank trod carefully. Dossiers were kept but seldom opened.

In the end he ruined himself. A great stylist, he had always known how to shine beside his eminent contemporaries. But his state was far poorer than fat Patiala or industrialized Mysore or ancient Jaipur. His exactions drove his people to revolt. The inhabitants of Alwar had never been a docile folk. Once, long before, there had been a purge of Muslims so savage that not only had every Muslim nose and ear been sent as gifts to a neighboring Muslim prince, but the bones of generations of the faithful dead had been dug up and shipped abroad. This time it was Muslim farmers, driven to despair by Sir Jai Singh's taxation and four years of drought, who took up the sword. The British squashed the rebellion; they did not think any the more highly of the maharajah for his having caused it.

By this time the maharajah had partially withdrawn into another world. He had hired a professor wise in such matters to determine the exact measurements of the headdress worn by the god Rama so that he might have it copied, believing himself to be the incarnation of that great deity. Alternating with such flights of afflatus came fits of purple fury when no one could come near him for fear of the pistol in the bottom drawer of his desk. Perhaps like Hamlet he was mad but north-northwest, however. He once summoned a famous astrologer from Bombay but jailed him as soon as he reached Alwar. After a few days he released the learned man and sent him home, after asking him, not without point, what sort of an astrologer he was who could not foresee his own dismal future. Sir Jai Singh's own brand of blindness led to his removal from the throne of Alwar in 1933 until the affairs of his state could be settled by a British official.

Sir Jai Singh made his home in Paris with a household of twenty-five to care for him. He died there on May 20, 1937, at the age of fifty-five, of apoplexy brought on, it was believed, by a fall in a squash court in the Bois de Boulogne and a broken hip. But Sir Jai Singh's imagination survived him. In Alwar there was a special automobile, golden inside and out. It was a big Lancaster custom-built in England to unusual specifications. It could rumble along at three miles an hour without overheating, to allow an escort of Alwar Lancers to trot in procession in front of it, or it could cruise at eighty on open roads. The driver and a companion sat in the open on gold cushions behind an ivory steering wheel. In back of them was a facsimile of the British coronation coach complete with royal carriage lamps, all gold, and decorated with gold crowns the size of soup plates on its doors. Behind this was a seat for two footmen.

When news came of the maharajah's death the car was made ready. It met the body, as the maharajah had ordered, at the border of the state. Dressed with shining taste, hands gloved as usual, the Maharajah Sir Jai Singh of Alwar was placed in his coach of majesty and driven for the last time through the streets of his capital. Dark glasses protected his dead eyes from the strike of the sun. It was said that as the golden hearse rolled by, his people honored him and wept. It was difficult to deny that though Sir Jai Singh had been a sadist, he was one of the few with a feeling for heroic comedy.

It could hardly be said, on the other hand, that the smiler with the knife was greatly mourned by his fellow Rajputs, who felt relief, if they felt anything, and settled back to enjoy what had by the 1930s become a ruling passion and a raison d'être for many princes. Polo demanded of its devotees all the dash and fire they had to spend and offered at least a chance of serious physical harm. The greatest match of all, the Thermopylae of polo, had been played at Delhi early in 1922 during the Prince of Wales's tour. It was the final of the Rutlam Cup between Jodhpur and Patiala, or to put it another way, between Rajputs and Sikhs, or another way still, between Sir Pratap Singh of Jodhpur and the Maharajah Bhupendra Singh of Patiala. Blood was involved. No one had been able to beat the Patiala team in a decade, but the Jodhpur team was at its peak and would be playing under the eyes of old Sir Pratap, who might not live to see another championship fight. Fifty leading princes were among the crowd and perhaps two hundred lesser ones, all eying Bhupendra Singh and Sir Pratap. The game began with a spurt of dust and a rattle of hoofs on the hard ground, and then it was all thunder and sweating flanks and the high sweet arc of the swinging stick. By the middle of the third chukker Patiala led by 3–0 and it began to look as if they were invincible. Then Jodhpur scored for the first time. In the last chukker the score stood at 5–5, with three minutes of play left. Everyone in the grandstand but Sir Pratap Singh was on his feet. Prince of Wales and Viceroy bounced up and down on their settee. Generals, maharajahs, civil servants with thirty years' seniority were yelling like schoolboys. Jodhpur scored the final goal and the bugle sounded the end of play. Sir Pratap Singh of Jodhpur stood up then with the tears bursting from his proud old eyes.

The most brilliant star in the galaxy of great Indian players of the 1930s was the young Maharajah Man Singh of Jaipur, better known as "Jai." The first time he took a team to England, in 1933, he was twenty-two and playing off a handicap of nine. His team set a record by winning every tournament it played in and fixed the Maharajah Man Singh's reputation as a sportsman for the rest of his life. His inheritance was already a proud one as head of the Kachhawa, or "tortoise," clan of Rajputs, who had established themselves in a terrain twice the size of New Jersey a thousand years before. Not all his ancestors had been heroes; one at least had been unmanned enough to promise half his dominion to a Muslim dancing girl and had been epitomized by his historian with "His life did not disclose one redeeming virtue amidst a cluster of effeminate vices, including even cowardice." The greatest of Jaipur's princes had been the Jai Singh who ruled from 1699 to 1744. He drove the Moguls out of Jaipur, left his great castle fort of Amber and in 1728 built the new city of Jaipur.

Jai Singh was a man of parts, a general of skill and determination, a man of honor in the tradition of Chitor, a lover of painting and architecture, a student of mathematics and science and the equal of any astronomer in Europe. He caused Euclid's *Elements* and Napier's *Logarithms* to be translated into Sanskrit and was able to correct certain errors in the calculations of his astronomical correspondents in Europe. The biggest of the five observatories which he built of stone and mortar still stands outside the city palace of Jaipur, having been renovated by a successor with fine marble and brass. In Brobdingnagian scale a gnomon ninety feet high with a flight of stairs up its hypotenuse serves the same purpose as the pin of a sundial; two hemispherical cups sunk into the ground and chased with symbols and notations are each the size of a big room; pillars, cones, curved buttresses pierced and incised, planes and arcs proliferate in a Chirico landscape as superhuman and alien as the heavens the contrivances were designed to measure. Jai Singh laid out the rest of his city in more acceptable terms after studying French and Italian plans. He made wide boulevards set in a simple geometry so that the angles drove in toward a square where a fountain brought plentiful water and where flower vendors had space to heap their piles of blazing marigolds and thread their necklaces of fresh jasmine. The buildings were painted a rusty pink and decorated with patterns of white, perhaps in imitation of the sandstone inlaid with white marble of older, richer times. The most arresting of them, a sugar-candy confection by a later ruler, was the Hall of the Winds, a five-story façade of curved, latticed windows looking strangely like a stone pipe organ. One seventh of the entire area of the city was taken up by the city palace, a maze of gardens and courtyards dominated by the seven-story mass of the maharajah's apartments. From the top of this the princes of Jaipur down to His Highness Man Singh could see, beyond the city walls, the ridge of hills to the east where, tenoned in the rock, squatted the Tiger Fort of Jaipur and beyond it the golden glint of the shrine of their sun god.

Beyond these again, commanding a defile in the hills that led to Delhi, brooded the ancient walled palace of Amber. It might have belonged to a Mogul emperor, with its alabaster pillars thick-spread as forest trees, its doors of sandalwood inlaid with ivory, its baths of creamy marble and walls so sown with tiny mirrors that they seemed of beaten pewter. After Jai Singh, Amber was not inhabited by any but custodians, but it retained two things vital to the house of Jaipur. In the palace there was a little temple where black Kali sat with serpents at her waist and human skulls for beads, the goddess who inspired the Thugs and at six o'clock each morning required the blood of a sacrificial goat. The princes of Jaipur made obeisance in this shrine as late as 1970 as part of the rituals of their installation.

Then, somewhere in the Jaigarh fort on a peak four hundred feet above the palace, the private treasure of the Jaipur princes lay hidden. It was thought to be a great weight of gold and jewels looted from Kabul by an ancestor who had fought for the Moguls and perhaps had added other valuables which the Moguls had not deigned to pocket. The hereditary guardians of this treasure were Minas, members of a primeval tribe that had been living in the Amber hills long before the Rajputs came. So tenacious and secretive were the Minas that no Rajput ever knew what wonders lay in their keeping. A maharajah was allowed to see the trove only once during his tenure and could select a single item from it. Man Singh's predecessor had chosen a bird of solid gold studded with rubies of extraordinary fire, so heavy that a woman could scarcely lift it. Man Singh kept it on his mantelpiece but was not himself considered old enough by the Minas to be invited to their fabulous lucky dip. He had been maharajah for twenty-five years when in 1947 the people of India took over its government, and still he had not taken his pick. It is said, though there is no proof of it, that he approached the Minas in their stronghold and pointed out what their choice might be: they could hand over the whole hoard to the ruling family (who had claims on it) or they might have to be prepared to surrender it to the new government of India. It was also said that when he died in 1970, the Maharajah Man Singh was the third-richest man in England.

There were many other precious things already in his possession. His jewels included a triple-stringed necklace of spinel rubies, the stones having been contributed by various Mogul emperors, and each bigger than a pigeon's egg, and three huge emeralds of which the largest weighed 490 carats. Even the goddesses in his temples wore 70-carat diamonds. Once a year in the time of a full moon he held a party on the roof of his palace unequaled for brilliance. White carpets were spread, white silk sheathed ledges and parapets, and a solitary chair of silver cushioned with white brocade was placed in the center. All were dressed in white, with plumes of egret feathers or white horsehair. The only jewels permitted, of course, were diamonds. But they were everywhere, spilling in shimmering rivers down the breast, piled in flickering cairns above the brow, ringing wrist and ankle and throat with bands of lunar fire. It was not the kind of occasion to attract the impecunious.

His Highness had many, many more possessions. His collection of thousands of miniature paintings and illuminated manuscripts, worth millions, he gave to the people. He had so many carpets of such antiquity and beauty that no attempt could be made to assess their total value; two hundred of them were masterpieces three hundred years old and of such exquisite workmanship that they contained two thousand five hundred and fifty-two knots to the square inch. A square foot of one of them would have occupied a weaver ten weeks, and some were big enough to cover a durbar hall.

To his credit, His Highness Man Singh lived without more ostentation than was natural to his position. Though he had come to maturity in times when it was inconceivable that the prerogatives and powers of princes could ever be curtailed, he was flexible enough to change with the times. He was astute enough to hire Sir Mirza Ismail, the Muslim Prime Minister who had kept Mysore so neat and tidy, and delegated power. Man Singh had first married a sister of the Maharajah of Jodhpur, then a daughter of another Maharajah of Jodhpur, and then in 1940 he met and married the younger sister of the Maharajah of Cooch Behar, a ruling house long noted for its advanced ideas about life. Her name was Aisha and she was one of the half dozen most beautiful women in the world.

By then Man Singh was an officer in the Life Guards and busy with the war. He was a good soldier, but the days of the furious Rajput charge had passed. When the war was over and India split apart, Man Singh was appointed Rajpramukh, or "President," of Rajasthan; when that duty ended he became ambassador to Spain for a while. In the meantime his wife Aisha fell in love with politics. She ran for the Indian Parliament on a conservative ticket that proposed an end to accepting foreign aid and foreign interference, relief for the overtaxed farmers, and a return to those original teachings of Gandhi that rejected much of Western materialism and mere technological sophistication, all flavored with a sort of Indian Goldwater taste. Aisha romped in with the biggest majority ever recorded by anyone, including that father of his country, Jahawarlal Nehru.

The maharajah had surrendered much, but he still had his polo. In 1957 his team won the gold cup at Deauville. Thirteen years later he was still taking every chance to play he could get. Early in June 1970 he was at Windsor, home ground of his close friend Prince Philip, Duke of Edinburgh. He had a bad fall and suffered concussion. By now he was, as *The Times* said, "certainly the most respected and popular figure in the polo world of India and England of the last forty years." He was fifty-eight; an age when bruises took longer to heal. His doctors warned him to keep off the polo grounds, but the season was running out. On Wednesday, June 24, 1970, the Maharajah Man Singh of Jaipur defied his doctors and his fate and cantered onto the green turf of Cirencester Park in the Cotswolds to ride for the Lavender Tigers against Rendcumb for the county cup, a gentler kind of polo than the battles he had won in youth, but pleasant enough. During the interval he collapsed and during the last chukker, before he could hear the final bugle of a game well played, he died. It was fitting enough and he would not have wished a better end, for he was, as he must have known despite his gaiety of heart and courage, the last of the Rajputs. There would be no more saffron chivalry on the hillside of Chitor.

Epilogue

◆⫷⫷⫷◆⫷⫷⫷◆⫷◆⫷⫷◆⫷⫷

The End of Glory

WITHIN THE Red Fort of Delhi, the Hall of Public Audience lay open on one side to gardens where once tame gazelles
had tiptoed in jeweled harnesses between suppliants come to
seek justice and feudatories come to pay homage to the foreign
rulers of India. Shah Jehan, its builder, had been the first to sit
on its marble dais. Aurengzeb, plain as a pilgrim, had handed
down his cold decisions from it. Nadir Shah, the Persian, had
held court in it before he stripped the fort of all its treasures,
and there the thankful British had sung hymns of praise to their
martial God after they stormed the city in September 1857. The
last Mogul, Bahadur Shah, had been tried there in rags, not
comprehending the whirl of words that banished him to Burma,
for having been a pawn of India's first nationalists.

So the Hall of Public Audience, echoing such occasions, was
a fitting location for the formal inception of the new Chamber
of Princes in 1921, a device which was thought to herald the
renaissance of the princely brotherhood. The princes assembled
on the lawns before the marble seat of Mogul authority in a

glowing patchwork of silk, velvet and brocade, as brilliant with jewels as if at a Mogul audience, to hear the Duke of Connaught inaugurate the Chamber in the name of the King-Emperor, whose tributaries they felt themselves to be. The gathering seemed at the time an impressive concentration of power, for between them the princes ruled great tracts of fertile land and more people than the entire white population of the British Empire; moreover, they had just demonstrated the considerable prowess of their private armies in the Great War, and the richest of them could easily have bought out more than one venerable duke. But the opening of the Chamber was to prove the last great public appearance en masse of the maharajahs.

The Chamber of Princes was one of the contrivances—a minor one—with which the British were seeking to control the ponderous movement toward self-government which their own ideas had set in motion throughout British India in the nineteenth century and which had gained impetus from the easy slogans of 1914 to 1918 about freedom, fighting for a better world, and the rights of man, with which the British government had had to prop up the morale of the British people. The postwar liberalism of the British government provided the climate for reform in India. Part of that reform was the attempt to bring the princes into a scheme of federation. The Chamber was the means by which the collective voice of the princes was to be heard. An imposing building was provided in New Delhi, the brand-new capital the British were constructing solidly enough to last for a thousand years, and the princes were encouraged to build themselves palaces nearby. A number did so, thus supplying the capital with buildings grand enough to house foreign embassies when the need arose within a couple of decades.

The Chamber of Princes had no executive powers. But it was hoped that it would become the forum in which some sort of unity could be forged as a preliminary to the formation of a coalition between the princes and the powerful Congress Party now vociferous in British India. There was a historic flaw in the concept. The princes had never been united: until the British imposed the peace of the sword over the subcontinent not much more than a century before, they had been at each other's throats. Until this moment, indeed, British policy had denied them all communication with one another about anything more dangerous than social matters or sporting occasions. The Chamber housed a very far from homogenous body. One scion of a conquering house might find an ancient tributary across the aisle. Even in modern times the self-interest of a die-hard Rajput might be very different from that of the sophisticated Maharajah of Mysore or the pious Maharajah of Travancore, while a Muslim prince's views must obviously differ in important ways from those of a Sikh prince or a devout Maratha. Some princes, notably the Nizam of Hyderabad, the strongest of them, disdained to go near the Chamber.

Far from becoming a melting pot, the Chamber and its secretariat served merely as a clearing house in which the princes aired and recorded their individual grievances and their fears that their rights might be infringed. There was unanimity on only one point—that their prerogatives must be protected and, if possible, extended. Their only safeguards, as they saw it, were the principle of paramountcy and their personal relationships, in most cases more mystical than practical, with the King-Emperor. They met twice a year and spent much time reinforcing these attitudes. In 1927 they hired some expensive English lawyers to examine the principle of paramountcy (by which the British, in return for a prince's recognition of their overriding interests, guaranteed to uphold him and his dynasty against all comers) to see whether it still obtained and whether it could be withdrawn. Wisely, the lawyers agreed with what the maharajahs themselves chose to believe—that the principle was immutable. Officials sympathetic to the princes pointed out at the time that history could not provide an instance of a single principle that could withstand the pressure of political necessity.

The next step in the grand scheme for Indian freedom was the three Round Table Conferences held in London from 1931 to 1932, where the princes were represented. They were still interested in the idea of federation, as the Maharajah of Bikaner announced in a speech when the first conference opened. The princes, he explained, were moved by three considerations: their devotion to the King-Emperor, a natural desire to assist the progress of their country and their countrymen in British India, and their belief that federation would benefit them and their subjects in the Native States. Beneath the maharajah's generous sentiments it was possible to detect, however, a rooted conviction that change must come slowly, if at all; his references to the struggling peoples of British India were tinged with the condescension of an autocrat for a conquered proletariat. The princes soon withdrew what little support they had given the idea of federation, and hardened their resistance to reform. Friends advised them not to do so, including one of their own most expert advisers, Sir Mirza Ismail, the perceptive and meticulous chief minister of Mysore, who pointed out: "The wisest course is to recognize and understand the new forces and adjust ourselves to them. Like all great forces, they can be wisely directed and controlled, if properly understood. They cannot be successfully dealt with by imitating the ostrich."

The maharajahs had some slight justification for feeling safe with their heads buried in their golden sand. Legal advice told them their position was inviolable; at none of the Round Table Conferences had there been the slightest intimation that paramountcy might lapse. When the Second World War arrived they did exactly what had come to be expected of maharajahs. They immediately offered men and money to the King-Emperor. Once more their troops fought in Africa, the Middle East, Asia and Europe, and one or two of the younger princes joined their squadrons in action. When the hiatus was over, it was discovered that the machinery of change was running at irresistible speed.

The postwar government of Britain was motivated by the purest of socialist ideals as far as its overseas possessions were concerned, unhampered by any precise knowledge of their nature. It cared only that they should be unshackled. The discussions of India's future took on a rather fevered air. It was obvious that the British would hand over power to the Congress Party, which was not only dominant but had many ties, spiritual and emotional, with the Labour government in power in London. The grand design was a Union of India in which both Hindu and Muslim interests would be represented and in which the princes would play a part. Gradually, however, practical difficulties began to ruffle the smooth seas of theory. Muslim fears of repression by a Hindu majority began to grow.

In March 1946, Prime Minister Clement Attlee dispatched a Cabinet mission of three men to Delhi, one of them the brilliant but ailing Sir Stafford Cripps. At their first session in India the members of the mission were shown a map delineating the Native States. They were shocked: not one of them had had the faintest idea of the size of the princes' territories, though two of the eminent gentlemen had been Cabinet ministers and the third was a leading judge. Not even by the time they left had the members begun to master the complexity of the princes' position. The judge had aged ten years under the strain of his responsibility, Sir Stafford was preoccupied by more important things, and the third member was anxious to get back to more familiar surroundings. The mission's chief concern had been the communal tension between Hindus and Muslims, which was both evident and severe enough to lead it to recommend dropping the idea of Union. From this eventually followed the partition of the subcontinent into two new nations.

As to the Native States, the mission restated what had already been said—that the British government could not retain its paramountcy because it could no longer keep in India the chief instrument of its power and the main guarantee of the princes' security, its large army. Many princes were cheered when the mission declared with finality that the British government could not and would not transfer paramountcy to the new government of India, even though the Congress Party had requested it. But not many princes understood the full implication of what followed. Paramountcy would therefore lapse, the mission explained, and the status of each state would revert to what it had been before its treaty with the British. The ingenuous took this to mean that the states would thus suddenly acquire sovereign rights; the more scholarly recalled that hardly any state had enjoyed real independence at the time of the treaty-making; and the perspicacious saw that the maharajahs had been left in the tiger's jaws. It was obvious that it was the nature of the Congress Party, pledged to egalitarianism and honestly committed to free the whole people of India, to swallow up the autocracies scattered like plums in a pudding as soon as it acquired power. The party had never disguised its intentions and was acting on unassailable principle. Legally, the British government acted correctly: technically it had left the princes with the choice of acceding to India or Pakistan or of reaching some political understanding with either of the new governments to allow them to remain independent. In practice, of course, the princes were left defenseless. When the Nizam of Hyderabad rightly demanded the return of the provinces his ancestors had ceded to the British, it was generally agreed that in principle he had right on his side. The only snag was that the residents of those provinces wished to be governed by the Congress Party, not by the Nizam.

All that remained was a somewhat academic discussion of the moral pros and cons of the British action. Morally the action had been indefensible and could only partially be excused by the fact that the British government of the day had no concept of what its obligations to the princes might be; that it had no sympathy for them had no bearing whatever on the issue. In effect, the debt the British owed the maharajahs for their continued support—and whatever good the British had done in India in the way of introducing democratic institutions and industrialization had depended at times on the power of the princes—was washed away in a flood of sentimentality and expediency. The plain truth was that the British public the Labour government represented wanted to wash its hands of India.

Lord Louis Mountbatten was sent to India as its last Viceroy to effect the transfer of power. He did so with all speed and hauled down the British flag on August 15, 1947. To the princes' astonishment he was inimical to their cause and called them, privately, "a bunch of nitwits." Between Mountbatten's arrival in India and the transfer date, the princes fought and lost their battle for survival. They had one ally, Sir Conrad Corfield, chief of the Political Department of the Government of India. Sir Conrad's whole career had been spent in India and he knew more about the Native States than anyone. For years he had tried to convince the princes that they must limit their conspicuous private spending and modernize their administrations. He had failed, but he was still determined that the princes should not be delivered to the Congress Party. Without Mountbatten's knowledge he culled from the secret files of the Political Department four tons of papers which spelled out the interesting vices enjoyed by certain of the princes, and burned them. He could not do much more, however. Against him were ranged Mountbatten, who was anxious that the states should accede as soon as possible to India or Pakistan and used his charm and authority to persuade the princes to sign the necessary instruments, and two strong men of the Congress Party, Sardar Vallabhbhai Patel and V. P. Menon. A few princes struggled briefly, but the only ones to withstand the pressure for any length of time were Kashmir and Hyderabad.

All but a few of the princes acceded to India for reasons of both geography and religion. The provisions of the instruments they signed were based on the Indian Independence Act of 1947, which had set up the new independent Dominion of India as of August 15, 1947, and which was itself an extension of the Government of India Act of 1935. This latter act had vested certain functions in any native government of India that might be formed in the rather nebulous future. By and large these functions were similar in nature to those exercised by the old central government in relation to the Native States. In 1947 it was thought, therefore, that the new government would be responsible for such things as defense matters, postal and telegraphic services, railroads and coinage without infringing too far on the prerogatives of the rulers. Indeed, the instruments of accession themselves contained certain safeguards. Article 5 of the standard instrument stipulated that the instrument's terms could not be varied without the ruler's acceptance conveyed by a supplementary instrument. Article 6 prohibited the new government from the compulsory acquisition of land within the state, except through the ruler acting in its behalf. Article 7 read: "Nothing in this Instrument shall be deemed to commit me in any way to acceptance of any future constitution of India or to fetter my discretion to enter into agreements with the Government of India under any such future constitution." Legally, this last article might have seemed the stoutest of bulwarks. In fact, it had no more strength than rice paper.

Whatever principles the government of India on the one hand and the princes on the other might have wished to follow in the warmth of freedom's dawn, in practice the princes shortly became pensioners of the government. They kept their palaces, private lands and family treasure. They no longer controlled the revenues of their states but they received annuities from the government, called "privy purses," on a scale generous enough for them to boast at least a semblance of their former style. These annuities were to diminish, roughly by half, whenever a maharajah's death passed on his throne to a successor. The princes were also permitted certain minor but traditional privileges; they kept their gun salutes, some household troops and their distinctive flags, and they remained immune from customs duties, prohibition laws and arrest on civil or criminal charges. A reasonably opulent life was still possible, particularly since the more astute among the richer princes had already established useful bank accounts in Switzerland and were developing financial interests in industries ranging from machine-tool manufacture through mining and textiles to moviemaking. One or two turned their least manageable palaces into hotels for American tourists. At first a handful of maharajahs retained some rags of seeming power but only the maharajahs of Mysore and Kashmir were appointed governors of their former states when the groupings were chaged.

The future—if there was a future for the maharajahs—lay with the heirs apparent. Some entered the foreign service, for which their education had fitted them, a few embraced politics, some naturally took an interest in their fathers' businesses, and a number joined the army. Of these soldiers perhaps the most

notable was Bhowani Singh, heir to Jaipur, who became adjutant
of the President's Bodyguard,* then commander of a battalion of
paratroopers; at the time of his accession as the fortieth Maharajah of Jaipur in 1970 he was colonel of a commando unit. He
was known by then in international society as "Bubbles." Of the
princes who entered politics, by far the most successful was
Karan Singh of Kashmir: the last maharajah to rule that state,
he was also the first prince to reach Cabinet rank in the government of India, where he served as Minister of Tourism and Civil
Aviation until Mrs. Indira Gandhi dissolved her parliament at
the end of 1970. In that parliament there were some twenty-five
members of former ruling houses, professing all shades of political opinion but possessing no political cohesion at all. Their
presence in the chamber of democracy hinted at something
significant, however. More than twenty years of rule by the
Congress Party, socialist in intent if not in effect, had not made
many noticeable changes in the dismal lives of the peasants of the
former Native States, so a maharajah, as the receptacle of folk
memories, was not without attraction to his erstwhile subjects. In
view of this potential appeal to the unsophisticated voter, the
princes seemed to possess at least some latent political power.
Only a few used it, but then it was startlingly effective. The
Maharani of Kolhapur defeated a general running on the Congress ticket. The beautiful and intelligent Maharani of Jaipur
won a larger majority than Pandit Nehru's own record. In addition, there were still some princes who were regarded by the
peasantry as religious leaders of a sort. It was the awareness of
this ancient awe that enabled the young Maharajah of Jodhpur
to conclude an election address in 1954 with "Enough of this
nonsense! Now let's go to the temple and think about God." In

---

* Formerly the Viceroy's Bodyguard. Dressed in long scarlet coats, white
buckskins, white gauntlets and gleaming black knee boots, its hand-picked
troopers were the equal of any mounted ceremonial unit on earth. In battle
they became pathfinder paratroopers. Sitting in his office, Bhowani Singh of
Jaipur was surrounded by photographs of previous adjutants, some of them
famous soldiers. Up to 1947 all the portraits were of Englishmen, thereafter of
Indians, but there was no sense of rupture in the continuity, particularly since
the adjutant's first gesture to a visitor was to offer him a cup of tea.

the temple the maharajah was a good deal more than a political candidate.

The threat of concerted political action from the princes was more apparent than real, however. No more unified than their fathers, the young princes of India were much more interested in the future than in the past. Yet the payment of the privy purses rankled more and more amid the socialist aspirations of the Indian government. By 1970 the annual dole amounted to a total of a little more than six million dollars (out of a budget of three billion), or less than a quarter of the cost of a modest dam. It was enough to make a pretext, if not an irrigation scheme. Beginning in May 1970, Prime Minister Indira Gandhi moved in earnest to abolish the privy purses, using various political expedients. Her legal right to do so was questionable, for the understanding between the government of India and the princes rested on the instruments of accession signed in 1947 by the ruling princes in their heirs' behalf as well as their own. Whether the Indian constitution of 1950 changed the relevant provisions of the instruments of accession, only the Supreme Court of India could decide. When the issue came before it at the end of 1970, the Court seemed not to accept Mrs. Gandhi's contention that she could cut off the privy purses. Though many observers judged the issue a spurious one, none could deny that it offered Mrs. Gandhi the best of pretexts for seeking a popular mandate, which she needed to assert better control over the divided Congress Party. On the night of December 26, 1970, Mrs. Gandhi dissolved parliament and three months later won a great victory at the polls in the biggest democratic vote ever recorded.

Thereafter no one could predict what the future of the princes might be. Though they still had recourse to the Indian courts and to the International Court at the Hague, a revitalized Mrs. Gandhi in power augured trouble. Certainly they might lose money, the Maharajah of Mysore the most with three hundred and fifty thousand dollars a year, the Nizam of Hyderabad about two hundred and seventy-five thousand dollars and the brand-new Maharajah of Jaipur one hundred and twenty-three thousand dollars. The Maharajah of Kashmir, who had long preferred to be known as Dr. Karan Singh, which he was entitled to as a doctor of philosophy, voluntarily surrendered his one hundred and forty-five thousand dollars a year during the parliamentary debates of 1970 and was properly cheered. For the rich princes, however, the privy purses were probably not a prime source of income. And in any case, what remained to them was more important than money and less perishable. The Maharajah Karni Singh of Bikaner inherited much of his redoubtable father's panache; the best shot in India, avant-garde in his thinking, the prince served as an independent member of parliament for fifteen years, at which point he remarked to an interviewer, "To me, being a maharajah is of no consequence. I am an Indian." As the prince spoke one of his servants was leaving his presence, backward, with as much reverence as had been shown the first Maharajah of Bikaner to come, sword in hand, to that desert place five hundred years before. For the servant at least, it would be a long time before the sun that was the father of Rajput princes ceased to shine.

Bibliography

No full scholarly history of the princes of India is available, though from time to time a state of the field, as it were, has been attempted. Colonel Malleson's famous work of 1875 stands alone as a serious work. For a more contemporary survey the researcher must therefore resort to autobiography, travelogue and periodical for secondary sources.

Among daily and weekly newspapers, I have drawn upon the files of the *Daily Telegraph* (London), the *New York Times*, *The Observer* (London), *The Sunday Times* (London), *The Times* (London) and the *Times of India*. I have also consulted numerous periodicals, notably the *Asiatic Review*, *Country Life*, *History Today*, the *Illustrated London News*, the *Indian States Forces Annual*, the *Indian State Railways Magazine*, *The Listener*, the *National Geographic Magazine*, *Orientations*, *The Sphere* and *Town*.

It is perhaps fair to warn the prospective student that very few books throw direct light on the history of the maharajahs and that the road to such a study is littered with the jagged shards of ancient inaccuracies.

ACKERLEY, J. R., *Hindoo Holiday. An Indian Journal*. London: Chatto, 1925.

ANGLESEY, the Marquess of (ed.), *Sergeant Pearman's Memoirs*. London: Cape, 1968.

ANONYMOUS, *Five Months with the Prince in India. Contains a glance at the Inner Life of the Inhabitants and Narrating the Chief Romantic and Picturesque Incidents in connection with the visit of the Prince of Wales*. London: James W. Allingham, 1876.

ANONYMOUS, *More Uncensored Recollections*. London: Eveleigh, Nash and Grayson, 1924.

ANONYMOUS, *Things I Shouldn't Tell*. Philadelphia: Lippincott, 1925.

ANONYMOUS, *Uncensored Recollections*. London: Eveleigh, Nash and Grayson, 1924.

ARCHER, W. G., *Paintings of the Sikhs*. London: Victoria and Albert Museum, Her Majesty's Stationery Office, 1966.

AYER, N. W. AND SON, INC., *The Histories of Some Famous Diamonds*. New York: Ayer, 1969.

BADEN-POWELL, LT. GEN. SIR ROBERT, *Memories of India*. Philadelphia: (n.d.).

———, *Pig-Sticking or Hog-Hunting. A Complete Account for Sportsmen—And Others*. London: H. Jenkins, 1924.

BAIRD, J. G. A. (ed.), *Private Letters of the Marquess of Dalhousie*. Edinburgh: Blackwood, 1911.

BALLANTINE, MR. SERGEANT WILLIAM, *Some Experiences of a Barrister's Life*. New York: Holt, 1882.

BARNES, MAJOR R. MONEY, *Military Uniforms of Britain and the Empire*. London: Seeley Service, 1960.

BARODA, H. H. the Maharani Chimnabai of, *The Position of Women in Indian Life*. London: Longmans, Green, 1911.

BARTON, SIR WILLIAM, *The Princes of India*. London: Nisbet, 1934.

BATTERSBY, H. F. PREVOST, *India under Royal Eyes*. London: G. Allen, 1906.

BEATSON, BRIG. GEN. STUART, *A History of the Imperial Service Troops of the Native States*. Calcutta: Office of the Superintendent of Government Printing, 1903.

BELL, MAJOR EVANS, *The Annexation of the Punjab and the Maharajah Duleep Singh*. London: Trübner, 1882.

BELLASIS, M., *Honourable Company*. London: Hollis and Carter, 1952.

BELOFF, MAX, *Imperial Sunset*, Vol. I, *Britain's Liberal Empire 1897–1921*. New York: Knopf, 1970.

BERNIER, F., *Travels in the Mogul Empire*. London: W. Pickering, 1826.

BHATTACHARYA, SACHCHIDANANDA, *A Dictionary of Indian History.* New York: Braziller, 1967.

BIGHAM, CLIVE, *Viceroys and Governors-General 1757–1947.* London: J. Murray, 1949.

BIRKENHEAD, EARL OF, *Halifax.* London: Hamish Hamilton, 1965.

BLUNT, SIR EDWARD, *The Indian Civil Service.* London: Faber, 1937.

BLUNT, W. S., *India under Lord Ripon. A Private Diary.* London: T. Fisher Unwin, 1909.

BOND, BRIAN (ed.), *Victorian Military Campaigns.* London: Hutchinson, 1967.

BOWRING, LEWIN B., *Haider Ali and Tippu Sultan and the Struggle with the Muselman Powers of the South.* Dehra Dun: EBD Publishing and Distributing, (n.d.).

BRISTOW, SIR ROBERT, *Cochin Saga. A History of Foreign Government and Business Adventures in Kerala, South India, by Arabs, Romans, Venetians, Dutch and British, together with the Personal Narrative of the Last Adventurer and an Epilogue.* London: Cassell, 1959.

BUCK, EDWARD J., *Simla Past and Present.* Bombay: The Times Press, 1925.

BUTLER, IRIS, *The Viceroy's Wife. Letters of Alice, Countess of Reading, from India 1921–1925.* London: Hodder, 1969.

Cambridge History of India, Vol. V, *British India 1497–1858;* Vol. VI, *The Indian Empire 1858–1947.* Delhi: S. Chand, 1968 and 1969.

CAMPBELL-JOHNSON, ALAN, *Mission with Mountbatten.* New York: Dutton, 1953.

CARMAN, W. Y., *Indian Army Uniforms Cavalry.* London: L. Hill (Books), 1961.

———, *Indian Army Uniforms Infantry.* London: Morgan-Grampian, 1969.

CASSERLY, MAJOR GORDON, *Life in an Indian Outpost.* London: T. Werner Laurie (n.d.).

CHAUDHURI, NIRAD C., *The Continent of Circe; Being an Essay on the Peoples of India.* London: Chatto, 1965.

CHUDGAR, P. L., *Indian Princes under British Protection. A Study of Their Personal Rule, Their Constitutional Position and Their Future.* London: Williams and Norgate, 1929.

COLLIER, RICHARD, *The Sound of Fury. An Account of the Indian Mutiny.* London: Collins, 1963.

CRANE, WALTER, *India Impressions. With Some Notes on Ceylon during a Winter Tour 1906–1907.* London: Methuen, 1907.

CROFT-COOK, RUPERT, *The Gorgeous East. One Man's India.* London: W. H. Allen, 1965.

CURZON OF KEDLESTON, the Marchioness, *Reminiscences.* London: Hutchinson, 1955.

CURZON OF KEDLESTON, the Marquess, *British Government in India.*

The Story of the Viceroys and Government House. 2 vols. London: Cassell, 1925.

———, *Leaves from a Viceroy's Notebook and Other Papers.* London: Macmillan, 1926.

DARLING, SIR MALCOLM, *Apprentice to Power. India 1904–1908.* London: Hogarth Press, 1966.

DASS, DIWAN JARMANI, *Maharajah.* Bombay: Allied Publishers, 1969.

DAVENPORT, WILLIAM, *India—A Personal Guide.* Garden City, N. Y.: Doubleday, 1964.

DEKOBRA, MAURICE, *The Perfumed Tigers. Adventures in the Land of the Maharajahs.* New York: Brewer and Warren, 1930.

DENYS, F. WARD, *Our Summer in the Vale of Kashmir.* Washington, D.C.: James William Bryan Press, 1915.

DEVEE, SUNITY, H. H. the Maharani of Cooch-Behar, *The Autobiography of an Indian Princess.* London: J. Murray, 1921.

DICKINSON, JOAN YOUNGER, *The Book of Diamonds.* New York: Crown, 1965.

———, *The Book of Pearls.* New York: Crown, 1968.

DILKS, DAVID, *Curzon in India,* Vol. I, *Achievement;* Vol. II, *Frustration.* London: Rupert Hart-Davis, 1969 and 1970.

DUFF, JAMES GRANT, *History of the Mahrattas.* 3 vols. Calcutta: R. Cambray, 1912.

DUNBAR, JANET, *Golden Interlude.* Boston: Houghton Mifflin, 1956.

EDEN, EMILY, *Portraits of the Princes and People of India.* London: J. Dickinson, 1844.

EDWARDES, MICHAEL, *Bound to Exile. The Victorians in India.* London: Sedgwick and Jackson, 1969.

———, *Everyday Life in Early India.* London: Batsford, 1969.

———, *Glorious Sahibs.* London: Eyre and Spottiswoode, 1968.

———, *The Last Years of British India.* London: Cassell, 1963.

———, *The Necessary Hell.* London: Cassell, 1958.

———, *The Orchid House. Splendors and Miseries of the Kingdom of Oudh 1827–1857.* London: Cassell, 1960.

EDWARDES, S. M. AND H. L. O. GARRETT, *Mughal Rule in India.* London: Oxford University Press, 1930.

FAYER, SIR J., *Notes of the Visits to India of Their Royal Highnesses the Prince of Wales and Duke of Edinburgh 1870–1875/6.* London: Kerby and Endean, 1879. Printed for private circulation only.

FITZE, SIR KENNETH, *Twilight of the Maharajahs.* London: J. Murray, 1956.

FITZROY, YVONNE, *Courts and Camps in India.* London: Methuen, 1926.

FORBES, ROSITA, *India of the Princes.* London: Travel Book Club, 1939.

FORSTER, E. M., *The Hill of Devi.* London: E. Arnold and Co., 1953.

FRASER, SIR ANDREW H. L., *Among Indian Rajahs and Ryots; a Civil Servant's Recollections and Impressions of Thirty-Seven Years of*

Work and Sport in the Central Provinces and Bengal. London: Seeley Service, 1911.

GALBRAITH, JOHN KENNETH, *Ambassador's Journal. A Personal Account of the Kennedy Years.* Boston: Houghton Mifflin, 1969.

GAUBA, KANHAYALAL L., *His Highness or the Pathology of Princes.* Lahore: Lion Press, 1945.

GAY, J. DREW, *From Pall Mall to the Punjab; or, With the Prince in India.* London: Chatto, 1876.

GEE, E. P., *The Wild Life of India.* New York: Dutton, 1964.

GHOSE, SAILEN, *Archives in India. History and Assets.* Calcutta: Firma K. L. Mulehopadhyay, 1963.

GOPAL, S., *The Viceroyalty of Lord Ripon 1880–1884.* London: Oxford University Press, 1935.

GORDON, HELEN CAMERON, *The Sunwheel, Hindu Life and Customs.* London: P. S. King, 1935.

GRIFFIN, SIR LEPEL H., *Ranjit Singh.* Oxford: Clarendon Press, 1892.

——, *The Rajahs of the Punjab, Being the History of the Principal States in the Punjab and their Political Relations with the British Government.* London: Trübner, 1875.

GRIFFITH, M., *India's Princes: Short Life Sketches of the Native Rulers of India.* London: W. H. Allen, 1894.

GUNTHER, JOHN, *Inside Asia.* New York: Harper, 1939.

Gwalior Today. Publicity Department, Government of Gwalior (n.d.).

HADFIELD, JOHN (ed.), *The Shell Guide to England.* New York: American Heritage Press (n.d.).

HALLIDAY, JAMES, *A Special India. Life in the ICS 1926–1947.* London: Chatto, 1968.

HAMILTON, LORD FREDERICK, *The Days before Yesterday.* London: Hodder, 1920.

HATCH, EMILY G., *Travancore. A Guidebook for the Visitor.* London: H. Milford, 1933.

HOLMAN, DENNIS, *Sikander Sahib.* London: Heinemann, 1961.

HONIGBERGER, JOHN MARTIN, *Thirty-Five Years in the East. Adventures, Discoveries, Experiments and Historical Sketches, relating to the Punjab and Cashmere; in connection with Medicine, Botany, Pharmacy &c. Together with an original Materia Medica; and a Medical Vocabulary in Four European and Five Eastern Languages.* London: H. Bailliere, 1852.

HOWARD, PHILIP, *The Royal Palaces.* Boston: Gambit, 1970.

HUXLEY, ALDOUS, *Jesting Pilate: An Intellectual Holiday.* New York: Doran, 1926.

HYDE, H. MONTGOMERY, *Lord Reading. The Life of Rufus Isaacs, First Marquess of Reading.* New York: Farrar, Straus, 1967.

Indictment of Patiala. Being a Report of the Patiala Enquiry Committee Appointed by the Indian States People's Conference. Bombay: The General Secretaries, The Indian States People's Conference, 1930.

IONS, VERONICA, *Indian Mythology.* London: P. Hamlyn, 1967.

ISMAEL, SIR MIRZA MUHAMMED, *My Public Life. Recollections and Reflections.* London: G. Allen, 1954.

JACKSON, STANLEY, *The Savoy. The Romance of a Great Hotel.* New York: Dutton, 1964.

JADHAVA, KHASHERAD, *Wake Up Princes.* Bombay: M. N. Kulkarni, 1920.

JAIPUR, H. H. the Maharajah of, *The Indian States Forces, their Lineage and Insignia.* London: L. Cooper, 1967.

JARDINE, DOUGLAS, *The Mad Mullah of Somaliland.* London: H. Jenkins, 1923.

JEHAN BEGUM OF BHOPAL, H. H. SULTAN, *An Account of My Life.* London: J. Murray, 1912.

———, *The History of Bhopal.* Calcutta: Thacher, Spink, 1876.

KAMAL, K. L., *Party Politics in an Indian State.* New Delhi: S. Chand (n. d.).

KARAKA, D. F., *Fabulous Mogul. Nizam VII of Hyderabad.* London: Derek Verschoyle, 1955.

KEENAN, JOHN L., *A Steel Man in India.* New York: Duell, Sloan and Pearce, 1943.

KINCAID, DENNIS, *The Grand Rebel. An Impression of Shivaji, Founder of the Maratha Empire.* London: Collins, 1937.

KIPLING, RUDYARD, *From Sea to Sea.* 2 vols. New York: Doubleday and Mc Clure, 1899.

———, *Rudyard Kipling's Verse. Definitive Edition.* Garden City, N.Y.: Doubleday, 1940.

LANE-POOLE, STANLEY, *Aurengzeb and the Decay of the Moghul Empire.* Delhi: S. Chand, 1964.

———, *Babar.* Delhi: S. Chand, 1964.

LATHAM, RONALD (trans.), *The Travels of Marco Polo.* Baltimore, Md.: Penguin Books, 1958.

LATIF, SYAD MUHAMMAD, *Lahore, Its History, Architectural Remains and Antiquities, with an account of its modern Institutions, Inhabitants, their Trade, Customs, etc.* Lahore: New Imperial Press, 1892.

LAWRENCE, SIR WALTER ROPER, *The India We Served.* London: Cassell, 1928.

DE LISLE, H. DE B., *Polo in India.* Bombay: Thacker, 1953.

LONGFORD, ELIZABETH, *Queen Victoria. Bound to Succeed.* New York: Harper and Row, 1965.

———, *Wellington. The Years of the Sword.* London: Weidenfeld and Nicolson, 1969.

LOTHIAN, SIR ARTHUR CUNNINGHAM, *Kingdoms of Yesterday.* London: J. Murray, 1951.

LOW, CHARLES, *Secret Asia.* London: Stanley Paul, 1939.

LOW, URSULA, *Fifty Years with John Company. From the letters of General Sir John Low of Clatto, Fife.* London: J. Murray, 1936.

LUNT, JAMES (ed.), *From Sepoy to Subadar. Being the Life and Adventures of Subedar Sita Ram, a Native Officer of the Bombay Army written and related by himself*. London: Routledge and Kegan Paul, 1970.

LYON, JEAN, *Just Half a World Away, My Search for the New India*. New York: Crowell, 1954.

MABBETT, I. W., *A Short History of India*. Australia: Cassell, 1968.

MACMUNN, LT. GEN. SIR GEORGE, *Vignettes from Indian Wars*. London: Sampson, Low, Marstone, 1932.

MACRORY, PATRICK A., *The Fierce Pawns*. Philadelphia: Lippincott, 1966.

MAGNUS, SIR PHILIP, *King Edward the Seventh*. New York: Dutton, 1964.

MALLESON, COL. G. B., *An Historical Sketch of the Native States of India in Subsidiary Alliance with the British Government*. London: Longmans, Green, 1875.

MALLET, VICTOR, *Life with Queen Victoria*, London: J. Murray, 1968.

McGUFFIE, T. H., *Rank and File. The Common Soldier at Peace and War 1642–1914*. New York: St. Martin's Press, 1966.

MEHTA, VED, *Portrait of India*. New York: Farrar, Straus, 1970.

MENON, V. P., *The Transfer of Power in India*. Princeton:Princeton University Press, 1957.

MENPES, MORTIMER, *Durbar*. London: A. and C. Black, 1903.

——, *India*. London: A. and C. Black, 1923.

MENZIES, MRS. STUART, *Lord William Beresford, V.C. Some Memories of a Famous Sportsman, Soldier and Wit*. London: H. Jenkins, 1917.

MISRA, REKHA, *Women in Mughal India 1526–1748*. Delhi: Munshiram Manoharlal, 1967.

MISRA, DR. V. C., *Geography of Rajasthan*. New Delhi: National Book Trust, India, 1967.

MITRA, S. M., *Anglo-Indian Studies*. London: Longmans, Green, 1913.

MONTAGU, EDWIN S., *An Indian Diary*. London: Heinemann, 1930.

MOON, PENDEREL, *Divide and Quit*. London: Chatto, 1961.

MORRIS, JOHN, *Eating the Indian Air. Memories and Present-Day Impressions*. New York: Atheneum, 1969.

MOSLEY, LEONARD, *Curzon. The End of an Epoch*. London: Longmans, 1960.

——, *The Last Days of the British Raj*. Bombay: Jaico Publishing House, 1965.

MUIR, RAMSAY, *The Making of British India 1756–1858*. Pakistan: Oxford University Press, 1969.

MUKHERJEE, SUJIT, *The Romance of Indian Cricket*. Delhi: Hind Pocket Books (P), 1968.

MUNSHI, K. M., *End of an Era; Hyderabad Memories*. Bombay: Bharatiya Vidya Bharan, 1957.

MUSGRAVE, CLIFFORD, *Royal Pavilion, an Episode in the Romantic*. London: L. Hill (n.d.).

NICOLSON, SIR HAROLD GEORGE, *King George V: His Life and Reign*. London: Constable, 1952.

NIGAM, N. K., *Delhi in 1857*. Delhi: S. Chand, 1957.

O'DWYER, SIR MICHAEL, *India As I Knew It 1885–1925*. London: Constable, 1925.

O'MALLEY, L. S. S., *The Indian Civil Service 1601–1930*. London: J. Murray, 1931.

OSBORNE, W. G., *The Court and Camp of Runjeet Sing*. London: H. Colburn, 1840.

PAL, DHARM, *Rajasthan*. New Delhi: National Book Trust, India, 1968.

PANDEY, B. N. (ed.), *A Book of India*. London: Collins, 1965.

———, *The Break-Up of British India*. London: Macmillan, 1969.

PANNIKAR, K. M., *The Founding of the Kashmir State*. London: G. Allen, 1953.

PANTER-DOWNES, MOLLIE, *Ooty Preserved*. London: Hamish Hamilton, 1967.

PARSONS, CONSTANCE E., *A Tour in Mysore State*. London: Oxford University Press, 1931.

PHADNIS, URSULA, *Towards the Integration of Indian States 1919–1947*. Bombay: Asia Publishing House, 1968.

POWELL, E. ALEXANDER, *The Last Home of Mystery*. New York: Century, 1929.

Prince of Wales's Eastern Book, The. A Pictorial Record of the Voyage of H.M.S. Renown 1921–1922. London: Hodder, for St. Dunstan's, 1922.

RAIJI, VASANT, *Ranji, The Legend and the Man*. Bombay: Vasant Raiji, 1963.

RAWLINSON, HUGH GEORGE, *Shivaji the Maratha, His Life and Times*. Oxford: Clarendon Press, 1915.

RAYMOND, JOHN (ed.), *Queen Victoria's Early Letters*. London: Batsford, 1963.

RICE, STANLEY, *Life of Sayaji Rao III*. 2 vols. London: Oxford University Press, 1931.

ROBERTS OF KANDAHAR, LORD, *Forty-One Years in India*. London: R. Bentley, 1897.

ROBOTHAM, W. A., *Silver Ghosts and Silver Dawn*. London: Constable, 1970.

ROUSSELET, LOUIS, *India and Its Native Princes*. London: Bickers, 1882.

ROY, JIT, *Shikar Tales by the Barrel*. Bombay: Pearl Publications, 1968.

RUDRA, DR. A. B., *The Viceroy and Governor-General of India*. London: Oxford University Press, 1940.

RUSSELL, W. H., *The Prince of Wales' Tour: A Diary in India*. London: Sampson, Low, Marston, Searle and Rivington, 1877.

RUSSELL, WILFRED, *Indian Summer*. Bombay: Thacker, 1951.

SEESODIA, THAKUR SHRI JESSRASINGHJI, *The Rajputs: A Fighting Race. A Short Account of the Rajput Race, Its Warlike Past, Its Early Connections with Great Britain and Its Gallant Services at the Moment at the Front*. London: East and West, 1915.

SEN, SIRDAR DHIRENDRA KUMER, *The Indian States: Their Status, Rights and Obligations*. London: Sweet and Maxwell, 1930.

SEN, N. B., *History of the Koh-i-noor*. Delhi: New Book Society of India, 1953.

SETON, GRACE THOMPSON, *Yes, Lady Saheb. A Woman's Adventurings with Mysterious India*. New York: Harper, 1925.

SHARMA, G. N., *Mewar and the Mughal Emperors*. Agra: Shiva Lal Agarwala, 1962.

SINGH, LT. COL. KESRI, *Hints on Tiger Shooting*. Bombay: Jaico Publishing House, 1969.

——, *The Tiger of Rajasthan*. Bombay: Jaico Publishing House, 1967.

SINGH, KHUSHWANT, *The Fall of the Kingdom of the Punjab*. Bombay: Orient Longmans, 1962.

——, *Ranjit Singh, Maharajah of the Punjab 1780–1839*. London: G. Allen, 1962.

SINGH, ST. NIHAL, *The King's Indian Allies. The Rajas and their India*. London: Sampson, Low, Marston, 1916.

SINHA, NARENDRA KRISHNA, *Ranjit Singh*. Calcutta: University of Calcutta Press, 1933.

SMITH, C. ROSS, *In Search of India*. Philadelphia: Chilton, 1960.

SMITH, R. BOSWORTH, *Life of Lord Lawrence*. 2 vols. London: Smith, Elder, 1883.

SPEAR, PERCIVAL, *A History of India*, Vol. II. Harmondsworth: Penguin Books, 1965.

STANFORD, J. K. (ed.), *Ladies in the Sun. The Memsahibs' India 1790–1860*. London: Galley Press, 1962.

STEEGMAN, PHILIP, *India Ink*. New York: Morrow, 1940.

SWINSON, ARTHUR, *North-West Frontier 1839–1947*. New York: Praeger, 1947.

TANDON, PRAKASH, *Punjabi Century 1847–1947*. Berkeley: University of California Press, 1968.

TAVERNIER, JEAN BAPTISTE, *Travels in India* (trans. by V. Ball). 2 vols. London: Macmillan, 1889.

THAPAR, ROMILA, *A History of India*, Vol. I. Baltimore, Md.: Penguin Books, 1966.

THOMPSON, E. J., *The Making of the Indian Princes*. London: Oxford University Press, 1943.

TOD, LT. COL. JAMES, *Annals and Antiquities of Rajasthan, or, The Central and Western Rajpoot States of India*. New York: Dutton, 1914.

TOTTENHAM, EDITH LEONORA, *Highness of Hindostan*. London: Grayson, 1934.

TOY, SIDNEY, *The Strongholds of India*. London: Heinemann, 1957.

TROTTER, CAPTAIN LIONEL J., *History of India under Queen Victoria*. 2 vols. London: W. H. Allen, 1886.

TWINING, E. F., *A History of the Crown Jewels of Europe*. London: Batsford, 1961.

TYNDALE-BISCOE, CANON CECIL EARLE, *Kashmir in Sunlight and Shade: A Description of the Beauties of the Country, the Life, Habits and*

Humour of Its Inhabitants, and an Account of the Gradual but Steady Rebuilding of a Once Down-Trodden People. London: Seeley Service, 1922.

———, *Tyndale Biscoe of Kashmir. An Autobiography.* London: Seeley Service (n.d.).

VAIDYA, SURESH, *Ahead Lies the Jungle.* Bombay: Jaico Publishing House, 1967.

WADDINGTON, C. W., *Indian India, As Seen by a Guest in Rajasthan.* London: Jarrolds, 1933.

WAKEFIELD, SIR EDWARD, *Past Imperative, My Life in India, 1927–1947.* London: Chatto, 1966.

WALEY, SIR SIGISMUND DAVID, *Edwin Montagu: A Memoir and an Account of His Visit to India.* London: Asia Publishing House, 1964.

WARDROP, MAJOR A. E., *Modern Pig-Sticking.* London: Macmillan, 1914.

VAN WART, R. B., *The Life of Lieutenant General H.H. Sir Pratap Singh.* London: Oxford University Press, 1926.

WEEDEN, REV. EDWARD ST. CLAIR, *A Year With the Gaekwar of Baroda.* Boston: Dana Estes, 1911.

WEST, CAPTAIN EDWARD W., *Diary of the Late Rajah of Kolhapur during His Visit to Europe in 1870.* London: Smith, Elder, 1872.

WHITE, T. H., *The Bestiary. A Book of Beasts.* New York: Putnam, 1954.

WILD, ROLAND, *The Biography of Colonel H.H. Shri Sir Ranjitsinhji Vikhaji, Maharajah Jam Sahib of Nawanagar.* London: Rich and Cowan, 1934.

WILLIAMS, PROF. L. F. RUSHBROOK (ed.), *A Handbook to India, Pakistan, Burma, Ceylon.* London: J. Murray, 1965.

WINDSOR, H.R.H. the Duke of, *A King's Story.* New York: Putnam, 1947.

WOODCOCK, GEORGE, *Faces of India. A Travel Narrative.* London: Faber, 1964.

WOODRUFF, PHILIP, *The Men Who Ruled India,* Vol. I, *The Founders;* Vol. II, *The Guardians.* London: Jonathan Cape, 1953 and 1954.

YEATS-BROWN, FRANCIS, *Lancer at Large.* New York: Garden City Publishing Co., 1939.

———, *Martial India.* London: Eyre, 1945.

———, *Pageant of India.* Philadelphia: Macrae-Smith, 1944.

YOUNGHUSBAND, SIR FRANCIS, *Kashmir.* London: A. and C. Black, 1917.

YOUNGHUSBAND, MAJ. GEN. SIR GEORGE and CYRIL DAVENPORT, *The Crown Jewels of Europe.* London: Cassell, 1919.

YULE, HENRY AND A. C. BURNELL, *Hobson-Jobson. A Glossary of Colloquial Anglo-Indian Words, and of Kindred Terms, Etymological, Historical, Geographical and Discursive.* New York: Humanities Press, 1968.

Index

✢《✧《✧《✧《✧《✧《✧《✧《✧《✧

Maharajahs are listed under title (e.g., Bikaner, Maharajahs of) rather than by family name.

About the Author

J o h n L o r d worked in India and London during
the preparation of *The Maharajahs*. Born in Lan-
cashire, England, in 1924, he is a producer for NBC
in New York.